The Role of Resources in Global Competition

Dramatic changes are taking place in the world of international business as we enter the twenty-first century. Increasing levels of international trade and foreign direct investment, the growth of huge multinational corporations and the emergence of new centres of economic prosperity are all evident. Businesses are faced with the challenge of having to survive and succeed in this competitive environment.

This book looks specifically at the question of how firms attain a sustainable competitive advantage (SCA) in a global environment characterised by above-average levels of geographic scope, marketing convergence and cross-national interdependencies.

The author:

- reviews international business literature;
- integrates insights from organisation theory, economics, strategic management and international business into a resource-based model of advantage;
- tests this model on a sample of firms in the automotive industry in Europe, the United States and Japan, with promising results;
- uses the results to provide an alternative to the largely positioning-based views of competitive advantage that prevail in current literature;
- discusses the implications of the study for research and practice.

This work will be of essential interest to academics and researchers in the fields of international strategy and international business.

John Fahy is Professor of Marketing at the University of Limerick. His teaching and research interests are in the areas of marketing strategy, global competition and electronic commerce, and he has published over 50 articles on these topics in journals including *Journal of Marketing*, *Journal of International Business Studies* and *Journal of Business Research*. He has extensive international experience, having had visiting appointments at Senshu University, Japan, Texas A&M University, US, Monash University, Australia and Aston University, UK. He has close links with industry through consulting assignments and his involvement in several training programmes, and is regularly invited to speak on business issues.

Routledge Studies in International Business and the World Economy

The Role of Resources in Global Competition

John Fahy

London and New York

First published 2001 by Routledge
11 New Fetter Lane, London EC4P 4EE

Simultaneously published in the USA and Canada
by Routledge
29 West 35th Street, New York, NY 10001

Routledge is an imprint of the Taylor & Francis Group

© 2001 John Fahy

Typeset in Britain by The Midlands Book Typesetting Company
Printed and bound in Great Britain by MPG Books Ltd, Bodmin

British Library Cataloguing in Publication Data
A catalogue record for this book is available from the British
Library

Library of Congress Cataloging in Publication Data

Fahy, John, 1962-
    The role of resources in global competition / John Fahy.
        p. cm.
    Includes bibliographical references and index.
        1. Competition, International.   2. Strategic management.
        3. Natural resources.   I. Title.
HF1414.F34 2001
658.8'8–dc21
                                                                2001019673

ISBN 0-415-23711-4

To Maeve,
The road goes on forever ...

Contents

Figures

Tables

Acknowledgements

I would particularly like to thank John A. Murray and P. Rajan Varadarajan, two people who played a big part in the development of the ideas presented in this book. Thanks also to a number of former colleagues at Trinity College, Dublin, including Patrick Butler, Martin Fellenz, Geoffrey McKechnie and David Shipley for their comments and insights. I am also grateful to Jim Bell, Francis Farrelly, Brendan Gray, Graham Hooley, David Jobber, Sheelagh Mataer and Tony Meenaghan for discussions that have helped to develop these ideas, and to several people who helped out with the completion of the research, including Padraic Delaney, Akira Gyobu, Jim Larragy, Myra O'Regan, Ruth Potterton and Richard and Mary Vail.

Some of the ideas presented in this book have also appeared in the form of journal articles elsewhere. Some aspects of the insights provided by the resource-based view of the firm (see Chapter 3) have appeared in the *Academy of Marketing Science Review* (2000), published by the Academy of Marketing Science, and the *Journal of European Industrial Training* (2000), published by MCB University Press. The conceptual model presented in Chapter 4 was also presented in the *Irish Marketing Review* (1998), published by Mercury Publications, while the methodology described in the Appendix also featured as part of an article that appeared in *Industrial Marketing Management*, published by Elsevier Science Inc. (1998).

competition. The globalisation of the business environment has been predicted for some time. For example, Toffler (1980) argues that the nation state is becoming obsolete in a global economy dominated by large transnational corporations, while Levitt (1983) has proposed that the combined forces of technology, communication and travel are helping to create markets that are increasingly homogeneous across countries.

Consequently, understanding the potential impact of a global environment on individual firms has become crucial. Opportunities present themselves in the form of new markets or the possibility of serving global markets from one or a few world centres. New competitors are emerging, often with different resource configurations or different perceptions on how the 'game should be played'. Institutional and political developments at a supranational level are increasingly impinging on the operations of individual firms. From a strategic management perspective, a central task facing executives is to chart a course for the organisation that enables it to gain and maintain a position of advantage over its competitors. The question of competition between firms has historically captured the interest of scholars, most notably in management and economics, and several conflicting views have emerged. This book seeks to integrate perspectives from a number of streams of literature including organisation theory, economics, international business and strategic management to further our understanding of how firms attain a sustainable competitive advantage in a global environment. A model of competitive advantage in a global environment is developed and a set of propositions is tested on a sample of firms in a global industry. The findings are reported and assessed in the context of the extant literature. The following sections provide an outline of the background to the book, the objectives of the research and an overview of how it was conducted.

BACKGROUND

Some developments in world trade

World trade since 1945 has been characterised by dramatic levels of growth in both its scale and scope. Since the end of the Second World War, trade has been growing at a faster rate than world output. For example, since 1950, world exports of manufactured goods have risen by a factor of sixteen compared with output growth of around six (*Economist* 1998). Dramatic shifts can also be seen in the direction of world trade and investment. In 1993, developing countries attracted a then record $70 billion in foreign direct investment (FDI), nearly twice the amount they received in 1991 and almost as much as the world's total FDI in 1986 (*Economist* 1995). This pattern has continued throughout the 1990s, with developing countries accounting for 45 per cent of foreign direct investment inflows in 1997 (*Economist* 1998). The geographical composition of trade has also shifted significantly with an increased percentage being accounted for by Japan and the other 'newly industrialized countries' of South and East Asia, while the relative importance of North America has declined and Western Europe has remained relatively constant (Grimwade 2000).

Important shifts in the industrial composition of world trade can also be observed. In 1955, over half of all world trade was in primary products, such as food, raw materials, ore and minerals, fuels and non-ferrous metals. By the mid-1990s, these products represented just 22 per cent of world merchandise trade. In contrast, manufactures have grown to account for the bulk of world trade and within this sector the biggest increases in trade shares have occurred in engineering products, which have grown from 21 per cent in 1955 to 38 per cent in 1995, while office and telecommunications equipment have grown from just under 1 per cent in 1955 to over 12 per cent in 1995 (Grimwade 2000). Trade in services has also grown dramatically, accounting for about 25 per cent of world trade in 1999 (WTO 1999). Equally important is the direction of trade within industries. In 1930, the United States held over 80 per cent of the world market for automobile production. By 1980, their share had dropped to just over 20 per cent, while Japan's had grown from 0 per cent in 1930 to over 28 per cent in 1980, and this despite the fact that by the 1980s, much of the production of automobiles in US plants was foreign-owned (Aliber 1993).

These evolving patterns of trade have coincided with the growth of some very large organisations. The United Nations estimates that the 100 largest multinationals, excluding those in banking and finance, accounted for $3.1 trillion of worldwide assets in 1990, or about 40–50 per cent of all cross-border assets (*Economist* 1993). Significant levels of consolidation have taken place in many sectors, such as pharmaceuticals, financial services, automobiles, telecommunications and media enterprises, leading to the formation of many large, globally scaled conglomerates. However, not all international trade is conducted by giant corporations. For example, Germany has many small to medium-sized companies or *Mittelstände* that have large market shares in their particular sectors and account for the bulk of Germany's trade surplus. These companies operate in businesses as diverse as measurement and control instruments for lengths and angles to cigarette machines to food for tropical fish (Simon 1992). These are typical of the international specialists identified by Mascarenhas (1999) that are resulting from falling trade barriers and corporate restructuring. Similarly, an analysis of US export statistics by Mahini (1990) found that the top 50 US multinational companies (MNCs) accounted for less than one third of all US exports in 1987.

The international business literature

The growth and diversity of world trade is mirrored by a growth in academic research addressing the management of firms operating across national boundaries. International business research is by no means a new field. It is possible to argue that it has its roots in trade theory (Ricardo 1817; Smith 1776) and although the focus of that research related to country competitiveness, it provided a foundation for later theorising on questions such as the location of international production (Dunning 1977). But it has been in the past three decades that the field has really begun to develop. Research by Nehrt, Truitt and Wright found that up to 1960, only sixteen research projects fitted their definition of international business research (Nehrt, Truitt and Wright 1970). By the time their study was concluded in 1968, over one hundred separate projects in the area were known to be under way. Since then the field has grown dramatically in terms of both breadth and diversity (Scholl-hammer 1994; Wright and Ricks 1994). Research activity has broadened across a greater range of functional areas and now also originates from a variety of geographic locations other than the United States (Thomas, Shenkar and Clarke 1994).

As the field has grown, four disciplines, namely economics, management, marketing and finance, have exerted a significant influence on its development (Chandy and Williams 1994). Consequently, two quite distinct paradigms can be observed. On the one hand, there is a well-established economics tradition, which has its roots in trade theory and has developed through contributions from industrial organisation economists (Caves 1971; Hymer 1960; Kindleberger 1969), transaction cost economists (Buckley and Casson 1976; Rugman 1981) and efforts by Dunning (1977; 1981) to develop an eclectic paradigm of international production. The primary focus of the economics paradigm has been on explaining the existence of the multinational company (MNC), though there has been little agreement on the issue between the different branches of economics. For example, industrial organisation economists have argued that MNCs exist to extend domestic monopolies across national borders in ways that overcome the inherent costs of doing business abroad. In contrast, transactions cost economists argue that MNCs exist because of the need to internalise value-adding activities in the absence of an effective external market mechanism.

The other major paradigm in the field, the management tradition, concerns itself less with the reasons why MNCs exist than with trying to understand how they can be managed effectively. For example, Porter (1986a), in what was perhaps a thinly veiled criticism of the economics tradition, commented that 'we know more about the problems of becoming a multinational than about strategies for managing an established multinational' (Porter, 1986a: 17).

Early management contributions concerned themselves with assessing how organisational structures change as firms internationalise (Chandler 1962; Fouraker and Stopford 1968) and with behavioural explanations of internationalisation (Aharoni 1966; Perlmutter 1969). Subsequent literature which has typically addressed core themes such as business strategy (Ghoshal 1987; Ohmae 1985; Yip 1989), organisational structure (Stopford and Wells 1972; Egelhoff 1982; Ghoshal and Nohria 1993) and the managerial processes of planning, coordination and control (Lorange 1976; Doz and Prahalad 1984; Hedlund 1986) represent initial efforts to inform the nature of management in multinational firms.

In summary, the international business literature is characterised by diversity in both its intellectual origins and in its focus of study. While such richness is desirable, it can also lead to problems. The simultaneous development of the economic and management paradigms has led to repeated calls for greater efforts to integrate perspectives within the field (Buckley 1991; Daniels 1991; Dunning 1989). The research to date adopting the management perspective has been criticised for its strongly functional orientation, reflected in contributions originating in disciplines such as finance, marketing, personnel and accounting (Wright and Ricks 1994). It is against this background of a rich but fragmented literature base that this research developed. The book seeks to deal with a core strategic issue facing firms, namely, how to gain a sustainable competitive advantage in a global environment, an issue which has to date received relatively little attention in the literature (Craig and Douglas 2000). And in doing so, it seeks to address the question in a way that takes account of both the management and economic traditions in international business.

OBJECTIVES OF THE BOOK

In virtually all economic analysis, differences between firms in the same line of business are repressed, whereas for researchers in the field of strategic management, firm heterogeneity is at the heart of their inquiry (Nelson 1991). One of the firm differences of central interest to management researchers and practitioners is that of performance. Why are some firms strong performers when measured along familiar dimensions such as sales growth, market share and return on investment while others struggle to survive or go out of business? Strategic management theory proposes that sustained superior performance is contingent on the ability of the firm to gain and retain a competitive advantage in the marketplace (Day and Wensley 1988; Ghemawat 1986; Porter 1985). While there is general agreement on the link between superior market/financial performance and the possession of a competitive advantage, there is somewhat less on what are the sources of advantage. For example, in the early 1980s, superior performance at the level of the firm was seen as contingent on the industry conditions in which the firm operated and how effectively the firm positioned itself within an industry (Porter 1980; 1985). However, by the second half of the decade, this view was being challenged by a number of authors who proposed instead that resource asymmetries between firms competing in the same industry is the key variable impacting on firm performance (Barney 1986a; Coyne 1986; Dierickx and Cool 1989). The rapid growth of this perspective in the early part of the 1990s led it to become known as the 'resource-based view' of the firm (RBV), a term originally coined by Wernerfelt (1984).

A review of the international business literature reveals that the question of sustainable competitive advantage in a global environment has been relatively neglected to date. Many of the issues of interest to international business researchers clearly can have a positive impact on performance, whether it be the transfer of domestic advantages to foreign markets (Hymer 1960), the effective arbitrage of financial and information opportunities in international markets (Kogut 1985a) or the development of effective coordination and control mechanisms between headquarters and subsidiaries (Doz and Prahalad 1981). But to date, the links between strategic action and superior performance have not been well delineated. In particular, there has been relatively little attention given to the question of sustained superior performance, which is somewhat surprising given that the sustainability of advantage and accruing returns have long been of interest in the field of strategic management. Sustainability of advantage is likely to be a particularly pertinent question in a business environment which is global, bringing with it greater levels of turbulence, uncertainty and complexity. Therefore, the primary focus of this book is on the question of how firms attain a sustainable competitive advantage in a global environment.

Underlying this overall objective are a number of sub-objectives. First, the term globalisation and its various connotations such as global strategy and global environment are used in a variety of ways by writers in the international business field. An initial sub-objective of the book is to propose a definition of what is meant by the term 'global environment' and to specify whether and how it differs from other frequently used terms such as the 'international environment'. Second, as noted earlier, a great deal has been written about firms trading internationally from the perspectives of both economics and management. Consequently, this book seeks to integrate and assess what is already known about global competition in order to build a reliable foundation for further conceptual and empirical work. Third, this book adopts a resource-based rather than an industry-based view of sustainable competitive advantage. However, the resource-based view of the firm (RBV) draws insights from both economics and strategic management and is also undergoing continued development with the emergence of new insights and points of clarification. A third sub-objective is to synthesise the extant RBV literature to provide an integrated picture of its origins, insights and status. Of particular relevance to this study is that the RBV literature has, with a few exceptions (e.g. Collis 1991; Fahy *et al.* 2000; Tallman and Fladmoe-Lindquist 1997), been exclusively domestic in its focus. It has not taken account of how a firm's resource configuration may be influenced by the country or countries in which it operates. A fourth sub-objective is to propose an extension of the resource-based view more accurately to describe the nature of competition in a global environment. Finally, one of the criticisms of the resource-based view is that, to date, its development has been largely conceptual rather than empirical in nature (Yeoh and Roth 1999). Some empirical contributions have begun to emerge, but its core propositions remain subject to verification, due in no small part to the difficulty inherent in measuring some of its key constructs (Godfrey and Hill 1995). A final sub-objective of the study is to develop a research design that facilitates an empirical test of propositions derived from the resource-based view of the firm. The objectives of the book are summarised in Table 1.1.

As academic disciplines grow and develop, it is argued that they should take stock of their progress from time to time (Thomas and Pruett 1993). In recent years, there have been several critical reviews of both the strategic management and international business fields. In a hard-hitting review, Bettis (1991) suggested that strategic management was caught in a normal science straitjacket, leading to what Daft and Lewin (1990) describe as 'incremental, footnote-on-footnote' research. Some of the problems identified within the field include research based on outdated concepts (what Bettis calls 'studying organisational fossils'), an ethnocentric focus and a lack of managerially relevant prescription (Bettis 1991). In looking at competition in a global environment, this book concerns itself with an issue that is both of current relevance and is, by definition, non-ethnocentric. Indeed, the importance of global competition as an area of research is demonstrated in a study by Lyles (1990), who found that a sample of strategic management experts rated it as the area likely to have the most impact on strategic research over the

Table 1.1 The objectives of the book

Overall objective
- To determine how a firm can attain a sustainable competitive advantage in a global environment

Sub-objectives
- To define what is meant by the term 'global environment'
- To review what is known about the nature of global competition
- To synthesise the literature on the resource-based view of the firm
- To extend the RBV to take account of competition in a global environment
- To develop a research design to test a resource-based model of SCA

---

next ten years and also as the topic likely to be of most relevance to prac-
tising managers. The passage of time has not disproved these predictions
and the emergence of an information society has only served further to
increase the global dimensions of modern business. Relevance in strategic
management research has also been a concern for some time. By looking
at the relationship between resources and advantage and the performance
implications of this relationship for firms operating in a global environment, the book seeks to meet such criteria as timeliness, innovativeness,
meaningfulness and actionability, which are among the dimensions of
practical usefulness that have been specified in the literature (Shrivastava
1987; Thomas and Tymon 1982).

Thomas and Pruett (1993) note that, by its very nature, the field of
strategic management is routinely exposed to a variety of perspectives
and consequently a fertile ground for multilectic inquiry. It is interesting to note that several reviews within the field of international
business have stressed the need for more integrative and interdisciplinary approaches to research (see for example, Buckley 1991; Daniels
1991; Dunning 1989; Dymsza 1984a; Ricks 1985; Sullivan 1998a, b;
Sundaram and Black 1992). Indeed, a review of twenty-seven years of
Journal of International Business Studies scholarship by Sullivan
(1998a) found that international business research activity has generated a significant downward trend in comprehensiveness, connected-
ness and complexity, further supporting the view that the field is
suffering from a 'narrow vision'. Calls for greater integration are not
surprising given the multidisciplinary nature of the international business field, drawing as it does from the social sciences such as
economics, political science, sociology, psychology, history and
anthropology as well as from the functional fields of business administration such as finance, marketing, production, personnel, accounting
and others (Dymsza 1984a; Toyne and Nigh 1998). Dunning (1989)
advocates an interdisciplinary approach in order to capture potential
synergies between the disciplines. He suggests that scholarly disciplines can be viewed as complementary assets and that the property
rights of the scholar may be more fully appropriated if combined with
insights from other disciplines. Daniels (1991) suggests that an interdisciplinary approach is likely to improve the relevance of research
because, as Van de Ven (1989) notes, 'impeccable micro logic is
creating macro nonsense'.

This book responds to these calls for greater interdisciplinarity. By
integrating strategic management and international business, it is
combining two fields that have a great deal in common due to their relatively young age (Bartlett and Ghoshal 1991) and their attention to core
themes such as product-market development and the commitment of
resources internationally (Negandhi and Savara 1989). Indeed, over the
years, reviews in the international business literature have suggested that

strategy questions such as strategic options for MNCs, studies of the internal dynamics of international businesses and performance-focused studies are key areas of research (see for example, Arpan, Flowers and Ricks 1981; Robinson 1981; Schollhammer 1994). By adopting the resource-based view of the firm as its theoretical base, this book brings to bear on the issue of global competition a perspective that is rich in both economic and management insights. Views from these two traditions are wedded together and applied to the problem of sustainable competitive advantage in a global environment. In short, the research adopts a theoretical perspective grounded in economics and management and applies it to the field of international business where perspectives on competition have, in the main, been informed by both international economists and international management theorists. The potential benefits likely to accrue from this integration of strategic management and international business have been highlighted by a number of authors (see for example, Bartlett and Ghoshal 1991; Root and Visudtibhan 1992). The benefits can run both ways. The theoretical strength of the disciplines underlying strategic management can inform our understanding of international business problems while at the same time, as Bartlett and Ghoshal (1991) note, recent work in the international business area has emerged to challenge established assumptions in the strategy field. In this context, the resource-based view of the firm holds some potential for furthering our understanding of global competition but at the same time is also likely to be advanced and improved by testing its propositions in a global context. As Ghoshal and Westney (1992) note, '(The study of) MNCs can be strengthened by a more systematic grounding in organisation theory and that the theory can be enriched by extension to one of the most complex forms of organisations currently in existence' (Ghoshal and Westney 1992: 2).

OUTLINE OF THE BOOK

The following chapter begins by defining what is meant by a global environment and by conducting a review of the international business literature to establish what is already known about the nature of global competition. The next phase involves a review of the literature falling within the realm of the resource-based view (RBV) of the firm to provide an integrated assessment of its insights and these are discussed in Chapter 3. The RBV is then applied to the question of global competition and a conceptual model and series of research hypotheses are proposed in Chapter 4. A methodology to test these hypotheses was devised and a mail survey was conducted on a sample of firms in the automotive components industry in Ireland, the United Kingdom, the United States and Japan. The results of this study are reported in Chapter 5. Finally, in

Chapter 6, conclusions are drawn regarding the nature of sustainable competitive advantage in a global environment, the limitations of the research are noted and its implications for practitioners, policy makers and researchers are outlined.

The review of the international business literature in Chapter 2 is conducted for two reasons. First, there has been a great deal of ambiguity in the use of terminology, with organisations operating across national borders being variously described as international firms, global firms, multinational enterprises and diversified multinational companies. The adjective 'global' is widely used but not in a very consistent manner. Therefore, it is essential to clarify exactly what is meant by the term 'global environment' for research purposes. It is defined as a business arena exhibiting above average levels of geographic scope, market convergence and cross-national interdependencies. As such it is viewed as a particular type of international environment with its own distinct competitive pressures. Perspectives from the organisation theory literature are used to delineate these competitive pressures. Global environments are considered to exhibit high levels of complexity/heterogeneity, rapid change, high volatility and high levels of perceived uncertainty, and, consequently, represent very difficult arenas in which to attain a sustainable competitive advantage.

The second purpose of Chapter 2 is to take stock of what is already known about the nature of competition in a global environment. Insights into this important question can be found within both the economic and managerial traditions in international business. Both have a long and illustrious history, and the chronological development of each tradition is reviewed and critiqued and points of similarity are noted. The economic paradigm has evolved from its roots in trade theory, through perspectives from industrial organisation and transaction cost economics, to more recent efforts to develop an 'eclectic paradigm' (Dunning 1977). The primary focus of attention in the economics literature has been on explaining the existence of MNCs, though views on this question vary between economists of the industrial organisation and transaction cost persuasions. Competition at the firm level has not always been of central interest and, where it is discussed, it is generally in the context of the rivalry between MNCs and firms in the host countries in which they operate. MNCs can out-compete these rivals through the extension of their domestic monopoly power (Hymer 1960) and/or through their multinationality, which enables them to exploit imperfections in factor markets (Dunning 1981). A rich and diverse management literature has been emerging since the 1960s and has generally concerned itself with core themes such as strategy, structure and process. It is distinguished by its recognition of changes in the business environment and, in particular, its discussion of MNCs as firms faced with the difficulty of reconciling the dual challenge of integration across countries and the need to be responsive to local country differences. But it is also notable for its lack of consensus on both the extent of environmental change and the appropriate organisational responses. Its largely contingency-based prescriptions to maximise possibilities for integration, to be locally responsive or to seek to combine both within complex organisational arrangements have neither been generally accepted nor empirically verified. In summary, though the economic and management literature has provided a diverse range of valuable insights, it has lacked consensus and is not without its gaps. In particular, it provides few guidelines on how a firm can attain a sustainable competitive advantage in a global environment.

The purpose of Chapter 3 is to examine and critique a recently emerging theory of sustainable competitive advantage, namely, the resource-based view of the firm (RBV). The complex relationship between the firm and its environment has long been a subject of debate in the organisation theory literature. Widely diverging perspectives exist, ranging from the view that organisations are at the mercy of their environments in a quasi-Darwinian sense which is favoured by population ecologists (e.g. Hannan and Freeman 1977) to the belief that firms can exercise strategic choices to influence their levels of resource dependence (Aldrich and Pfeffer 1976). The resource-based view of the firm, which is rooted in models of monopolistic competition originating in the 1930s, also adopts a voluntaristic orientation and sees individual firms as being able to influence their destinies through the strategic choices they make regarding their resource portfolios. The RBV has been warmly embraced in the strategic management literature. It has contributed to an ongoing swing away from the industry as the focus of analysis and has been at the forefront of growing levels of attention being paid to the firm's internal strengths and weaknesses (Hoskisson *et al.* 1999).

Contributions falling within the parameters of the resource-based view have grown dramatically since the late 1980s. The literature is characterised by diversity in its orientation and insights and by inconsistency in the use of nomenclature and terminology. Chapter 3 synthesises the extant literature and presents an integrated model highlighting the relationships between resources, managerial choices and sustainable competitive advantage (SCA). A competitive advantage is defined as an advantage one firm has over a competitor or group of competitors in a given market, strategic group or industry and is sustainable if the resources underlying it possess characteristics that prevent its duplication. Key resources, then, are those that are inimitable, immobile and non-substitutable which, in turn, is a function of properties such as tacitness, complexity, specificity, regulatory protection and economic deterrence. Resources that possess these barriers to duplication and provide value to customers which can be appropriated by the firm are a source of SCA. However, the process is not automatic and the firm's management plays an important role in the relationship between resources and advantage. Management exercises a range of strategic choices regarding resource identification, their development and protection and their deployment in product markets which influences the level of advantages and the rents attained.

In Chapter 4, the resource-based view of the firm is adopted as a theoretical lens to examine the question of sustainable competitive advantage in a global environment. The RBV is an appealing framework given that resources are central to many of the perspectives on global competition such as trade theory and industrial organisation, yet their role has not been examined in any systematic manner to date. The fundamental logic of the RBV, which is that firms gain an SCA by deploying difficult-to-duplicate resources in ways that create value for customers, still holds in the global context. However, some important conceptual extensions to the basic model are necessary. The resource pool available to the firm is extended to take account of the presence of country-specific resources (CSRs) as well as firm-specific resources (FSRs) and to recognise that these resources are located in both the country of origin and in host countries in which the firm operates. The Bartlett and Ghoshal typology of strategic orientation is integrated into the model as a frame for describing the alternative approaches to the moderating role of management in the process by which resources are converted into advantages. From the revised model and the conceptual integration of the strategic management and international business literature, a series of ten research hypotheses is proposed.

These hypotheses were tested on a sample of firms in the automotive components industry. This industry was selected primarily because it exhibits the characteristics of a global industry illustrated by the presence of global customers with largely universal needs, global competitors, pressures for cost reduction and investment/technological intensity. It is also an attractive choice because it is characterised by relatively open competition, which is important given that the research is concerned with resource-based as opposed to monopoly-based advantages. The findings of the research are reported in Chapter 5. In terms of resources, firm-specific advantages such as quality systems, design/engineering know-how, reputation, the expertise of management people and the ability to work with customers are all considered to be essential. At a broad level, firm-specific resources were found to be more important than country-specific resources. More specifically, firm-specific capabilities are considered more important than intangible assets or tangible assets and advanced country-specific resources are perceived to be more important than basic country-specific resources. These findings strongly support the hypotheses and the analysis of the resource pool provides evidence that some resources are more important than others in terms of gaining an SCA, which is a central proposition of the resource-based view of the firm.

An analysis of the firm's strategic orientation reveals the presence of all four types, namely, multinational firms, international firms, global firms and transnational firms in this global industry. In fact, multinationals and transnationals account for over 50 per cent of the sample while less than 10 per cent class themselves as global. However in this study, few significant relationships were found between the firm's strategic orientation and its resource pool. Global firms were found to attach high levels of importance to country-specific resources, in particular, access to labour at low cost and government incentives such as tax reductions, but in general other propositions were unsupported.

The fortunes of the automotive components industry are closely linked to those of the automotive business, which went through a period of recession during the first half of the 1990s. Consequently, pressure from vehicle manufacturers depressed profitability levels in the supply industry. This study found that profitability levels, though low, have been rising steadily since 1990. Consistently top performers in terms of profitability, market share and sales growth are compared with consistently poor performers using discriminant analysis. Top performers are distinguished by the significantly higher levels of importance that they attribute to capabilities and intangible assets. This finding suggests that these difficult-to-duplicate resources are important sources of sustainable competitive advantage, which strongly supports predictions derived from the resource-based view of the firm.

In the final chapter, these findings are considered. The question of performance heterogeneity is one that is of central importance to both the study and the practice of strategic management. Conflicting views exist concerning the relative importance of a firm's resource endowments versus the industry context in which it operates. In the international business literature, attention to the latter has been dominant. The challenges facing managers are largely framed in terms of the conflicting desire for efficiencies generated by the cross-border integration of operations with the need for adaptation and local responsiveness. Superior performance is seen as being related to the effective management of this conflict and the development of strategies, structures and processes that fit with given industry conditions. Evidence to support this position has been largely anecdotal. This book provides support for an alternative view of performance heterogeneity based on the deployment of difficult-to-duplicate resources in ways that create value for customers. In the context of the global automotive components industry, the deployment of firm-specific capabilities and intangible assets is positively correlated with sustained superior levels of profitability and market share. This finding has similarities with the industrial organisation perspective on international business, which stresses the importance of the firm-specific advantages of MNCs. Shifting the focus from industry conditions to the nature of the firm's resource endowments represents a promising avenue for understanding the nature of performance heterogeneity in a global environment.

The study has several important implications for practice, policy making and further research. Strategies in the marketplace should seek to utilise resources that cannot be imitated, hired away or substituted for by competitors. These types of resource decisions set the firm on a path trajectory that ultimately influences its survival and prosperity. Though its specific concern is with competition at the level of the firm, the RBV also has important policy implications. Country competitiveness can be seen in terms of the competitive advantages of its firms. Government investments and regulatory decisions can positively influence the international competitiveness of its firms. Policy makers should also examine the role of the country's stock of resources in terms of its ability to compete in the market for mobile foreign investment. Again, more difficult-to-duplicate national resources enable countries to command a greater share of FDI, with a consequent impact on employment and living standards. Finally, a number of research directions are outlined. The benefits of an interdisciplinary approach to research such as the integration of complementary perspectives, the addition of richness to debates and recommendations and the clarification of important constructs are highlighted. The emergence of the RBV as a theory of competitive advantage in international business is noted, as is its possible application in other aspects of international business research. However, future research needs to take account of a number of conceptual and empirical issues. The RBV has much in common with other disciplines such as evolutionary economics, and trends towards a general broadening of its theoretical base are evident in the literature. At the same time, this study indicates that some of its core propositions are in need of further validation, such as the relative importance of particular groups of resources and the process by which resources are converted into positions of advantage. Much work remains to be done, but the RBV represents a compelling approach to understanding performance heterogeneity.

2 Perspectives from international business

INTRODUCTION

This book focuses on the question of how firms attain a sustainable competitive advantage in a global environment. It is appropriate to begin by examining the relevant literature in the field of international business. This review has two main purposes. First, it is necessary to clarify exactly what is meant by the term 'global environment'. A great deal of ambiguity exists in the use of terminology, with the adjective 'global' being interpreted in different ways by different authors. These interpretations are examined and a definition of global environment is proposed. Second, it is necessary to take stock of what is already known about the nature of competition in a global environment to provide a foundation for further work. As noted in Chapter 1, the international business literature is a broad and diverse body of thought that has grown dramatically in the past three decades. A selective review of this literature is conducted, focusing on the question of competition between firms. The findings of this review are presented, an assessment of the current state of knowledge is made and some conclusions are drawn.

THE GLOBAL ENVIRONMENT

One of the features of the international business literature has been its tendency to use a variety of terms when describing organisations and the strategies/structures that they adopt. To some extent the terminology has evolved over the years as the nature of international business has changed, though most terms are still in common usage. In the 1960s, the labels 'multinational' and 'international' seemed to predominate when organisations operating across national borders were described. In 1969, Kindleberger (1969) distinguished between three types of firms, namely, national firms with international operations, multinational firms and international corporations. The use of the word global became popular in the 1980s, driven by the work of influential writers like Levitt (1983) and the much-publicised strategic choices of firms like Saatchi and Saatchi and British Airways. In the late 1980s, the popular work of Bartlett and Ghoshal (1987a, b; 1989) set out distinct explanations of international, multinational and global firms and proposed a new form – the trans-national. However, usage of the label 'transnational' can be found as far back as 1964 (Kircher 1964), where it was taken to mean firms exhibiting high levels of international ownership and control. Other variations on these descriptions have been used, including multidomestic, multi-national enterprise (MNE) and the diversified multinational company or DMNC (Doz and Prahalad 1991). And it appears that the search goes on, with a new description, the supranational, making an appearance at the 1996 Strategic Management Society annual conference (Hamel and Prahalad 1996).

Difficulties with the use of terminology are compounded by incon-sistent application, particularly with regard to the adjective 'global'. For most of the past two decades, discourse on concepts like globalisation and the global environment has been ubiquitous in business circles. Whether in the mass media, at academic and business conferences or in academic journals and the business press, discussion on these issues has tended to occupy some space and time. However, there appears to be little agreement on what exactly global means. For example, the 'global marketplace' has been used to describe the diverse international market for goods and services (Douglas and Craig 1989), while the term 'global participation' has been used to describe any kind of presence in a foreign market (Particelli 1990). A 'global strategy' has been taken by many to mean an emphasis on the integration of business decisions across national borders (Levitt 1983; Porter 1986a), yet others have used it interchangeably with strategies that do not stress cross-border integra-tion (Agthe 1990; Kim and Mauborgne 1988; Moss Kanter and Dretler 1998; Rabstejnek 1989). Another recent contribution suggested that some of the motives for global strategies include access to strategic markets, dodging trade barriers and availing of investment incentives (Aaker 1998). But the early internationalisation literature highlights these as typical of the motives underlying initial decisions to expand abroad (Aharoni 1966).

Clarification of exactly what is meant by the use of the adjective 'global' when referring to the business environment has therefore become essential. A review of the literature demonstrates that the global environment has three distinguishing features (see Figure 2.1). First, there is the growing worldwide scope of business, which is illustrated by some of the recent developments in world trade described in Chapter 1. Firms are sourcing supplies, locating production, searching for markets and encountering competitors in many diverse locations around the world (Drucker 1986; Gluck 1982; Peters 1990; Prahalad and Lieberthal 1998). Second, there is the increasing convergence of world markets,

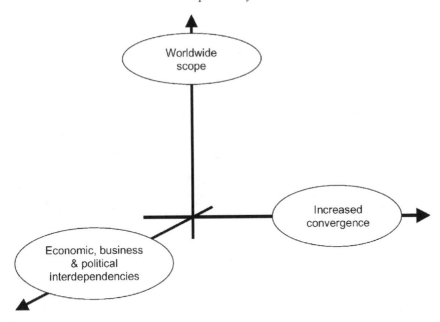

Figure 2.1 The characteristics of a global environment

resulting in greater levels of demand homogeneity and product availability (Levitt 1983; Lewis and Harris 1992; Ohmae 1985). And finally, there are the increasing economic, political and business interdependencies that exist across national boundaries (Dicken 1992; Kobrin 1991; Kogut 1985a; Lewis and Harris 1992).

In the literature, a variety of drivers have been identified that are playing a role in shaping the development of this global environment. These include variables which are exogenous to the firm, such as technology (Levitt 1983; Ohmae 1985; Porter 1986a, b; Quelch and Klein 1996), travel and communications (Doz 1987; Henzler and Rall 1986; Levitt 1983; Ohmae 1985), converging income levels (Gluck 1982; Ohmae 1985; Henzler and Rall 1986; Doz 1987; Jain 1989), trade agreements (Henzler and Rall 1986; Porter 1986a, b; Yip 1989), the dominance of the English language (Ohmae 1989a) as well as endogenous variables such as the need to amortize high R&D costs (Gluck 1982; Lewis and Harris 1992; Ohmae 1985; Porter 1986a, b), the pursuit of economies of scale (Doz 1987; Porter 1986a, b; Yip 1989), shortening product life cycles (Henzler and Rall 1986) and strategic intent (Doz 1987; Hamel and Prahalad 1989). Lewis and Harris (1992) argue that, despite the setbacks which may occur from time to time such as protectionism or stalled trade talks, there exists a virtuous cycle of globalisation where international innovation transfers lead to the increased convergence of economic bases and interdependencies, which in turn accelerates the rate at which further transfers can take place. Indicative of the development of a global environment is the speed with which innovations are transferred globally (Ohmae 1985; Peters 1990) and the difficulty that exists in trying to identify the countries of origin of products ranging from cars to breakfast cereals (Sera 1992). The growth of web-based businesses has led some commentators to go as far as talking about the end of geography, whereby products and competitors from any part of the world are simply a click away (Hamel and Sampler 1998).

In short, the global environment can be defined as any business arena exhibiting above average levels of geographic scope, market convergence and cross-national interdependencies. Globalisation is the *process* by which geographic scope, convergence and interdependence is increasing. It is an ongoing and, in the opinion of many authors, an unstoppable process (Dicken 1992; Levitt 1983; Lewis and Harris 1992; Naisbitt and Aburdene 1990). This raises the question of whether the environment being faced by companies today is different from that which existed when Hymer wrote his seminal work in 1960. Or, as some authors argue, are the effects of globalisation overstated and lacking sufficient empirical evidence (Doz 1987; Shoham 1995)? Here the common distinction in organisation theory between the general and the task environment (Bourgeois 1980a) becomes important. Bourgeois (1980a) defines the general environment as comprising broad social, political, economic, demographic and technological trends and there is little dispute in the literature that these forces are undergoing a process of globalisation. A task environment, which is influenced by developments in the general environment, is analogous to the notion of industry as used by economists and management writers. A review of the literature demonstrates the presence of a view that some task environments or industries have become more subject to global influences than others. Industries that have been identified as exhibiting strong global characteristics include, for example, aircraft (Doz 1987; Hout, Porter and Rudden 1982), chemicals (Chakravarthy and Perlmutter 1985; Levitt 1983) and semiconductors (Kobrin 1991; Porter 1986a).

Therefore, the global environment can be seen as a subset of the more general international business environment, the latter being a label favoured by many authors (Czinkota, Rivoli and Ronkainen 1989; Hibbert 1997; Rugman and Hodgetts 1995). This approach is similar to that which has been adopted for definitions of global firms and global marketing. For example, Bartlett and Ghoshal (1989) distinguish global firms from international, transnational and multinational firms. Global firms, in their view, are those that build global-scale facilities to produce standard products that are shipped worldwide under a tightly controlled central strategy. In the marketing literature, Jeannet and Hennessey (1998) distinguish global marketing from export marketing, international marketing, multinational marketing and pan-regional marketing. In their view, a global marketing strategy involves the creation of a single strategy, encompassing many markets and aimed at leveraging commonalties across markets. The pros and cons of this approach have been the subject of intense debate in the marketing literature (see for example, Boddewyn, Soehl and Picard 1986; Douglas and Wind 1987; Hampton and Buske 1987; Huszagh, Fox and Day 1986; Kashani 1989; Rau and Preble 1987; Robinson 1986). But while the global environment is a subset of the international business environment, it is also an important locus for academic research. If the trends documented in Chapter 1 continue and the predictions of many writers such as Lewis and Harris (1992) and Naisbitt and Aburdene (1990) come to pass, then a greater number of task environments will exhibit global characteristics. It is also a very challenging business environment, as shown below.

In the organisation theory literature, the concept of the environment has occupied a great deal of attention and there is an extensive body of work that seeks to define its important characteristics (Aldrich 1979; Dill 1958; Duncan 1972; Emery and Trist 1965; Lawrence and Lorsch 1967; Thompson 1967). Reviewing this literature, Bourgeois (1980a) identifies four salient aspects of an environment, namely, its level of complexity/heterogeneity (low–high), its rate of change (slow–rapid), its volatility (low–high) and managerial perceptions of its level of uncertainty (low–high). An analysis of the literature on the global environment leads to the conclusion that it is characterised by high levels of complexity/heterogeneity, rapid change, high volatility and high levels of perceived uncertainty. For example, Naisbitt (1994) posits that there exists a number of 'global paradoxes' such as (i) the bigger and more open the world economy becomes, the more small and middle-sized companies will dominate and (ii) as the global economy gets larger, its component parts get smaller. The view that such paradoxes exist reflects the heterogeneity and complexity of the global environment. The pace of change has been stressed by many writers (Ohmae 1985; Peters 1990), and managers have been urged to respond quickly or face dire consequences. And the evidence of a lack of agreement concerning the appropriate organisational responses, which is highlighted in the following section, is indicative of a great deal of uncertainty. As such, the global environment represents a demanding arena in which to attain a sustainable competitive advantage. The aim of this book is to attempt to contribute to our understanding of how firms succeed in doing so and it is appropriate that our analysis should begin by taking stock of what is already known. This is the focus of the next section.

PERSPECTIVES ON COMPETITION IN THE INTERNATIONAL BUSINESS LITERATURE

In Chapter 1, it was noted that there are two dominant traditions in the international business literature, namely, those rooted in economics and those rooted in management theory. Both have different origins and different foci and both provide insights into the nature of competition. In this section, the chronological development of these two strands of literature is outlined and critiqued separately. Many of the contributions reviewed pre-date the emergence of global environments. However, this does not mean that the insights provided by the early literature are irrelevant in that context. Other contributions would not claim to address the kind of environment described above and do not use the language of global competition, but equally, this does not mean that the insights provided by this literature are invalid either. Therefore, to avoid confusion throughout this section, the term 'international competition' is used to describe any form of competition between firms in different countries. Where the term 'global competition' is used, it refers to the subset of competition in a global environment. Similarly, the economic agent responsible for international competition is most frequently described as the multinational company (MNC) and this label is used in a general sense throughout the chapter, though it is recognised that, in the work of some authors, the MNC is afforded a very specific meaning. The section concludes by noting points of similarity between the economic and managerial traditions and an assessment of the current state of knowledge is made.

The economic perspective on international competition

The economic paradigm of international business has a long and illustrious history. A wide range of reviews of this literature are available (see, for example, Buckley 1983; Calvet 1981; Dunning 1993a; Hennart 1982; Kogut 1989; Robock and Simmonds 1983; Robinson 1981, to name but a few). Indeed, what Casson (1987) describes as 'second generation literature' reviewing the reviewers is also available (for example, Kay 1983). The development of the economic paradigm has been characterised by a shifting of units of analysis and by differing theoretical perspectives. Early contributions were concerned with explaining trade patterns and capital flows using the country as the unit of analysis. The late 1950s and 1960s saw a shift of focus to the economic agent responsible for trade and capital flows, namely, the multinational company (MNC). This literature sought to explain the existence of the MNC and spawned a range of theoretical perspectives that continues to deal with this fundamental question. In the mid 1970s, Buckley and Casson (1976) were able to claim that there was still no established theory of the MNC. By the 1990s, Buckley (1990) suggested that such a core theory now existed, though it was not without its problems. The intellectual evolution of the economic perspective is summarised in Table 2.1 and subsequent paragraphs will elaborate on the key stages in its development.

Table 2.1 Evolution of the economic perspective on international competition

Perspective	Key insights	Major contributors
Trade theory (location theory)	Absolute and comparative advantage, factor endowment theory	Heckscher (1919), Ohlin (1933), Ricardo (1817), Rybczynski (1955), Samuelson (1948), Smith (1776)
An industrial organisation perspective (market imperfections theory)	Factor and product markets are imperfect, MNCs possess firm-specific advantages, FDI originates in oligopolistic industries. FDI may be horizontal, vertical or both and may be defensive	Caves (1971; 1974), Graham (1978), Hymer (1960), Kindleberger (1969), Knickerbocker (1973)
A transactions cost perspective (internalisation theory)	Intermediate product markets are imperfect and characterised by transaction costs. Firms may internalise these imperfect markets. Internalisation across borders gives rise to MNCs	Brown (1976), Buckley (1988), Buckley and Casson (1976), Casson (1979; 1985; 1987; 1991), Hennart (1982), Horaguchi and Toyne (1990), Hymer (1968), McManus (1972), Rugman (1981; 1986), Teece (1981; 1986a)
The eclectic paradigm	Multinational production is explained by a combination of ownership advantages, internalisation advantages and location-specific advantages	Dunning (1977; 1981; 1988a, b)

Trade theory

Though recent developments in the scope and complexity of international business have rendered many of its fundamental assumptions impractical, classical trade theory provides a good starting point from which to examine the evolution of the economic paradigm. With the country as the unit of analysis, trade theory explains the existence of international trade in terms of absolute and comparative advantages. It posits that countries focus on the production and trade of goods where absolute or comparative cost advantages are held. The Heckscher–Ohlin theory of factor endowments (Hecksher 1919; Ohlin 1933) extended this concept by holding that a country has a comparative advantage in the commodity that uses extensively the country's abundant factor. Trade theory relies on a series of assumptions, including: (i) countries have perfect goods and factor markets; (ii) the factors of production, namely, labour and capital, are locationally immobile; (iii) production functions are internationally identical; (iv) all enterprises are price takers operating under conditions of atomistic competition; and (v) there are no barriers to trade and no transactions costs (Dunning 1988a; Rugman 1981). With the country as its unit of analysis, trade theory has little to say, explicitly, about inter-firm competition. By implication, however, it does suggest that the superiority of a firm in one country over those in another is related to the country-specific resources available to the firm, an issue which has recently been revisited with some interest (Dunning 1993b; Porter 1990). This implies that the competitive advantage of firms is related to the comparative advantages of their country of origin.

The industrial organisation perspective (market imperfections theory)

Subsequent work by economists in the Bain/Mason industrial organisation (IO) tradition (Bain 1968; Mason 1939) moved the focus from the macro-level of the country to the micro-level of the firm and switched attention from trade patterns to foreign direct investment (FDI) patterns. Hymer (1960) had noted that foreign investment tended to be concentrated in specific industries worldwide rather than in specific countries, suggesting that these capital flows could not be explained by the search for the best interest rates as contended by the factor endowment hypothesis. Hymer proposed that FDI was driven by a desire to counter competition in foreign markets and to appropriate fully the returns deriving from advantages developed domestically (Hymer 1960). Firms operating in foreign markets faced disadvantages *vis à vis* local competitors, including the latter's greater familiarity with local conditions, political and exchange risks, and the travel and communication costs incurred in conducting foreign business (Caves 1971; Hymer 1960). To overcome these disadvantages, it was argued that firms must possess idiosyncratic advantages that generate economic returns over and above their opportunity costs when used in foreign markets (Graham 1978). These advantages may derive from imperfections in goods markets (e.g. product differentiation, seller concentration), factor markets (proprietary technology, managerial skills) and government-imposed restrictions (tariffs) (Kindleberger 1969). Caves (1971) outlined how imperfections in the market for goods such as product differentiation and seller concentration helped to explain horizontal and vertical foreign direct investment. Firms that successfully develop differentiated products possess specific marketing capabilities which can be transferred to foreign markets at little or no cost and enable the appropriation of returns more effectively than via the market mechanism. Seller concentration is a key driver of backward vertical foreign direct investment because of the need to remove uncertainty surrounding important factor inputs and because of the possibility to control key sources of supply creating a barrier to entry for new firms. Further drivers of FDI were also identified, including defensive activity (Graham 1978; Knickerbocker 1973) and mimetic activity or 'follow the leader' reasons (Kindleberger 1969).

In terms of the issue of international competition, the principal focus of the Bain/Mason IO perspective has been on the rivalry between the multinational firm and firms located in host countries. It provides a view on how the former overcomes the inherent disadvantages of doing business abroad, which is based on the possession of idiosyncratic advantages. The unequal distribution of advantages between firms in different countries is itself a sufficient condition for foreign direct investment (Hymer 1960). The particular firm-specific advantages can include knowledge, information or techniques (Caves 1971), technological expertise or entrepreneurial skills (Graham 1978), ownership of a brand name, possession of special marketing skills, patented technology, favourable access to sources of finance, team-specific managerial skills, plant economies of scale and economies of vertical integration (Kindleberger 1969). Aside from these unique firm-specific advantages, Caves (1971) points out that a further advantage of the multinational company is its ability to buy factors of production either in the home or host country, allowing it the opportunity to trade at two different sets of factor prices which harks back to the insights provided by trade theory.

Achieving superior returns from these advantages is deemed to be a function of the possession of monopoly power in the firm's home country and the extension of this power into foreign markets. Hymer notes that the kinds of abilities which lead to international operations will most often be possessed only by a few firms (Hymer 1960). He argues that if many firms possess the ability, then it is probably not too difficult to acquire even for local firms which, given that they have special advantages of their own because of their nationality, will be likely to predominate. This is supported by Caves (1971), who suggests that firms which invest abroad will be relatively large, will face relatively few competitors at home and will be in a better position than domestic rivals to overcome barriers to entry. This last point is supported by empirical research (see Gorecki 1976; Shapiro 1983). Firms transfer these advantages to foreign markets via direct investment rather than the market mechanism primarily to protect their monopoly power (Teece 1981), though it may also be due, in some cases, to the unique characteristics of the advantage (Caves 1971).

The transaction cost perspective (internalisation theory)

Transaction cost analysis is a branch of economics that has developed from the seminal work of Coase (1937) and its earliest applications in the field of international business are to be found in McManus (1972) and Buckley and Casson (1976). Similar to industrial organisation theorists, these writers also used empirical anomalies in foreign direct investment patterns as a rationale for their approach. An extensive review of FDI by Buckley and Casson (1976) found that (i) capital flows rejected the factor endowment hypothesis, (ii) most multinationals were either horizontally or vertically diversified, (iii) multinationality was a characteristic of concentrated industries and (iv) that it tended to be greater the larger the firm, all of which had previously been observed by Bain/Mason IO theorists. Similarly, using empirical data on foreign investment in Canada, McManus (1972) noted substantial variation in the levels of inward FDI among industries and also that foreign subsidiaries operating in Canada tended to be industry leaders in terms of productivity and size. However, transaction cost theorists provided a different explanation for these patterns and also argued that an additional finding, namely, that multinationality tended to be greater in industries characterised by high research and skill intensity, was inadequately explained by conventional Bain/Mason IO models (Buckley and Casson 1976). Transaction cost theorists argue that the existence of the multinational firm can be easily explained within the conventional transaction cost framework. This framework adopts a systems approach, viewing businesses as a range of activities, including R&D, production, marketing, the training of labour, the building of a management team etc. All these activities are inter-dependent and connected by flows of intermediate products. Because markets for these intermediate products are imperfect, there is an incentive to bypass them by creating internal markets. Internalisation carries certain costs such as coordination and communication costs; hence the optimum scale of the firm is where the costs and benefits of further internalisation are equalised (Coase 1937). The transaction cost perspective operates just as easily for an inter-county or inter-state firm, implying that the multinational firm is simply a special case of the domestic multi-plant firm (Buckley and Casson 1976; Casson 1991; McManus 1972).

In addition, the transaction cost framework provides alternative explanations for vertical and horizontal foreign direct investment. Internalisation of tangible intermediate products in a multi-stage production process gives rise to a vertically integrated producer. Vertical integration takes place across nations due to the failure of intermediate product markets for reasons such as uncertainty regarding continuity of supply. This is particularly accentuated when the trading relationship requires the development of transaction-specific assets giving rise to high switching costs (Teece 1986a). The level of integration is determined by the interplay of savings in production costs against transportation costs incurred, or industrial policy restrictions such as requirements for subcontracting. When the intermediate product is supplied from a less developed country where the necessary infrastructures to support market processes are absent or poorly developed, significant efficiency gains can accrue (Teece 1981). Internalisation of intangible flows of know-how gives rise to a horizontally integrated producer (Buckley and Casson 1976; Teece 1981). Transaction costs in the market for know-how means that it is more efficiently transferred through a governance structure than through the market (Teece 1986a). Again, the extent of horizontal integration will be determined by the interplay of benefits accruing from the exploitation or collection of know-how (both motivations empirically established by McClain 1983) versus coordination and communication costs (Buckley and Casson 1976; Teece 1981). Both vertical and horizontal integration are possible within the same firm (Teece 1981) and firms will internalise to achieve efficiency gains unattainable in the market (McManus 1972; Teece 1981).

In terms of the issue of international competition, the transaction cost perspective emphasises efficiency over market power. It identifies a number of sources of the transaction costs faced by multinational firms, including those that are (i) policy-related (locational imperfections), such as tariffs, quotas, currency restrictions, subsidies and tax incentives (Rugman 1981), (ii) factor-related, such as in the market for managerial and technical know-how (Johnson 1970; Magee 1977) and (iii) those that are transaction-related, including search costs (Rugman 1981; Teece 1986a), the costs of defining the obligations of the parties or the absence of futures markets and contract enforcement (Buckley and Casson 1976; Rugman 1981), bilateral concentration of market power (Buckley and Casson 1976) and buyer uncertainty and imperfect information (Buckley and Casson 1976; Teece 1986a). Though the focus of this perspective is primarily on explaining why multinational firms exist, its implications for competition are that efficiency-derived advantages can be gained by minimising transaction costs. For example, the location of activities is driven by least-cost considerations (Buckley 1988) and is determined mainly by an interplay of comparative advantage, barriers to trade and regional incentives to internalise which may make it optimal to locate different stages of production in different nations (Buckley and Casson 1976).

The eclectic paradigm

A further influential contribution is Dunning's 'eclectic paradigm of international production' (1977; 1988a, b). The main contention of the eclectic paradigm is that it is necessary to take account of three types of advantages, namely ownership advantages, internalisation advantages and locational advantages in order to fully explain international production patterns (Dunning 1977). In its original form (Dunning 1997), the eclectic paradigm emphasised firm-specific or ownership advantages in a similar fashion to economists in the Bain/Mason tradition. The capability of a home country's enterprise to supply either a foreign or domestic market from a foreign production base was considered to be dependent on the possession of certain resource endowments not available to or utilized by another country's enterprises. These ownership advantages could be of three kinds. First are those that also provide a domestic advantage, such as size (economies of scale), monopoly power (access to markets or raw materials) or resource capability and usage (exclusive possession of intangible assets such as patents, trademarks, management skills etc.). Second are those that a branch plant in a home country has over a *de novo* entrant and reflect access to parental advantages. Third, there are the advantages arising from multinationality *per se*, such as the more and the greater the differences between the economic environments in which the enterprise operates, the better placed it is to take advantage of different factor endowments and market situations. Internalisation is pursued either to fully exploit the advantages or avoid the disadvantages of the market and may give rise to either vertical or horizontal integration. In general terms, Dunning (1977) contends that some trade will take place where only location advantages exist, such as trade between an industrialised and a non-industrialised nation. Trade between industrialised nations is based more on ownership advantages, presupposing that these are combined with home- or host-country locational advantages. Where they are combined with host-country locational advantage, foreign production takes place. Thus, the eclectic paradigm rests on the possession of unique advantages, the internalisation of those advantages and their use in conjunction with immobile locational advantages in home or host countries.

In this way, the eclectic paradigm provides an over-arching view of international competition, taking account not only of rivalry in host countries but also the reciprocal effects of competition on source countries. It re-affirms the importance of firm-specific or ownership advantages as a key motivation for decisions to expand internationally as well as being a potential source of superior returns in foreign markets, which was initially identified by the Bain/Mason IO perspective. It also concurs with transaction cost theorists on the merits of internalisation for the protection of these unique advantages and the potential for efficiency gains through the reduction of transaction costs. But it also adopts the external, macro-perspective of trade theory to give attention to the variable factor endowments of home and host nations.

Concluding comments on the economic paradigm

The evolution of the economic paradigm has been nothing if not controversial. On the one hand there is the conflict between economists of the Bain/Mason industrial organisation and transaction cost traditions and on the other there are the competing claims for a general theory of the

MNC. In terms of the former, Buckley and Casson (1976) argue that one of the weaknesses of the Bain/Mason IO perspective is its idea that possession of an intangible asset is taken as given and fails to account for the cost of acquisition of these advantages, thus overstating the firm's profitability and not providing an explanation of why firms invest in these advantages. Firm-specific advantage is therefore viewed as a short-run and static phenomenon as it is only in the short run that endowments of propriety knowledge are fixed (Buckley 1983). Furthermore, Buckley (1983) questions the fundamental IO view that a local firm possesses inherent advantages over the MNC, particularly when the latter is an experienced international competitor. However, reacting to the view that internalisation represents a new theory of the MNC, Kindleberger finds all its key concepts such as appropriability, transaction costs and coordination within the firm rather than the market to be either implicit or explicit in the Hymer/Kindleberger framework (Kindleberger 1984).

Competing claims of a general theory have been made by the eclectic paradigm and internalisation theory. The selection of the term 'eclectic' implies an attempt to develop a general theory, as does its incorporation of perspectives from industrial organisation, transactions cost and location theory. However, transactions cost theorists claim that internalisation theory alone is sufficient to explain FDI (Rugman 1981) and that the separation of ownership and internalisation advantages leads to double counting (Buckley 1988; Itaki 1991). However, recent research has suggested that the electic paradigm may be a more powerful predictor of international market entry mode than the transactions cost approach (Brouthers, Brouthers and Werner 1999). The controversy is likely to continue but may be best summarised by McClain (1983), who argues that all the perspectives concur that firms possess advantages which overcome the costs of operating in a foreign environment, that the market for these advantages is imperfect, providing a motivation for internalisation and that 'one cannot blame workers in our knowledge-based industry for trying to establish a modicum of product differentiation' (McClain 1983: 296).

In conclusion, it can be argued that the question of international competition has not always been the central concern of the economic paradigm. However, its extensive and diverse literature provides a great deal of insight, either explicitly or implicitly, into this question. For example, its reviews of foreign direct investment patterns demonstrate that successful international competitors are likely to be few in any given industry, are likely to be relatively large and likely to possess and extend monopoly powers into foreign markets. It focuses attention on the possession of firm-specific advantages as a prerequisite for competing effectively abroad and on the relationship between these advantages and the firm's country of origin. Furthermore, it demonstrates that effective exploitation of advantages is related to the firm's choice of governance mechanism. However, the economic paradigm represents only half the picture. Equally influential have been a diverse range of contributions from management theorists, which are reviewed in the next section.

The management perspective on international competition

The earliest management perspectives on the question of international competition appeared during the 1960s. Some of these initial contributions had a distinctly economic flavour. For example, Vernon's (1966) international product life cycle thesis was founded on the simple dynamic of the changing equilibria of demand and supply. He proposed that the location of production varied with the stage of the product's life cycle. Uncertainty at the early stages of development required the location of production close to the market, with the imperative for flexibility outweighing the cost considerations. As the product matured, production could be moved to progressively lower-cost countries and could ultimately result in re-imports from these countries, challenging the Heckscher–Ohlin theorem by suggesting that underdeveloped countries could become the production site for high-income products.

However, the management perspective began to distinguish itself through an increasing emphasis on the behavioural aspects of international competition. For example, Perlmutter's EPRG framework proposed four attitude types – ethnocentrism, polycentrism, regiocentrism and geocentricism – that influenced the goals, philosophies and involvement of firms in foreign markets (Perlmutter 1969). Evidence of these differing managerial philosophies has subsequently been found to affect strategic planning processes (Chakravarthy and Perlmutter 1985), marketing activity (Jain 1989) and strategic activity (Taggart 1998). Behaviouralism was also central to Aharoni's (1966) typology of *initiating forces* underlying expansion into foreign markets. He identified a range of forces, including internal drivers such as the motivation of a senior executive and external drivers such as market opportunity, which he considered critical to the decision to internationalise. Furthermore, he developed a framework of the stages and influences in the decision-making process which determined acceptance or rejection of foreign investment proposals (Aharoni 1966) and which subsequently spawned a body of literature examining a 'stages model' of international involvement (Johanson and Wiedersheim-Paul 1975; Johanson and Vahlne 1977; Welch and Luostarinen 1988).

In contrast to the economic paradigm, the management perspective does not demonstrate clear chronological stages in its development. A number of themes were in evidence in the literature appearing in the 1960s and these have developed and evolved over time as the nature of international business has changed. Therefore, the evolution of management thought is reviewed on a thematic basis (see Table 2.2). Strategic

Table 2.2 Evolution of the management perspective on international competition

Decade	Business strategy	Organisational structure	Managerial process
1960s	Chandler (1962), Fayerweather (1969)	Chandler (1962), Fouraker and Stopford (1968), Kircher (1964)	Perlmutter (1969)
1970s	Prahalad (1975)	Stopford and Wells (1972), Wells (1972)	Doz (1976), Heenan and Perlmutter (1979), Lorange (1976), Prahalad (1975; 1976)
1980s	Bartlett and Ghoshal (1987a, b; 1989), Doz (1980; 1987), Ghoshal (1987), Kogut (1985a, b), Levitt (1983), Morrison and Roth (1989), Ohmae (1985; 1989a, b), Porter (1986a, b), Prahalad and Doz (1987), Wortzel (1991)	Bartlett (1986), Bartlett and Ghoshal (1987a, b; 1989), Daniels, Pitts and Tretter (1984; 1985), Egelhoff (1982; 1988a, b), Hamel and Prahalad (1983), Lemak and Bracker (1988)	Baliga and Jaeger (1984), Bartlett (1983; 1986), Bartlett and Ghoshal (1987a, b; 1989), Doz (1980; 1986), Doz and Prahalad (1981; 1984), Dymsza (1984b), Hedlund (1986), Lorange (1989), Prahalad and Doz (1987)
1990s	Bartlett and Ghoshal (1992), Birkinshaw, Morrison and Hulland (1995), Carpano, Chrisman and Roth (1994), Collis (1991), Hagigi, Manzon and Mascarenhas (1999), Hu (1995), Johansson and Yip (1994), Johnson (1995), Luo (1999), Morrison and Roth (1992; 1993), Palich and Gomez-Mejia (1999), Prahalad and Lieberthal (1998), Rennie (1993), Sundaram and Black (1992), Yip (1992), Yip, Johansson and Roos (1997)	Bartlett and Ghoshal (1990), Birkinshaw and Morrison (1995), Ghoshal and Bartlett (1990), Ghoshal and Nohria (1993), Hu (1992), Leong and Tan (1993), Malnight (1996), Morrison and Roth (1993), Nohria and Ghoshal (1997), Padmanabhan and Cho (1999), Sundaram and Black (1992)	DeNero (1990), Doz and Prahalad (1991), Ensign (1999), Ghoshal and Nohria (1993), Gupta and Govindarajan (1991; 2000), Hamilton and Kashlak (1999), Herbert (1999), Kostova (1999), Malnight (1995), Martinez and Jarillo (1991), Muralidharan and Hamilton (1999), Nobel and Birkinshaw (1998), Rosenzweig and Singh (1991), Roth, Schweiger and Morrison (1991), Sullivan (1992); Sundaram and Black (1992), Theuerkauf (1991)

management literature, generally, identifies three core themes in its analysis of organisations, namely the issues of strategy, structure and managerial processes (Galbraith and Nathanson 1978; Miles and Snow 1978). In line with this scheme, the management perspective on international competition is reviewed under these three broad headings in the following paragraphs.

International business strategy

International business strategy was initially framed in terms of balancing the conflicting demands of unification and fragmentation (Fayerweather 1969) and these conflicting pulls have appeared in various guises right up the global/local debate of today (Naisbitt 2000; Oliver 2000; Sanchez 1998). Fayerweather (1969) proposed that the pressure for fragmentation was driven by the unique combinations of economic, cultural, nationalistic and other characteristics found in different markets while firms sought to remain unified to retain economies and synergies. These pressures were revisited in the 1970s, labelled as the conflict between integration and responsiveness (Prahalad 1975) and as the conflict between the economic and political imperatives (Doz 1980). Responsiveness to national differences in tastes, industry structures, distribution systems and government regulations (the political imperative) created a pull for market-to-market differentiation while efficiencies and cost savings (the economic imperative) represented a pull towards integration. More recently, the integration/responsiveness (IR) framework was extended to show how this conflict exists at increasingly micro-levels of analysis, from the industry to the firm to particular functions and to tasks (Ghoshal 1987). Several normative implications are proposed. Industries may be characterised by an inherent pull towards integration or responsiveness, implying that successful strategies require a fit with industry determinants. On the other hand, firms may retain the strategic choice to pursue integration or responsiveness and the IR framework demonstrates how such strategies can be operationalised through functions and tasks.

The decade of the 1980s was marked by a distinct shift in emphasis towards the integration end of the IR spectrum. It was during this period that the term 'global' became popular and was used initially to describe how consumer markets in different countries were becoming increasingly homogeneous, driven by technological advances and greater levels of communication and travel (Levitt 1983). It was suggested that firms should respond to this development by seeking to maximise the possibilities for functional integration across countries (Gluck 1982; Levitt 1983; Ohmae 1985). Firms were advised to expand their worldwide scope, to locate elements of the value chain wherever it was most efficient to do so and to design products in a way that appealed to the maximum number of customers throughout the world (Gluck 1982). The benefits accruing from the standardisation of products and practices were asserted to be economies of scale in production, distribution, marketing and management, allowing the firm to offer quality products at low prices. Other authors were more circumspect and adopted a Bain/Mason industrial organisation perspective, suggesting that the appropriate level of integration is related to the globalisation potential of the industry (Henzler and Rall 1986; Hout, Porter and Rudden 1982; Malnight 1996; Porter 1986a, b; Yip 1989; Yip and Coundouriotis 1991). Initially this idea was framed in terms of a frequently used dichotomy between the global and the multidomestic firm (Hout, Porter and Rudden 1982), with the former emphasising integration and the latter emphasising responsiveness, depending on the industry context. Subsequent contributions suggested a typology of strategic types based around 2 × 2 matrices using the integration/responsiveness dimensions as the discriminating variables (Henzler and Rall 1986; Porter 1986a, b; Yip 1989). These typologies implied that an integrated or global business strategy was only possible in certain industries. Such a strategy called for a concentrated configuration of value chain activities in the most efficient world locations or a high level of coordination between activities or both (Porter 1986a, b). Additional strategy levers such as market participation and competitive moves could be used to facilitate integration (Yip 1989), though some authors did concede the possible necessity for occasional local adaptation (Henzler and Rall 1986). In short, a number of descriptions of what constituted a global business strategy were proposed during the 1980s, which while exhibiting some differences, emphasised the importance of integration across countries. These descriptions of a *global* strategy are summarised in Table 2.3.

Support for the integration perspective was not widespread, however. At a conceptual level, some authors had a very different view of the world that was rooted in the differences rather than the similarities across borders (Doz 1980; Doz, Bartlett and Prahalad 1981; Doz and Prahalad 1980; Moss Kanter and Dretler 1998; Palich and Gomez-Mejia 1999; Naisbitt 2000). For example, the uneven distribution of comparative advantages worldwide created arbitrage opportunities for firms that operated in multiple countries (Kogut 1983, 1984, 1985a, b; Rangan 1998). It is proposed that substantial gains could accrue to a firm that is in a position to engage in production shifting, tax minimisation and financial market and information arbitrage in response to international comparative dynamics. Flexibility in an uncertain environment is also central to the arguments of Feiger (1988), who, in addition to production shifting and transfer pricing, proposes diversifying sourcing to match with sales in order to minimise foreign currency risks. However, recent research by Rangan (1998) has found that the ability of multinationals to operate flexibly is constrained by past actions. Still another approach

Table 2.3 Perspectives on global business strategy

Gluck	1982	Companies must become international, configuring their value chain wherever it is most efficient to do so and designing products in ways that appeal to the maximum number of customers in a world industry
Hout, Porter and Rudden	1982	Subsidiaries of companies in different parts of the world are closely integrated to compete against worldwide competitors in distinct industries or industry segments, which gives rise to benefits of either reduced unit costs or preemptive moves into new markets
Levitt	1983	Companies should seek to standardise products and practices in order to attain the benefits of economies of scale in production, distribution, marketing and management to be in a position to offer quality products at the lowest price (HPV and LDC)
Ohmae	1985	Because the needs of consumer segments are becoming homogeneous throughout the Triad, it is essential that companies simultaneously launch new products in all three areas
Henzler and Rall	1986	Using an *integration* strategy, the company builds an integrated, worldwide value-added chain, exploiting economies of scale in R&D and production, but tailoring the downstream elements to local conditions to compete on HPV or LDC
Porter	1986a, b	A company attempts to achieve a position of global cost leadership or differentiation either through a concentrated configuration of value chain activities, or coordination among dispersed value chain activities, or both
Yip, Yip and Coundouriotis	1989, 1991	A process of worldwide integration where the firm manipulates five global strategy levers, namely, market participation, global products and services, location of value added activities, global marketing and global competitive moves to maximise integration and efficiency

focused on product flexibility through a broad product portfolio, allowing for economies of scope in investments in technology and distribution channels (Hamel and Prahalad 1985). Furthermore, the integration hypothesis was being tested in a significant volume of empirical work with inconclusive results. For example, at the industry level, a longitudinal study of the white goods sector in Europe discovered a trend towards market fragmentation rather than standardisation, favouring responsive strategies (Baden-Fuller and Stopford 1991), though more recent research in this industry suggests that global strategies are becoming increasingly appropriate (Segal-Horn, Asch and Suneja 1998). Other research sought to determine the extent of the association between global integration and firm performance measured in financial terms. Despite the fact that much of this research was conducted in what were specified as global industries (i.e. industries favouring integration), the findings failed to provide convincing evidence of an associative link (Morrison and Roth 1992; Morrison, Ricks and Roth 1991; Roth 1992; Roth and Morrison 1990; Roth, Schweiger and Morrison 1991). Associations between standardisation/integration and performance were also tested at the marketing functional level and, here also, strong evidence of a causal relationship was missing (Samiee and Roth 1992; Szymanski, Bharadwaj and Varadarajan 1993).

One response to the uncertainty surrounding what was the appropriate strategic response to environmental change which began to emerge towards the late 1980s was the view that the global/local dichotomy was too simplistic to capture the full complexities of international business strategy (Ghoshal 1987). Strategic decisions, it was felt, required consideration of a variety of factors. For example, Ghoshal (1987) proposed that strategy could be considered in terms of the interplay of the strategic objectives of (i) achieving efficiency, (ii) managing risks and (iii) innovation, learning and adaptation with potential sources of competitive advantage deriving from national differences, scale economies and scope economies. Some writers who had previously advocated a global approach to strategy were beginning to emphasise the importance of local dimensions and to recommend 'insiderisation' (Ohmae 1989a, b) while the rhetoric of the literature aimed at practitioners became one of 'think global, act local' (*Fortune* 1989; Koepfler 1989; Theurerkauf, Ernst and Mahini 1993). These views focused interest on a possible multi-dimensional approach to international business strategy, in line with a trend away from unidimensional approaches in the strategy literature generally (Gilbert and Strebel 1989). A new normative approach to managing firms, termed the 'transnational solution', was proposed, advocating that management seek to combine and balance global integration, market responsiveness and an ability to maximise learning opportunities (Bartlett and Ghoshal 1987a, b; 1989; 1992; Lipparini and Fratocchi 1999; Lorenz 1989; Sullivan and Bauerschmidt 1991). Firms pursuing a 'transnational strategy' were viewed as operating in a highly inter-dependent manner, seeking to maximise efficiencies and learning while at the same time remaining sufficiently flexible to respond to local conditions and opportunities. Over the years, while some literature acknowledges that firms exhibit the traits of transnationals (Lorenz 1989; Malnight 1996; Taylor 1991), empirical research suggests that the transnational remains an ideal type (Leong and Tan 1993), though one recent study conducted in China concludes that the transnational outperforms the other strategic types (Luo 1999).

In summary, the distinguishing feature of strategy literature has been its recognition of the nature of the environment in which firms operate. It has recognised how the competitive environment has been changing and has proposed the emergence of a global environment. It has high-lighted that multinational firms face a difficult challenge in trying to reconcile the conflicting pressures for organisational integration and efficiency with the need for local autonomy and responsiveness to host-country conditions. This dilemma has also been to the fore of the organisation structure and managerial process literature, which has been closely related to the strategy discourse as it has developed.

International organisational structure and managerial processes

The literature on international organisational structure has built on the foundation of the seminal work of Chandler (1962), which emphasised the need for congruence between structure and strategy. An extensive analysis of how the structure of the multinational enterprise evolves with its strategy was proposed by Stopford and Wells (1972) and Wells (1972). This research, based on a study of 187 large, US MNCs, proposed that four forms of organisation structure could be observed, depending on the relative mix of foreign product diversity and the percentage of overall sales obtained abroad. Firms with relatively low levels of both foreign product diversity and foreign sales were characterised by an international division structure. As foreign product diversity increased, firms moved to worldwide product divisions while increases in the percentage of foreign sales tended to be accompanied by area division structures. Where both foreign product diversity and foreign product sales were high, firms organised on the basis of either matrix or mixed structures of product and area divisions. Empirical support for these relationships was found in subsequent studies (Daniels, Pitts and Tretter 1984; Franko 1976).

In the 1980s, the growth of foreign manufacturing and the arguments for greater integration in international business strategy prompted further study of organisational structures. International divisional structures and area divisions were typically associated with autonomy and flexibility and suited to locally responsive strategies while worldwide product divisions were seen as providing central coordination, maximising economies of scale and suited to integrated strategies. Firms structured on the basis of area divisions tended to have higher levels of foreign manufacturing than firms with worldwide product structures (Egelhoff 1988a). Egelhoff's (1988a) study, spanning large MNCs in both Europe and the US, found only partial support for the contention by Stopford and Wells (1972) that MNCs with area division structures exhibit a higher percentage of foreign sales than those with product division structures. He proposed extending the original Stopford and Wells model to incorporate foreign manufacturing as a third discriminating variable in the measurement of MNC structures (Egelhoff 1988a).

Over one-third of the firms in the Egelhoff study had some form of matrix or mixed structure and the continuing growth of complex organisations (Vernon 1977) represented a further area of study. The proponents of the transnational solution (Bartlett 1986; Bartlett and Ghoshal 1989) or differentiated network (Nohria and Ghoshal 1997) suggested moving beyond the matrix structure to thinking instead of the firm as an interorganisational network (Ghoshal and Bartlett 1990). The distinguishing features of the transnational structure are that (i) it builds and legitimises multiple, diverse internal perspectives, (ii) its physical assets and management capabilities are distributed internationally but are interdependent and (iii) it requires a robust and flexible internal integrative process (Bartlett 1986). The transnational shares many of the structural traits of Hedlund's (1986) heterarchy. The heterarchical MNC has many centres, which have different roles, are involved in strategy formulation as well as implementation, and are integrated by normative rather than coercive control, where information about the whole is contained in each part and where coalitions with other firms are frequent (Hedlund 1986).

Over the past two decades there has been increasing concern that the focus of attention on the formal structure of the firm may be misplaced (Bartlett 1983; Bartlett and Ghoshal 1990; Beer and Davis 1976; Ghoshal and Nohria 1993). For example, using the case of a leading US multinational, Beer and Davis (1976) highlighted the failure of major structural changes implemented through inappropriate processes and superimposed on unresolved power and inter-group conflict. A study of ten large, diverse and successful MNCs found that each had retained the simple structure of the international division and had focused on improving managerial processes rather than re-organising in response to continued growth (Bartlett 1983), suggesting that seeking the correct formal structure may not be a recipe for success. A significant body of thought has emerged since on the process of managing large MNCs (see Doz and Prahalad 1991 for a review). As thinking regarding the MNC evolved from that of an organisation with autonomous subsidiaries to a more globally integrated organisation, it has been accompanied by changing perspectives on the key processes of planning, coordination and control (Bartlett, Doz and Hedlund 1990).

Initially, the planning problem was framed in terms of the strategic need of the MNC to reconcile the conflicting pressures of adaptation and integration (Lorange 1976). This kind of approach typically led to the development of typologies of planning systems that match the organisational structure (Lorange 1976) or strategic predisposition (Chakravarthy and Perlmutter 1985) of the MNC. Thus, for example, the planning system of an MNC with a worldwide product structure will emphasise integration, and planning costs will be borne largely by the worldwide business division (Lorange 1976). Likewise, strategic predispositions towards integration or responsiveness underlie the four types of planning systems, namely, top–down planning, bottom–up planning, portfolio planning and dual structure planning proposed by Chakravarthy and Lorange (1984). Planning models in the 1980s sought to account for both the trend towards greater integration (Lorange 1989) and concern with managing greater complexity (Bettis and Hall 1981; Naylor 1985; Wind and Douglas 1981). Some empirical evidence also emerged which argued that strategic planning systems may be a source of competitive advantage for MNCs (Coates 1989), though this is likely to be influenced by the cultural divergence between headquarters and subsidiaries (Herbert 1999).

The early literature on coordination and control was also framed in terms of the need to reconcile the conflicting demands for integration and responsiveness (Doz 1980; Doz, Bartlett and Prahalad 1981). The need to shift emphasis from integration to responsiveness and vice versa, over time, and when dealing with different aspects of the organisation, required what Doz (1980) called an administrative coordination strategy. His research of twelve European MNCs found that functional and administrative managers, who generally do not have specific integration/responsiveness biases, were used as a means to achieve coordination between national and product managers, though this process did increase the risks of strategic paralysis, fragmentation and bureaucratisation (Doz 1980). Control was viewed as a key issue in the case of MNCs emphasising subsidiary autonomy due to the pursuit of nationally responsive strategies (Doz and Prahalad 1981). This theme has also been revisited recently by Muralidharan and Hamilton (1999), who argue that control mechanisms should evolve as the subsidiary matures. The successful acquisition of control by headquarters was considered to involve changes in the cognitive and strategic orientations of subsidiary managers (Doz and Prahalad 1981). Three classes of mechanisms were proposed to achieve these changes, namely, data management mechanisms, managers' management mechanisms and conflict resolution mechanisms, with the selection of the various mechanisms contingent on individual situations (Doz and Prahalad 1981; 1984). The transfer of managers within the MNC as a source of control was explored by Edstrom and Galbraith (1977). Their view was that some MNCs used management transfer to socialise managers, creating international, verbal communication networks permitting personal, yet decentralised, control suitable to a locally responsive strategy. The nature of managerial coordination and control processes in firms classed as transnationals was also explored (Bartlett and Ghoshal 1989). It was argued that the task of headquarters became one of managing interdependencies and coordinating the complex linkages of the transnational such as strategic objectives and operating policies, flows of supplies, components and funds and, finally, the collection, storage and redistribution of the company's accumulated information, knowledge and experience. The task of subsidiary managers became that of communicator of opportunities and threats in the local environment, defender of the national perspective and advocate of the country organisation's interests (Bartlett and Ghoshal 1989).

In a manner similar to the strategy literature, perspectives on structure and process have evolved over time. The issue of fit has been central to thinking in the area following the direction initiated by Chandler (1962), including internal fit between strategy, structure and process and external fit with the environment in which the firm operates. The complexity of this environment and the efforts to take account of both pressures for integration and responsiveness has led to the emergence of some complex organisations with complex management processes such as Hedlund's (1986) heterarchy and Ghoshal and Bartlett's (1990) inter-organisational network. The implications of the different strands of management literature for competition in a global environment are examined in the following paragraphs.

Concluding comments on the management perspective on international competition

The management perspective on global competition is represented by an extensive body of literature. It is rich and varied in its content and has helped to specify the challenges of global competition as well as likely organisational responses to it. Contributions have been largely conceptual but, since the late 1980s, a growing body of empirical work has been emerging. To a certain extent, it has been a 'hot topic' in the management literature, leading to many of its contributions taking on the characteristics of the management fads so strongly criticised by Eccles and Nohria (1992) and Hilmer and Donaldson (1996). But it has also dealt with the pressing problems facing managers who have to contend with a rapidly changing business environment.

The main contribution of the management perspective has been this recognition of environmental change. From the outset, it has recognised that MNCs face a conflict in trying to reconcile pressures for organisational integration and efficiency while at the same time remaining sufficiently flexible to respond to local contingencies. It has documented how the environment has been changing and how there exists the possibility that different firms may face different types of environment. But it has also shown a clear lack of consensus regarding both the exact scale of environmental change and the appropriate level of organisational response. Some authors strongly advocate the emergence of increasingly homogeneous markets worldwide (Levitt 1983; Ohmae 1985), others argue to the contrary (Doz 1987; Robinson 1986), while others adopt a middle ground, acknowledging the potential existence of global segments of homogeneous demand (Guido 1992; Jain 1989; Kale and Sundharshan 1987; Riesenbeck and Freeling 1991). Suggested organisational responses have ranged from greater levels of integration and efficiency (Henzler and Rall 1986; Yip 1989) to greater organisational flexibility (Kogut 1985a). Increasingly complex strategic and organisational arrangements have been proposed as the solution to the problem of how to succeed in the rapidly changing international business environment (Bartlett and Ghoshal 1989; Hedlund 1986).

It also appears that this focus on the environment has not served the management perspective well in regard to the question of competition. It has led to the literature exhibiting a very deterministic flavour (Henzler and Rall 1986; Hout, Porter and Rudden 1982; Malnight 1996; Porter 1986a, b; Prahalad and Doz 1987; Yip 1989; Yip, Johansson and Roos 1997), suggesting that successful strategies necessitate both an understanding of, and a level of fit with, environment conditions. But, to date, there is no agreement that such fit leads to superior performance; nor is there adequate empirical evidence that adopting an integrated strategy leads to superior performance in a global industry (Morrison and Roth 1992; Samiee and Roth 1992). At the same time there is little consensus on the extent of environmental change and the appropriate organisational responses. So while there is a rich and varied set of perspectives available, there is little clarity on, for example, the question of how firms might attain a competitive advantage. Furthermore, there is little examination or agreement on how advantages gained might be *sustained* over a period of time. In fact, though much of the literature suggests that strategic initiatives or changes in structure and process might be performance enhancing, it tends to stop short of saying that such initiatives will lead to an advantage over competitors. This suggests that understanding how a sustainable competitive advantage can be attained remains an important research question and one that is of major relevance to practitioners. Before moving on to examine this question in more detail, some concluding comments will be made on the management and economic perspectives.

A comparison of the economic and management perspectives

The economic and management perspectives on international competition represent two quite distinct traditions. The economic paradigm has a longer history, rooted in the trade theory literature of the past two centuries. More explicit attention began to be paid to issues at the level of the firm by industrial organisation economists such as Hymer and Kindleberger writing in the 1960s. Management contributions within the domain of international business also began to emerge during the 1960s but only grew rapidly in the 1980s as the debate concerning the globalisation of world markets intensified. The focus of the two traditions is also quite different. As noted earlier, economists have been largely concerned with explaining why MNCs exist, and different views on this question have been put forward as noted earlier. Management writers have been more concerned with the complexity involved in managing multinational firms and with proposing solutions to managerial problems relating to strategy, structure and process.

Unfortunately, at times it appears that economists and management theorists have been guilty of talking past each other, a problem that is not unusual in academic disciplines (Ghoshal and Moran 1996). Several areas of commonalty and overlap can be identified. Similar concepts have been discussed but labelled differently in the two fields. For example, in 1960, Hymer identified the homogenisation of consumer tastes around the world, an issue subsequently taken up with some enthusiasm by Levitt (Levitt 1983). Bain/Mason industrial organisation economists including Graham (1978) and Knickerbocker (1973) labelled certain kinds of FDI as 'defensive'. This reappeared in the 1980s in the managerial literature labelled as cross-subsidisation (Hamel and Prahalad 1985). And at a very core level, Dunning (1988b) sees close similarities between Porter's (1986a, b) notions of configuration, coordination and competitive advantage and the economic concepts of location, internalisation and ownership advantage respectively.

Some reviews of the literature have argued for greater levels of mutual recognition. For example, Kogut (1989) notes that much of what is written in management is rooted in economics, though this is not always acknowledged by management writers. Over the years, several economists have argued that greater attention to managerial issues would enhance the economic paradigm (Calvet 1981; Dunning 1993b; Hymer 1960; Teece 1986a) though, to date, these calls do not appear to have been greatly heeded. For example, in 1993 Buckley argued that it was time to search for ways of 'bringing management back in' to economic analysis (Buckley 1993). He proposed that this could be done within the confines of internalisation theory, where the roles of managers include identifying market imperfections, making internalisation decisions, creating market imperfections to generate rents and using internalisation as a strategic weapon to increase the transactions costs of competitors (Buckley 1993). The existence of such common ground, which has been inadequately explored to date, means that the interface of economics and strategic management represents a fertile arena for the kind of interdisciplinary inquiry described in Chapter 1.

This chapter has reviewed what both traditions have had to say about the question of international competition. It demonstrates that there is a rich and diverse set of opinions but also that there is little overall consensus. In seeking to understand why MNCs exist, economists tend to focus on the question of competition between MNCs and the firms in the host countries in which they do business. In this regard, the literature concentrates on understanding the advantages that MNCs have over host firms and the sources of these advantages. Industrial organisation theorists have identified a range of advantages which may originate in an MNC's home-country operations such as a brand name or marketing skills that it can use to try to outcompete local firms (Kindleberger 1969). Transactions cost theorists demonstrate how the firm's governance mechanisms may enable it to attain cost advantages (Teece 1981). Dunning's eclectic paradigm recognises that MNCs could gain advantages from their choice of production locations and also due to their multinationality, which enables them to exploit imperfections in product markets (Dunning 1981). By contrast, much of the focus of the management literature has been outward, examining the changing business environment and its likely potential impact. This has played an important role in delineating the challenges which MNCs face and will continue to face. But it has also led to a somewhat deterministic pattern of argument in which increasingly complex solutions to the difficult problem of international competition are advocated. A strongly positioning-based approach to strategy (Porter 1996) has been adopted and firms are advised to strive for efficiencies (low cost), responsiveness (differentiation) or a combination of both. By focusing on sustainable competitive advantage in a global environment, this book tries further to bridge the gap between the more internal economic perspective and the outward-looking management literature in which both the sources of advantage as well as the competitive context in which they are deployed are considered.

CONCLUSION

This chapter has two main purposes. First, in the context of a great deal of ambiguity in the literature, a definition of the term 'global environment' is proposed. It is defined as a business arena exhibiting above-average levels of geographic scope, market convergence and cross-national interdependencies. It is noted that such environments are characterised by high levels of complexity/heterogeneity, rapid change, high volatility, high levels of perceived uncertainty and, as such, represent difficult arenas in which to attain a sustainable competitive advantage (SCA). In that context, the second purpose of the chapter is to take stock of what is already known about the nature of competition in a global environment. A review is conducted of the relevant streams of literature in the field of international business. A great deal of richness and diversity can be observed, but it is also noted that the literature is not without its gaps. In particular, it is concluded that no clear explanation has emerged to show how a sustainable competitive advantage can be attained in a global environment. In the midst of various perspectives, some confusion and at times contradiction, a good theory of SCA is necessary. One theory that has come to the forefront of the debate on competitive advantage in recent years is the resource-based view of the firm (RBV). In the next chapter, an analysis of the origins, insights and current status of the resource-based view of the firm is provided.

3 The resource-based view of the firm (RBV)

INTRODUCTION

In this chapter, a synthesis of the relevant literature in organisation theory, economics and strategic management is conducted with the objective of providing an integrated analysis of the origins, insights and current status of the resource-based view of the firm (RBV). The chapter opens by noting that the RBV is just one of a number of theories of the firm, and a review of its differences and similarities with a variety of competing perspectives is presented. The subsequent section, which is the core of the chapter, focuses in detail on the logic of, and the insights provided by, the resource-based view. It demonstrates that certain key resources combined with managerial choices play a central role in sustaining superior performance. To date, however, the majority of 'resource-based' contributions have been of a conceptual rather than empirical nature. The empirical work that has taken place is reviewed briefly and some outstanding research issues are identified. The chapter concludes by reaffirming the merits of the resource-based view of the firm as a theoretical framework for examining the issue of sustainable competitive advantage in a global environment.

ORIGINS, ORIENTATION AND DEVELOPMENT

The question of what is the appropriate unit of analysis for business phenomena has long interested organisation theorists. A basic unit of analysis which is common to a variety of social sciences, including economics, sociology, psychology and anthropology, is exchange (Toyne 1989) and this is the level of analysis on which transactions cost economics, with its implications for international competition outlined in Chapter 2, is built. However, the most frequently considered unit of analysis is the firm, or the organisation as it is more commonly referred to in organisation theory. The interaction between a firm and its environment is most usually viewed as an open system (Emery 1969), with dynamic flows in both directions to the extent that the distinction between firms and environments has itself been questioned (Perrow 1967). A broad range of theories, originating in economics, politics and sociology, has sought to shed light on the nature of this relationship. Morgan (1986) uses the metaphor of the six blind men and the elephant to suggest that the various theories have contributed important but only partial explanations of this overall relationship. Several attempts have been made to develop over-arching schemes that integrate various theories, most notably, Astley and Van de Ven (1983), Barney and Ouchi (1986) and Hrebiniak and Joyce (1985).

In Figure 3.1, a further scheme is proposed, which builds on the work of Astley and Van de Ven (1983) but also incorporates additional theories not included in their model. The vertical axis draws a distinction between theories that adopt a top–down versus a bottom–up approach. 'Top–down' theories describe universal forces which determine the nature of events, while 'bottom–up' theories, on the other hand, think of reality as an aggregation of specifics. This is usually treated as a macro versus micro distinction (Astley and Van de Ven 1983). The horizontal axis depicts the separation of assumptions between strategic choice and environmental determinism, an issue that is at the core of much organisation theory (see, for example, Aldrich 1979 and Lawless and Finch 1989).

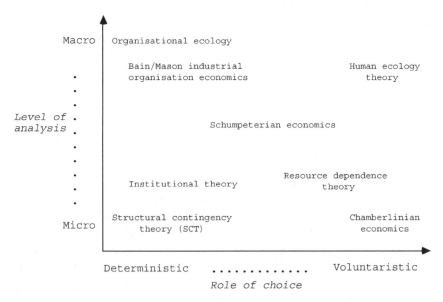

Figure 3.1 Perspectives on the firm/environment relationship

Note: This figure does not aim to include all extant theories of the relationship between the firm and the environment but rather incorporates several major schools of thought from the disciplines of economics, sociology and politics to demonstrate the richness and diversity of perspectives on the relationship.

The question of whether these voluntaristic and deterministic views are competing has been the subject of some debate (Hrebiniak and Joyce 1985), but for the purposes of exposition they are depicted separately in the proposed scheme. The competing theories are mapped as occupying a position in a theoretical space rather than the more common 2 × 2 matrix approach (Astley and Van de Ven 1983) to show that the boundaries between the theories are not clear cut but rather share points of common interest.

The resource-based view in the context of the firm/ environment relationship

The earliest acknowledgement of the potential importance of firm-specific resources is to be found in the work of economists such as Chamberlin and Robinson in the 1930s (Chamberlin 1933; Robinson 1933), which was subsequently developed by Penrose (1959). Rather than emphasise market structures, these economists highlighted firm heterogeneity and proposed that the unique assets and capabilities of firms were important factors giving rise to imperfect competition and the attainment of super-normal profits. For example, Chamberlin (1933) identified that some of the key capabilities of firms included technical know-how, reputation, brand awareness, the ability of managers to work together and, particularly, patents and trademarks, many of which have been revisited in the recent strategy and marketing literature (Day 1994; Hall 1992). Penrose's work also provides other penetrating insights into the nature and role of resources in the firm. For example, she distinguishes resources from services, arguing that it is never resources themselves that are inputs into the production process, but rather the services that they can render. In other words, services yielded by resources are a function of the way in which the resources are used, in that exactly the same resource if used for different purposes or in different ways or in combination with other resources provides a different service or set of services. Penrose (1959) sees this distinction as the source of uniqueness of each individual firm, and it is a distinction that has many parallels with the separation of resources and capabilities that characterises much of the strategy literature (see, for example, Hill and Jones 1998).

Given that its origins are in a view of the world favoured by economists of the Chamberlin/Robinson tradition (Seth and Thomas 1994), the resource-based view of the firm adopts a very particular perspective on the nature of the relationship between the firm and its environment. It is most appropriately located in the micro-voluntaristic 'corner' of Figure 3.1. Its central assumption of firm heterogeneity contrasts with that of branches of industrial organisation economics of the Bain/Mason tradition. In other words, its focus of interest is on individual firms, rather than groups or populations of firms, that it views as being able to control their own destiny and meet competitive challenges through choices made regarding the development and deployment of idiosyncratic resources. It departs from neoclassical microeconomics and Bain/Mason industrial organisation, which attempt to characterise the behaviour of the representative firm (Hill and Deeds 1996) and focuses instead on firm heterogeneity (Carroll 1993; Nelson 1991). On the issue of exchanges between the firm and its environment, it places primary emphasis on economic as opposed to social or political exchanges. This is in keeping with its economic origin, which views organisational actors as rational beings maximising their self-interests.

These points aside, it has been argued that the resource-based view of the firm provides an illuminating generalisable theory of the firm (Mahoney and Pandian 1992). Building on the view that good science is good conversation, Mahoney and Pandian (1992) argue that the resource-based view effectively sustains the conversation within strategic management and between strategic management and branches of economics. Thomas and Pollock (1999) support this position by noting that the resource-based view incorporates elements of the spatial competition, strategic group, management cognition and network streams of research in strategic management. Mahoney and Pandian (1992) contend that it informs the discussion of issues such as distinctive competencies and diversification strategy within strategic management as well as sharing perspectives with major branches of organisational economics, including evolutionary (Schumpeterian) economics, transaction cost economics, property rights theory and positive agency theory. Mahoney and Pandian also argue that a further strength of the resource-based view is its ability to complement industrial organisation economics, which emphasises external industries and product markets. Similarly, Conner (1991) shows how the resource-based view shares at least one commonalty and one difference with five major branches of economics, including neoclassical perfect competition, Bain/Mason IO, the Chicago school, Schumpeterian economics and transaction cost economics. Indeed, the resource-based view also shares common assumptions with theoretical perspectives from outside the discipline of economics, as shown in Table 3.1. This is not to suggest that it represents an integrated or unifying theory of the firm, but its ability to 'sustain the conversation' with a variety of perspectives allied to its own unique insights on firm heterogeneity makes it an important foundation upon which to build further research.

The development of the resource-based view within strategic management

Until the late 1980s, the resource-based view was characterised by a rather fragmented process of development. Though, as noted above, the

Table 3.1 The RBV and theories of the firm/environment relationship

Assumptions of the RBV	Org. ecology	Bain/ Mason	Instit. theory	SCT	Human ecology	Res. depend.	Cham. econ.	Sch. econ.
Firm heterogeneity	Yes	Yes		Yes		Yes	Yes	Yes
Strategic choice						Yes	Yes	Yes
Firms acquire/accumulate resources	Yes	Yes	Yes		Yes	Yes	Yes	
Above-normal returns possible					Yes	Yes	Yes	
Innovation key to survival/prosperity	Yes							Yes
Equifinality				Yes	Yes	Yes	Yes	Yes

Key:
Org. ecology – Organisational ecology theory
Bain/Mason – Bain/Mason industrial organisation economics
Instit. theory – Institutional theory
SCT – Structural contingency theory
Human ecology – Human ecology theory
Res. depend. – Resource dependence theory
Cham. econ. – Chamberlinian economics
Sch. econ. – Schumpeterian economics

concept of resources was central to the contributions of economists such as Chamberlin (1933), Robinson (1933) and Penrose (1959), these insights did not initially coalesce into a unified body of thought within economics. Similarly, as the discipline of strategic management developed, the issue of resources received attention but was not afforded pride of place in its early models. Frameworks in strategic management which emerged in the 1960s and 1970s from the Carnegie Institute of Technology and the Harvard Business School typically gave equal weighting to the firm/its resources as well as to the industrial context in which it operated. In contrast to economics, strategic management saw itself as being primarily normative, seeking to develop a practically useful set of concepts which managers could use to manage (Ansoff 1965). Models of these strategic decisions typically proposed a rational process of setting objectives, followed by an internal appraisal of capabilities and an external appraisal of outside opportunities open to the firm, leading to a decision to expand or diversify (the strategic decisions) based on the level of synergy between existing products/capabilities and investment prospects (Ansoff 1965). Implicit in this model of strategic management is the idea that the firm/its resources and its industry environment are of equal importance and that managers should strive to achieve an optimal fit between them.

A more complete illustration of this issue of fit is to be found in the Learned, Christensen, Andrews and Guth (LCAG) framework (Learned *et al.* 1969; Andrews 1971). The LCAG framework extended earlier thinking to incorporate not only the firm's strengths/weaknesses and the opportunities/threats in the environment but also the personal values of key implementers and broader social expectations, all four of which are interrelated. Additionally, the sequence of activities was altered somewhat. Determination of a suitable strategy was posited to begin with the identification of environmental opportunities. The ability of the organisation to avail of these opportunities was constrained by its resource and competence base. Subsequent strategic choices accounted for the personal values of implementers and the organisations' responsibility to society (Learned *et al.* 1969). However, the idea that the firm's strengths and resources are of equal importance to industry opportunities and threats is again implicit. The core concepts of analysis, rationality and fit in these early models are reflected in the structure and content of subsequent literature (Hofer and Schendel 1978; Powell 1992) and provide the foundation for some of the current strategic management texts in general use (Hill and Jones 1998; Thompson and Strickland 1998).

In the 1980s, the work of Porter (1980), which was grounded in Bain/ Mason industrial organisation (IO), led to a shift away from firm resources to emphasise the industry quadrant of the LCAG framework (Hoskisson *et al.* 1999). Porter sought to answer the question of why some industries seemed to be inherently more profitable than others, allowing the attainment of long-run, above-normal profits. He proposed that the answer lay in understanding industry structure, which could be analysed in terms of five key forces, namely the rivalry among existing competitors, the threat of entrants and of substitutes and the bargaining power of buyers and of suppliers. Firms could earn monopoly rents either by selecting industries which were 'structurally attractive' or by manipulating the forces driving competition in their favour through the selection of generic competitive strategies (Porter 1980). This deterministic focus on industry conditions was reflected in much of the subsequent thinking in strategic management (see, for example, strategic groups (McGee and Thomas 1986), barriers to entry (Karakaya and Stahl 1989), competitive analysis (Prescott and Smith 1987) and key success factors (de Vasconcellos E Sa and Hambrick 1989)). The normative implications of Porter's model were essentially contingency-based. He suggested a typology of generic strategic alternatives, the suitability of which was dependent on the industry's structure and stage of development.

However, in the later part of the 1980s, a growing body of empirical work testing Porter's ideas began to cast doubt on their validity. Researchers observed performance differences not only between firms in the same industry (Cubbin 1988; Hansen and Wernerfelt 1989; Rumelt 1991) but also within the narrower confines of strategic groups within industries (Cool and Schendel 1988; Lewis and Thomas 1990). Hansen and Wernerfelt's (1989) study assessed the relative impact of economic and organisational factors on firm performance and found that organisational factors explain about twice as much of the variance in firm profit rates as economic factors. Rumelt's second sample of some 2,800 business units incorporating four-year longitudinal data showed that business-unit effects explained 44 per cent of the variance in business-unit profitability while industry effects explained a mere 4 per cent. This built on earlier work (Rumelt 1982), which found that firm effects explained up to six times more performance variation. Rumelt's research supported similar findings from the same Federal Trade Commission Line of Business database by other researchers (see Schmalansee 1985; Wernerfelt and Montgomery 1988) and his findings have been further validated through the use of a different methodology by Powell (1996). Stretching the time frame from four to thirty years, Cubbin (1988) concluded that there were no persistent industry effects. Similarly, within the tighter confines of strategic groups, Cool and Schendel (1988) found performance differences between strategic group members in the US pharmaceutical industry by analysing data from 1963 to 1982. These findings were supported by Lewis and Thomas's (1990) study of the UK retail grocery industry.

These empirical findings coincided with, and complemented, a conceptual swing away from the industry as focus of interest. The beginnings of this swing can be seen in the work of economists such as Wernerfelt (1984) and Barney (1986a) and management theorists such as Coyne (1986). Indeed, Wernerfelt's (1984) work gave a hint of the richness that lay in analysis of the firm in that he described his article as a 'first cut at a huge can of worms'. This article was also the first to adopt the expression 'resource-based view of the firm' and its significance is evident in that it was awarded the *Strategic Management Journal* best-paper prize in 1994 for reasons such as being 'truly seminal' and 'an early statement of an important trend in the field' (Zajac 1995). What followed was something of an explosion of interest, reflected in the diverse range of contributions based on insights from both economics and management (Amit and Schoemaker 1993; Barney 1986a, b, 1989, 1991, 1996; Black and Boal 1994; Collis 1991, 1994; Collis and Montgomery 1995; Conner 1991; Conner and Prahalad 1996; Coyne 1986; Dierickx and Cool 1989; Ghemawat 1986; Grant 1991a; Hall 1989, 1992, 1993; Lado, Boyd and Wright 1992; Lippman and Rumelt 1982; Mahoney and Pandian 1992; Peteraf 1993; Reed and DeFillippi 1990; Rumelt 1984, 1987; Wernerfelt 1989; Williams 1992). In summary, the perceived importance of the firm and its resources has varied as the strategic management discipline has developed and reached something of a crest in the late 1980s and early 1990s. In the next section this extensive body of literature is reviewed to provide an exposition of the assumptions and insights of the resource-based view of the firm.

THEORETICAL INSIGHTS OF THE RESOURCE-BASED VIEW

While in 1991 Collis (1991) could claim that no coherent body of theory had emerged to summarise the resource-based view and ongoing contributions continue to provide additional nuances, its fundamental tenets are currently quite well established. The basic logic of the resource-based view is relatively simple. It starts with the assumption that the desired outcome of managerial effort within the firm is a sustainable competitive advantage (SCA). Achieving an SCA allows the firm to earn economic rents or above-average returns. In turn, this focuses attention on how firms achieve and sustain advantages. The resource-based view contends that the answer to this question lies in the possession of certain key resources, that is, resources having the characteristics of value, appropriability and barriers to duplication. An SCA can be obtained if the firm effectively deploys these key resources in its product markets. Therefore, the RBV emphasises strategic choice, charging the firm's management with the important tasks of identifying, developing and deploying key resources to maximise returns. In summary, the essential elements of the resource-based view are: (i) sustainable competitive advantage and superior performance; (ii) key resources; and (iii) strategic choices by management. Each of these elements is examined in detail in the following sub-sections.

Sustainable competitive advantage and superior performance

The pursuit of competitive advantage is an idea at the heart of much of the strategic management literature (see, for example, Coyne 1986; Day and Wensley 1988; Ghemawat 1986; Hall 1993; Pitts and Lei 1996; Porter 1985; Williams 1992). Indeed, Aharoni (1993a) argues that whatever its different definitions, strategy entails an attempt by a firm to achieve and sustain competitive advantage in relation to other firms. The prominent role given to competitive advantage may derive from the economic and militaristic origins of the strategy literature (Whittington 1993). Early classical economists give pride of place to the idea of the rational economic man inherently pursuing his own self-interests (Smith 1776) and therefore strategy could be seen as an elaborate game of move and counter-move, bluff and counter-bluff as businesses sought to gain positions of advantage (von Neumann and Morgenstern 1944). This idea of seeking to achieve positions of advantage through success in competitive battles has a very strong militaristic flavour. Indeed, the word strategy itself is related to the ancient Greek word *stratos*, meaning army (Cummings 1993) and military metaphors such as leadership, planning and implementation are very prevalent in the strategic management literature (Whittington 1993) and have also been popularised in the strategic marketing literature (Kotler and Singh 1981).

However, while the notion of competitive advantage remains central to the strategy literature (Ghemawat 1986), clear definitions of the concept are rare. For example, Coyne (1986) appears to propose the answer in an article entitled 'Sustainable competitive advantage – What it is and what it isn't', but instead focuses on the conditions necessary to achieve an SCA and on the implications of the possession of such advantages for strategic choices. Indeed, the literature generally gives much greater attention to how advantages might be attained and maintained rather than clarifying exactly what a competitive advantage is. Understanding the concept is further complicated by the fact that it is frequently used interchangeably with terms like 'distinctive competence' (Day and Wensley 1988). One approach that has been adopted in the literature has been to think of advantage in terms of attaining positions of superiority on dimensions such as differentiation or delivered cost (Bharadwaj, Varadarajan and Fahy 1993; Day 1994; Day and Wensley 1988; Hunt and Morgan 1995; Porter 1980; 1985). However, this approach has not accounted for conceptual and empirical work which has argued that differentiation and low cost are not mutually exclusive; superior-performing firms appear to excel in both (Baden-Fuller and Stopford 1992; Gilbert and Strebel 1989; Hall 1980).

Understanding competitive advantage requires an analysis of its constituent elements. Advantage can be viewed as a relative concept (Hu 1995; Kay 1993, 1994). In other words, advantage is deemed to be meaningful only when compared to another entity or set of entities. In addition, Hu (1995) argues that advantages are also relative to an arena or context and that what counts for an advantage in one context (such as a national market) may not be so in another (international market) and may indeed be a disadvantage. A competitive advantage, then, is an advantage one firm has over a competitor or group of competitors in a given market, strategic group or industry (Kay 1993). Any given firm may have many kinds of advantages over another firm, such as a superior production system, a lower level of wages and salaries, an ability to deliver better customer service and so on. However, when describing competitive advantage, the strategy literature has tended to focus implicitly on advantages on which customers place some level of value. This point is developed explicitly by Coyne (1986), who proposed that the advantage must be in some 'product/delivery attribute that is a key buying criterion for the market'. Similarly, Kay (1993) defines competitive advantage as 'the ability of a firm to add more value than another firm in the same market'. Such a view of competitive advantage suggests that in any given competitive context, whether it is a market, strategic group or industry, more than one firm can have a competitive advantage. For example, if four firms are competing on the same value dimension in the same market, company A might have a competitive advantage over company B but B could also have a competitive advantage over company C. Kay (1993) argues that the marginal firm in the industry is the relevant benchmark when no explicit comparator (such as company B) is stated. In the above example, companies A, B and C can be said to have competitive advantages and company A has the greatest competitive advantage. In summary, as value is its essential element, the potential for competitive advantage resides in the firm's outputs and the relative importance of these outputs in given product markets (Williams 1992). The strategic management literature would appear broadly to concur that a firm's output can deliver value to customers if it is relatively more differentiated, delivered at relatively lower cost, or both.

Also of interest to researchers has been the issue of whether these advantages are sustainable or can be made to be sustainable. The terms 'sustained advantage' (Barney 1991) and 'sustainable advantage' (Grant 1991a) both appear in the literature, but can be interpreted in the same way. Sustainability does not refer to a particular period of calendar time; nor does it imply that advantages persist indefinitely (Gunther McGrath, MacMillan and Venkataraman 1995), but rather depends on the possibility and extent of competitive duplication. Industry studies have typically reported the rapid imitation of competitive moves and the difficulty of maintaining advantages. For example, Ghemawat (1986) claims (i) that competitors secure detailed information on 70 per cent of new products within one year of their development, (ii) that patenting fails to deter imitation and (iii) that between 60 per cent and

90 per cent of all production process improvements quickly diffuse to competitors. Particular businesses such as the financial services industry are cited as an example of where sustainable advantages are difficult to attain due to the rapid imitation of new products (Bhide 1986). The resource-based view of the firm posits that advantages can be sustainable (that is, resist erosion) if they are derived from key resources possessing certain defining characteristics, a point that is developed in more detail later.

Finally, gaining a competitive advantage through the provision of greater value to customers can be expected to lead to superior performance measured in conventional terms such as market-based performance (e.g. market share, customer satisfaction) and financial-based performance (e.g. return on investment, shareholder wealth creation) (Bharadwaj, Varadarajan and Fahy 1993; Hunt and Morgan 1995). Research by Buzzell and Gale (1987), Jacobsen (1988) and Jacobsen and Aaker (1985) has argued that market share and profitability are both outcomes of the efforts by firms to secure cost and differentiation advantages. Extant marketing literature emphasises a link between the delivery of value to customers and levels of customer satisfaction, leading to potential market-share and profitability gains (Kotler 1988). Where the advantage is sustained, superior performance levels can be expected to persist in a manner analogous to the notions of super-normal profit or rent in economics.

The economics literature holds that, given strong competitive pressures, high rationality will prevail and economic rents will dissipate (Schoemaker 1990). However, two exceptions are identified, namely, monopoly rents and Ricardian rents (Peteraf 1993). Monopoly rents accrue to the deliberate restriction of output by firms facing downward-sloping demand curves in industries characterised by barriers to entry, whether legal or otherwise (Peteraf 1993). As Kay (1993) puts it, it is possible for firms to generate persistently large returns without having a competitive advantage other than the absence of competitors, in other words, operating in non-contestable markets (Baumol, Panzer and Willig 1982). Rents also accrue in circumstances where resources are limited or quasi-limited in supply (Ricardian rents). If resources were not limited, increased production by new entrants would shift the supply curve outward, forcing marginal firms to leave the market (Peteraf 1993). It is the persistence of these superior returns accruing to scarce resources that is the central concern of the resource-based view of the firm. The development of the RBV has been instrumental in improving our understanding of why resource supply might be limited or why resource heterogeneity might persist. It has also informed the question of how resources are converted into competitive advantages to enable the realisation of sustained superior performance. This issue will be examined in detail below.

The characteristics of key resources

The list of resources in any given firm is likely to be a long one. One of the principal insights of the resource-based view of the firm is that not all resources are of equal importance or possess the potential to be a source of sustainable competitive advantage. Much attention has focused, therefore, on the characteristics of advantage-creating resources. For example, in describing whether a firm's culture can be a source of sustained competitive advantage, Barney (1986b) proposes that it can if it meets three conditions, namely that the culture is valuable, rare and inimitable. In a more general discussion of resources, Barney (1991) adds a further condition, namely that resources must also be non-substitutable. Similarly, Grant (1991a) points to four characteristics of resources that are important determinants of competitive advantage, namely, durability, transparency, transferability and replicability. Collis and Montgomery (1995) extend the list to five to include inimitability, durability, appropriability, substitutability and competitive superiority. Finally, Amit and Schoemaker (1993) produce a list of eight defining characteristics, including complementarity, scarcity, low tradability, inimitability, limited substitutability, appropriability, durability and overlap with strategic industry factors. In the interests of parsimony, these conditions, tests and characteristics have been grouped under the three headings of value, appropriability and barriers to duplication.

Value

We noted earlier that value to customers is an essential element of competitive advantage. Therefore, for a resource to be a potential source of competitive advantage it must be valuable or enable the creation of value. In the words of Barney (1991), it must permit the firm to conceive of or implement strategies that improve its efficiency and effectiveness by meeting the needs of its customers. By implication, this means that though the resource may meet some other tests, such as being immobile or inimitable, if it does not enable the creation of value it is not a potential source of competitive advantage. This also implies an important complementarity between the resource-based view and environmental models of competitive advantage (Barney 1991; Collis and Montgomery 1995). The firm must identify those resources which are overlapping or congruent with the strategic industry factors (SIFs) prevalent at the present time and likely to be important in the future (Amit and Schoemaker 1993; Miller and Shamsie 1996), if advantage is to be attained.

Appropriability

Once value is derived from a resource, the key question becomes who appropriates it. The value created is invariably subject to a host of potential claimants, such as customers, suppliers, employees, share-holders and the government (Collis and Montgomery 1995; Kay 1993). Appropriation of value becomes a particular problem where property rights are not clearly defined. While the firm may be effective in appropriating the value from its physical and financial assets, it may be less so in the case of intangible assets such as brand names or copyrights (Grant 1991a). Of particular interest from a resource-based perspective is the appropriation of the value created by the firm's human resources. Employee mobility means that it is risky for a firm to be dependent on the specific skills of a few key employees who may also be in a position to bargain with the firm to appropriate a major part of their contribution to the value-added (Grant 1991a). However, this bargaining power is tempered by the relationship between the individual's skills and the organisational routines (Grant 1991a; Nelson and Winter 1982) or what Wernerfelt (1989) describes as 'team effects', where the company can pay employees their individual value but reap the larger joint values. Companies must therefore guard against the dissipation of value-added, and appropriability is the ability to turn added value into profit (Kay 1993).

Barriers to duplication

The inability of competitors to duplicate a given firm's bundle of resources or their deployment is one of the defining issues within the resource-based view of the firm and one that has been the subject of much attention. Resource heterogeneity is a fundamental assumption within models of imperfect competition and the RBV is concerned with understanding the persistence of this heterogeneity. Barney (1991) puts it slightly differently when he lists rareness as being one of the key characteristics necessary before a resource has the potential to generate sustainable competitive advantage. If a resource can be easily duplicated and is therefore not rare, it will not have the potential to generate an SCA. Understanding what prevents the duplication of value-creating resources is a key concern but one that has been complicated by the inconsistent and at times conflicting use of terminology in the literature. Several overlapping classification schemes dealing with barriers to duplication have been proposed, including asset stock accumulation (Dierickx and Cool 1989), capability gaps (Coyne 1986), capability differentials (Hall 1992; 1993), *ex-post* limits to competition (Peteraf 1993), isolating mechanisms (Rumelt 1984; 1987), uncertain inimitability (Lippman and Rumelt 1982) and causal ambiguity (Reed and DeFillippi 1990) (see Table 3.2).

Simply put, barriers to resource duplication can be said to exist if the resource is inimitable or imperfectly imitable, immobile or imperfectly mobile and non-substitutable or imperfectly substitutable. The classification schemes presented in Table 3.2 are concerned primarily with the

Table 3.2 Alternative classifications of barriers to resource duplication

Author	Barriers to resource duplication
Lippman and Rumelt (1982)	Uncertain inimitability
Reed and DeFillippi (1990)	Complexity, tacitness and specificity
Rumelt (1984; 1987)*	Communication good effects, economies of scale, information impactedness, producer learning, reputation, response lags
Coyne (1986)	Business system gaps, managerial gaps, position gaps, regulatory gaps
Hall (1992; 1993)	Cultural differentials, functional differentials, positional differentials, regulatory differentials
Dierickx and Cool (1989)	Asset erosion, asset mass efficiencies, causal ambiguity, interconnectedness of asset stocks, time compression diseconomies

* Some of Rumelt's isolating mechanisms have been omitted because they are external to the firm. Advertising and channel crowding are industry conditions. Buyer evaluation costs and buyer switching costs are industry features.

Source: J. Fahy, 'Strategic marketing and the resource-based view of the firm', *AMS Review.*

question of inimitability, which has been given most attention in the literature. However, the development of weak typologies has not helped efforts to illuminate the question of inimitability. For example, Barney (1991) proposes that resources will be imperfectly imitable if one or a combination of three factors are present: (i) the resource is dependent on unique historical conditions; (ii) causal ambiguity exists; and (iii) the resource is socially complex. However, it is possible to conceive of a single resource that may exhibit all three characteristics.

Perhaps a useful starting point in explaining inimitability is Grant's (1991a) idea of transparency. The most basic problem a competitor might have is an information problem, whereby the competitor is unable to identify the reason behind a given firm's success. This is essentially the concept of causal ambiguity (Reed and DeFillippi 1990) or uncertain imitability (Lippman and Rumelt 1982), where there is ambiguity concerning the connections between actions and results. Lippman and Rumelt (1982) suggest that uncertainty regarding which factors are responsible for superior performance explains efficiency differences between both incumbents and potential new entrants despite free entry. This uncertain imitability gives rise to rents which may even accrue to atomistic price takers, thus not arising from market power or restricted entry. Reed and DeFillippi (1990) also note that the ambiguity may be so great that not even managers within the firm understand the relationship between actions and outcomes.

In seeking to explain the causes of such ambiguity, Reed and DeFillippi (1990) shed light on the characteristics of resources that may prevent their imitation by competitors. They suggest three characteristics of resources that can simultaneously be sources of ambiguity and advantage, namely, tacitness, complexity and specificity. Tacitness is a characteristic of skill-based activities (Polanyi 1967) and refers to an inability to identify or codify a pattern of activities. Skilled activities are based on learning by doing that is accumulated through experience and refined by practice (Reed and DeFillippi 1990). It is implicit in the notions of information impactedness and producer learning (Rumelt 1987), and time compression diseconomies (Dierickx and Cool 1989). Complexity results from the interconnectedness of asset stocks (Dierickx and Cool 1989), the social relationships within the firm (Barney 1991) and from co-specialised assets (Teece 1986b); that is, assets that must be used in connection with one another. It resides in the large numbers of technologies, organisation routines and individual or team-based experiences that go to make up an organisation (Reed and DeFillippi 1990). It suggests that few individuals, if any, have sufficient breadth and depth of knowledge to grasp the overall performance package (Nelson and Winter 1982). This information is then immobile even though employees may be recruited by competitors. Specificity is the idea that transactions within the firm and with its external constituents are idiosyncratic to individual firms (Williamson 1975; 1985). Such transactions have a time dimension (Dierickx and Cool 1989) and this path dependence of an individual firm's activities is exceedingly difficult to identify and replicate (Barney 1991; Collis and Montgomery 1995; Dierickx and Cool 1989).

Even where resources are clearly identified and understood, their imitation may be prevented through the legal system of property rights (Coyne 1986; Hall 1992, 1993). Resources such as patents, trademarks and copyrights may be protected through intellectual property laws and competitive advantages may accrue from other regulatory activities such as the granting of operating licences (Coyne 1986). In addition, transparent resources may not be imitated due to the presence of economic deterrents (Collis and Montgomery 1995; Rumelt 1984, 1987). For example, imitation may be deterred by a pre-emptive sizeable investment that is not, though it could be, replicated by a competitor due to the likelihood of the follower not receiving an adequate return on investment.

In summary, resources are likely to be inimitable or imperfectly imitable where their relationship with advantage is poorly understood and/or they possess the characteristics of tacitness, complexity, specificity, regulatory protection and economic deterrence. However, it must also be impossible for a competitor to hire away a value-creating resource. In other words, the resource must also be immobile or imperfectly mobile. Much of the literature focuses on identifying the kinds of resources that are likely to be less mobile. Grant (1991a) proposes that some resources may be geographically immobile due to the costs of relocation. However, more significant barriers to mobility exist where the resources are firm-specific, where property rights are not well defined, where transaction costs are high and/or where the resources are co-specialised (Peteraf 1993). These are also the kinds of traits closely associated with inimitability. Consequently, the resource-based view of the firm places a premium on resources that are accumulated within the firm (Dierickx and Cool 1989; Peteraf 1993; Teece, Pisano and Shuen 1997) as many of these resources, subject to path dependencies, possess barriers to both imitability and mobility.

Finally, the resources must also be non-substitutable. Peteraf (1993) and Collis and Montgomery (1995) note how the Porter five-forces model (Porter 1980) has focused attention in the strategy literature on the threat of substitutes. Barney (1991) points out that though a firm may not be able to imitate or acquire a competitor's resources, it may be able to pursue the same strategy by either substituting similar resources or different resources in an effort to match the competitor's advantage.

To summarise, a firm's resources are a source of sustainable competitive advantage if they possess the three key characteristics of market value, appropriability and barriers to duplication. A further trait gaining some attention in the literature recently has been durability of the resource (Amit and Schoemaker 1993; Collis and Montgomery 1995; Grant 1991a). For example, Grant (1991a) notes that the life span of technological resources is getting much shorter due to the pace of innovation, though resources such as corporate and brand reputation appear to be much more durable. However, as long as a resource is valuable, appropriable and resists duplication it enables the firm to attain a sustainable competitive advantage. Should the resource be durable, the advantage may last for a longer period subject to the efforts of competitors to duplicate it.

Identifying key resources

The current business literature is replete with discussion that attributes the superior performance of firms to strengths such as customer service excellence, design capability, managerial know-how and teamwork. At any given time an organisation is likely to have a wide range of resources at its disposal. From a resource-based perspective, the normative challenge facing firms is to identify and deploy those resources that meet the criteria set out above.

Once again, the literature is not short of classification schemes for the resource pool within the firm and again there is the potential for a great deal of confusion arising from the inconsistent use of terminology. For example, the term 'competencies' appears frequently in the literature, sometimes preceded by the adjectives 'core' or 'distinctive', sometimes not, sometimes used interchangeably with the term 'capabilities', which, in turn, is used interchangeably with the term 'skills', which is frequently preceded by the adjective 'core'. Approaches to classifying resources vary considerably. Traditionally, resources tended to be classified on the basis of physical characteristics, leading to distinctions being drawn between financial resources, physical resources, human resources, organisational resources and technological resources (Hofer and Schendel 1978). Alternatively, using an organisational process approach, Lado, Boyd and Wright (1992) classify the firm's 'competencies' into those which are resource-based, transformation-based, output-based and managerially based, while Williams (1992), concentrating on the question of imitability, groups together what he terms slow-cycle resources, standard-cycle resources and fast-cycle resources. And finally, in arguing for a return to a broader definition of resources, Baghai, Coley and White (1999) identify four categories, namely, operational skills, privileged assets, growth-enabling skills and special relationships.

However, a basic distinction can be made between resources that arise from what the organisation *has* versus those arising from what it *does* (Hall 1992). This is sometimes labelled as the difference between a firm's resources and its capabilities (Amit and Schoemaker 1993; Grant 1995; Hill and Jones 1998) or as the difference between its assets and its competencies (Hall 1992). Resources or assets are typically further sub-divided into those that are tangible and those that are intangible (Grant 1995; Hall 1992). For the purposes of consistency we use the term 'resources' as an all-embracing one. Resources are then sub-divided into three groups, namely, tangible assets, intangible assets and capabilities as shown in Table 3.3, which also notes points of commonalty with the existing, diverse range of classification schemes used in the literature.

Table 3.3 A classification of the firm's resource pool

Author	The firm's resource bundle		
	Tangible assets	*Intangible assets*	*Capabilities*
Wernerfelt (1989)	Fixed assets	Blueprints	Cultures
Hall (1992)		Intangible assets	Intangible capabilities
Hall (1993)		Assets	Competencies
Prahalad and Hamel (1990)		Core competencies	
Itami (1987)			Invisible assets
Amit and Schoemaker (1993)			Intermediate goods
Selznick (1957); Hitt and Ireland (1985); Hofer and Schendel (1978)			Distinctive competencies
Irvin and Michaels (1989)			Core skills

Source: J. Fahy, 'Strategic marketing and the resource-based view of the firm', *AMS Review.*

Tangible assets

Tangible assets refer to the fixed and current assets of an organisation that have a fixed long-run capacity (Wernerfelt 1989). Examples include plant, equipment, land, other capital goods and stocks, debtors and bank deposits. Tangible assets have the properties of ownership and their value is relatively easy to measure (Hall 1989). The book value of these assets is assessed through conventional accounting mechanisms and this value is usually reflected in the balance sheet valuation of companies. The other defining characteristic of tangible assets is that they are transparent (Grant 1991a) and relatively weak at resisting duplication efforts by competitors. For example, though plant or land may be geographically immobile, each is relatively imitable and substitutable.

Intangible assets

Firms may also possess intangible assets. A variety of such assets has been identified, including trademarks, patents, copyright, registered designs, contracts, trade secrets, networks, databases and brand and company reputation (Hall 1992; Williams 1992). It is the presence of these intangible assets that accounts for the significant differences that are observed between the balance sheet valuation and the stock market valuation of publicly quoted companies (Grant 1991a; Hall 1989, 1992; Rumelt 1987). These differences are particularly pronounced in industries such as pharmaceuticals where patents are critical, consumer goods industries where trademarks and brand reputation are critical, and service firms where company reputation is critical (Grant 1991a). Intangible assets have relatively unlimited capacity (Wernerfelt 1989). For example, Nayyar (1990) demonstrates how service firms can diversify on the basis of reputation where consumers face significant information acquisition costs. Firms possessing intangible assets can leverage their value by using them in house, renting them (e.g. a licence on a patent) or selling them (selling a brand and its inherent reputation). Wernerfelt recommends using them in house as renting can be difficult to police (Wernerfelt 1989).

Intangible assets are relatively resistant to duplication efforts by competitors due to either regulatory or position gaps or differentials (Coyne 1986; Hall 1992, 1993). Intellectual property is afforded legal protection though this is frequently violated, particularly in international markets. Databases, networks and reputation are examples of asset stocks (Dierickx and Cool 1989); the inherent complexity and specificity of their accumulation hinders imitability and substitutability in the short run.

Capabilities

Capabilities have been described by a variety of terms, including skills (Klein, Edge and Kass 1991), invisible assets (Itami 1987) and intermediate goods (Amit and Schoemaker 1993). In Hall's (1992) terms, they are the 'doing' as opposed to the 'having' in a company, but he restricts capabilities to personnel within the firm. Indeed, an emerging body of literature has recently adopted the resource-based perspective to evaluate the strategic importance of an organisation's human resources (Boxall and Steeneveld 1999; Kamoche 1996; Lado and Wilson 1994; Lepak and Snell 1999; Pfeffer 1994; Richard 2000; Ulrich and Lake 1991). More broadly, Grant (1991a) draws on Nelson and Winter's (1982) notion of organisational routines to demonstrate that capabilities can be people-based or based on the interaction between people and other resources. For example, one of Walmart's claimed unique capabilities is its logistics system (Irvin and Michaels 1989; Stalk, Evans and Schulman 1992). This system is essentially a collection of tangible assets, namely, 14 computerised facilities and a fleet of 6,500 trucks. However, the reason that the company's overall logistics capability cannot be duplicated is related to the way that these tangible assets are linked with the firm's people and its organisational routines. In this sense the essence of capabilities is interaction, resulting in Amit and Schoemaker's (1993) description of capabilities as intermediate goods in the production process. Generally speaking, capabilities is a broad category incorporating individual skills and learning within the firm as well as interactions such as teamwork, organisational culture and trust between management and workers.

Capabilities do not have clearly defined property rights as they are seldom the subject of a transaction (Hall 1989), resulting in a difficulty in their valuation. They have limited capacity in the short run due to learning and change difficulties, but have relatively unlimited capacity in the long run (Wernerfelt 1989). Capabilities possess significant barriers to duplication. Individual skills can be highly tacit, making them imperfectly imitable and imperfectly substitutable though top-performing individuals may be hired by competitors. Where capabilities are interaction-based, they are even more difficult to duplicate due to causal ambiguity. The RBV literature has tended to favour capabilities as the most likely source of sustainable competitive advantage. However, Collis (1994) argues against making this case too forcefully. He notes that capabilities are susceptible to erosion as the firm adapts to external or competitive changes, to replacement by a different capability and to being surpassed by a different capability. A summary of the key characteristics of the three categories of resources is provided in Table 3.4.

The role of strategic choices by management

Is was noted earlier that a sustainable competitive advantage arising from resource heterogeneity can be expected to lead to superior performance levels or rent. However, to ensure that the level of such returns is not

Table 3.4 Characteristics of key resources

| Type of resource | Characteristic of resource | | |
	Value	Appropriability	Barriers to duplication
Tangible assets (TAs)	Fixed long-run capacity. Property rights defined. Book value measurable	Value relatively easy to appropriate	Relatively easy to duplicate. Immobile and may be protected by economic deterrence. Relatively inimitable and substitutable
Intangible assets (IAs)	Relatively unlimited capacity. Property rights defined. Value difficult to measure	Value relatively easy to appropriate	Relatively difficult to duplicate due to regulatory and accumulation-related barriers
Capabilities (Cs)	Capacity limited in the short run but relatively unlimited in the long run. Property rights not well defined and value difficult to measure	Value relatively difficult to appropriate	Significant barriers to duplication caused by causal ambiguity, tacitness, complexity and specificity

overstated it is also necessary to take account of the cost of resource deployment. Rumelt (1987) has argued that the classical concept of rent applies in a static world and proposes an alternative, entrepreneurial rent (or Schumpeterian rent – Mahoney and Pandian 1992), which he defines as the *ex-post* value or payment stream of a venture minus the *ex-ante* cost of the resources combined to form the venture. Rents of greater than zero are likely to be the result of *ex-ante* uncertainty (Rumelt 1987). The *ex-ante* cost of resources (labelled *ex-ante* limits to competition by Peteraf 1993) is developed at length in Barney (1986a). He analyses the cost of resource deployment or strategy by introducing the concept of the strategic factor market, that is, a market where the resources necessary to implement a strategy are acquired. If this market is perfectly competitive, then the cost of acquiring strategic resources will approximately equal the economic value of those resources once they are used to implement product-market strategies (Barney 1986a). However, he adds that strategic factor markets are likely to be imperfect because managers tend to have differing expectations about the future value of a strategy, reflecting the uncertainty of the competitive environments facing them. Above-normal returns can then be earned by firms who have superior insight into the likely value of a strategy and consequently pay less than the full economic value necessary to implement it. This can be due to more accurate expectations, good fortune or both (Barney 1986a).

This argument is rejected to some extent by Dierickx and Cool (1989), who contend that very many resources, such as reputation and trust, are accumulated within the firm and cannot be bought and sold in factor markets. They argue that as these resources are non-tradable the only option for realising their value is to deploy them in product markets. Barney (1989) counters by claiming that the logic still holds and that, in the case of accumulated resources, the cost of accumulation must be accounted for, which he again sees as being a function of the firm's expectations or good fortune. Indeed, he concurs on the importance of accumulated resources by suggesting that a firm is likely to be better informed about the true future value of its own resources than competitors. Once again, this illustrates the importance put on accumulated resources by proponents of the resource-based view due to the combination of likely value to the firm as well as barriers to imitability and mobility.

The foregoing dialogue highlights another key point, which is the moderating role played by managers in the process by which resources lead to sustainable competitive advantages. Resources in and of themselves do not confer a sustainable competitive advantage (Thomas and Pollock 1999). As Kay (1993) puts it, a resource only becomes a competitive advantage when it is applied to an industry and brought to a market. Consequently, Williams (1992) describes the managerial role as specifically one of converting resources into something of value to customers. Other contributors typically see the managerial role as a multifaceted one. For example, Aaker (1989) identifies four activities, including the identification of relevant resources in the industry, the identification of resources within the firm, the development of these resources and the neutralising of competitors' resources. Recommending a sequential approach, Grant (1991a) suggests first identifying key resources, then selecting a strategy which best exploits them and finally investing to replenish the firm's resource base. In summary, the managerial role can be seen as one of identifying, developing, protecting and deploying its resource base (Amit and Schoemaker 1993).

The initial task facing managers is to try to identify the resources possessing the potential to generate sustainable competitive advantage. The prescriptive managerial literature provides guidelines as to how this might be done. For example, Prahalad and Hamel (1990) propose that resources must meet three conditions, namely, that they (i) provide potential access to a wide variety of markets, (ii) are relevant to the key buying criteria of customers and (iii) are difficult to imitate. In short, key resources are those that meet the three criteria of value, appropriability and barriers to duplication outlined earlier. However, the task of resource identification is a potentially very difficult one due to the problem of causal ambiguity (Lippman and Rumelt 1982; Reed and DeFillippi 1990), which hinders understanding of the relationship between resources and advantage.

Once key resources are identified, the literature recommends the ongoing development and protection of these resources (Stevenson 1976; Wernerfelt 1989). The task of resource development is illustrated by Dierickx and Cool's (1989) concept of asset stocks and flows. They argue that asset stocks, such as R&D capability or reputation, cannot be adjusted instantaneously but are accumulated through a consistent pattern of resource flows or investments. Where investment patterns lack consistency, the stock depreciates. Some authors provide a sequential framework for firms to follow in the development of resources, suggesting that the process must begin at the top of the company and penetrate into the deeper levels (Irvin and Michaels 1989). Furthermore, resource development is of central importance as its path dependency can provide a strong barrier to duplication. Other models of the resource-based view (Bharadwaj, Varadarajan and Fahy 1993; Day and Wensley 1988) propose a re-investment of profits in the development of the resource base, in other words after the resource has been deployed and an advantage realised. This is the task Grant (1991a) describes as filling resource gaps, which he sees as having an important time dimension as the firm tries to equip itself with the resources necessary to achieve competitive advantages in the future. Resource development for the future is also central to the concepts of strategic intent (Hamel and Prahalad 1989) and dynamic resource fit (Itami 1987). Therefore, resource development can be viewed as an ongoing process of consistently building resource stocks within the firm and continuing to rebuild these stocks as they are used up. Similarly, some resources will need ongoing protection from the imitative efforts of competitors. This is perhaps most relevant in the case of resources protected within the legal framework, where firms may need to show a determination to enforce their legal rights. Resources that possess inherent barriers to their duplication due to their inimitability, immobility and non-substitutability may not require such vigorous defence.

However, in terms of realising the potential for sustainable competitive advantage and superior performance, the critical managerial challenge relates to how the firm's key resources are deployed, in essence, its strategy in the marketplace. In actual practice, cases have shown that resource deployment involves changes to the organisation's structure and that long-term success may be contingent on organisational learning capabilities (Moingeon *et al.* 1998). The literature on strategy, whether described as business or competitive strategy, is an extensive one incorporating sometimes quite different views of what strategy is (see, for example, Chrisman, Hofer and Boulton 1988 and Hax and Majluf 1988 for reviews). One interpretation of strategy, which has held from the early work of Ansoff (1965) and Andrews (1971), is that strategy is concerned with matching the firm's strengths with the opportunities and threats presented in the marketplace. The resource-based view of the firm adopts this perspective on strategy. For example, Amit and Schoe-maker (1993) note that the applicability of a firm's resources to a partic-ular industry setting, or what they call an overlap with a set of strategic industry factors, will determine the available rents. Other authors, such as Lado, Boyd and Wright (1992), go even further, suggesting that firms should not seek solely to meet industry success factors but also to try to create new ones, generating a Schumpeterian-type revolution in the industry. By taking account of industry conditions, Collis and Mont-gomery (1995) claim that the resource-based view has helped to integrate the strategy field, which has emphasised industry factors (Porter 1980) and firm factors (Prahalad and Hamel 1990) at different stages in its development.

However, developing a match between the firm's resources and the success factors in an industry is a very demanding task. It was noted earlier that returns from strategic efforts are linked to managerial expec-tations about the value of the strategy where more accurate expectations can be expected to lead to more positive outcomes (Barney 1986a). The accuracy of expectations is influenced by friction forces or the properties of both the organisational actors and the environment or system in which they operate (Schoemaker 1990). Organisational actors are charac-terised by bounded rationality, impacting on their ability to frame prob-lems, gather intelligence, arrive at conclusions and learn from experience (Russo and Schoemaker 1989; Schoemaker 1992). The environments about which choices should be made are characterised by uncertainty and complexity concerning aspects such as technological changes and the rules of the game (Amit and Schoemaker 1993; Schoemaker 1990). Furthermore, Barney (1986a) notes that environmental analysis is unlikely systematically to generate expectational advantages because the methodologies for collecting this information and the conceptual models for analysing it are both in the public domain.

In summary, the resource-based view posits that the firm's manage-ment team assumes responsibility for identifying, developing, protecting and deploying value-generating resources. Given the practical difficulties of these tasks, good-quality top management in itself can possibly exhibit the characteristics of a key resource. For example, Castanias and Helfat (1991) contend that superior management skills, which they classify as generic skills, industry-related skills and firm-related skills, can be sources of rent. In particular, managerial skill can exhibit barriers to imitation because they are intangible and difficult to codify (Castanias and Helfat 1991). They may also be the result of a long period of learning by doing or of the manager's set of experiences or dominant logic (Prahalad and Bettis 1986), which is path-dependent and potentially very difficult to imitate. However, where the important skills possessed by managers are industry-specific (Castinas and Helfat 1991), managerial mobility may be a problem, raising the issue of the appropriability of value. This risk of mobility rises when managerial skills are not linked to other actors in the organisation, or what Wernerfelt (1989) describes as 'team effects'. Castanias and Helfat (1991) note that the greater the ability of top managers to collect their earned rents through remuneration packages, the greater the incentive to generate these rents, with the result that highly compensated managers may appropriate all the rent that they create.

Towards a conceptual model of the resource-based view of the firm

In conclusion, the resource-based view assumes the existence of firm heterogeneity and resource heterogeneity within firms as well as the possibility of sustained superior performance or economic rent. It provides a set of insights into the relationships between key resources available to the firm, managerial choices with respect to those resources and the levels of competitive advantage and performance attained by the firm in the marketplace. One of its key insights is that not all resources are of equal importance in terms of achieving a sustainable competitive advantage. Rather, it is only those resources that possess the characteristics of value, appropriability and barriers to their duplication by competitors. The latter characteristic is particularly important in ensuring that whatever advantages are achieved are also sustained. Advantages arising from intangible assets and capabilities are, therefore, likely to be more sustainable. Key resources in and of themselves do not necessarily create a competitive advantage. The management of the firm plays an important moderating role in this process. Strategic activities that must be undertaken by management include the identification of key resources, the development and protection of these resources and their appropriate deployment in product markets. None of these tasks is easy, emphasising the central role of strategic choice in the model. The effective deployment of key resources enables the achievement of sustainable competitive advantage. SCA is measured in terms of value delivered to customers, which is generally thought of as being either high perceived value or low delivered cost or both. SCA, in turn, gives rise to sustained superior performance measured in terms of market-based or financial-based performance and analogous to the economic notion of entrepreneurial rent.

Aspects of this set of relationships have been modelled elsewhere in the literature. For example, Day and Wensley (1988) document a sequential process whereby sources of advantage (superior skills and resources) lead to positional advantage (superior customer value or lower relative costs), which in turn leads to performance outcomes (market share and profitability) and the sequence is completed when profits are re-invested to sustain advantage. The same basic logic underlies a contingency model of competitive advantage in service industries developed by Bharadwaj, Varadarajan and Fahy (1993), which details the sources of advantage, barriers to imitation and the moderating effects of the characteristics of services and services industries. A conceptual model that builds on these contributions and summarises the discussion in this section is presented in Figure 3.2. Despite its origins in models of imperfect competition developed in the 1930s, the resource-based view of the firm is a relatively new perspective, having only gained a critical mass in the late 1980s (Wernerfelt 1995). Its development to date is characterised by an emphasis on conceptualisation. The empirical research that has taken place is briefly reviewed in the next section.

EMPIRICAL ASSESSMENT OF THE RESOURCE-BASED VIEW

Though the literature suggests that much remains to be done in terms of the empirical validation of the propositions put forward by the resource-based view (Godfrey and Hill 1995; Miller and Shamsie 1996; Rouse and Daellenbach 1999; Yeoh and Roth 1999), recent years have seen some progress in this area. The emerging empirical work broadly falls into one of three categories. First, some work has begun to emerge which tests aspects of the RBV illustrated in the model in Figure 3.2, such as how resources are developed within the organisation and the relationship between resources and competitive advantage. This line of research is of most direct relevance to this study and is summarised in Table 3.5 and discussed in the following paragraphs. Second, there is an emerging stream of research which uses the resource-based view to inform the

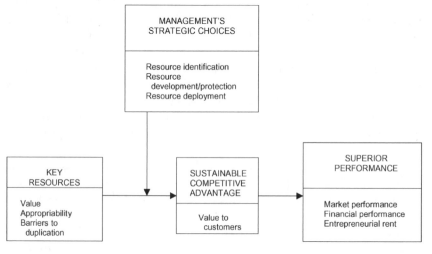

Figure 3.2 A resource-based model of sustainable competitive advantage

Table 3.5 Selected empirical research on the resource-based view of the firm

Author	Aspect of the resource-based view examined	Sample	Main findings
Brush and Artz (1999)	The contingencies which define valuable resources in the veterinary services sector	193 veterinary practices in the US	Ability to retain clients has strong performance implications; service properties moderate the relationship between resources and performance
Capron and Hulland (1999)	The redeployment of key marketing resources following horizontal acquisitions	253 mergers and acquisitions between 1988 and 1992	Highly immobile resources are more likely to be redeployed than less immobile resources. General marketing expertise has the most impact on market share and profitability
Collis (1991)	Relevance of the resource-based view to competition in a global industry	Primary and secondary analysis of the bearings industry	Superior performance can be explained in terms of the possession of key resources
Gunther McGrath, MacMillan and Venkataraman (1995)	The process by which resources are developed	160 project initiatives in 40 firms in 16 countries	The comprehension and deftness of an organisational sub-unit influences its level of competence
Hall (1992)	The relative importance of intangible resources in terms of overall business success	95 chief executives from select industry sectors in the UK (Response rate = 11%)	Company reputation, product reputation and employee know-how were considered to be the most important in terms of overall success
Helfat (1994)	Whether R&D has the characteristics of a rent-producing resource	Secondary data on 26 firms in the US petroleum industry from 1974 to 1981	Evidence of intra-industry differences in R&D expenditure
Henderson and Cockburn (1994)	R&D capabilities as a source of competitive advantage	Primary and secondary data on 10 major pharmaceutical firms in America and Europe	Both 'component' and 'architectural' competence have a positive influence on research productivity

Table 3.5 (continued)

Author	Aspect of the resource-based view examined	Sample	Main findings
Levinthal and Myatt (1994)	Factors influencing the development of a firm's resource endowments	The US mutual fund industry	Resource development is influenced by market activity and by managerial choices regarding markets
Maijoor and Van Witteloostuijn (1996)	Impact of resources on performance at the strategic group and industry level	Longitudinal data from 1967–1990 on the audit industry in the Netherlands	Large audit firm and its partners appropriate the rent in the industry by strategic regulation of the demand and supply sides of the market
Makadok and Walker (2000)	To examine the antecedents and consequences of forecasting ability in the mutual funds industry	206 money-market mutual funds (MMMFs) between 1975 and 1994	Forecasting ability leads to higher levels of appropriable economic returns; it both increases and is increased by firm size
Marcus and Geffen (1998)	How competences are developed	The electricity generation industry	Macro-environmental variables and firm-specific capabilities both contribute significantly to the creation and acquisition of competences
Mascarenhas, Baveja and Jamil (1998)	How competencies are developed	12 leading multinational companies	Identified competencies fall into three major groups: technological know-how, reliable processes and close relationships with external parties
Miller and Shamsie (1996)	The relative impact of property-based and knowledge-based resources on performance	7 major Hollywood studios from 1936 to 1965	Environmental context moderated the impact of resources on performance with periods of stability favouring property-based resources and periods of uncertainty favouring knowledge-based resources

Table 3.5 (continued)

Author	Aspect of the resource-based view examined	Sample	Main findings
Roth (1995)	The relationship between the CEO and resources located in different countries	74 chief executives in medium-sized firms in 9 selected industries (Response rate = 24%)	Some significant relationships were observed between CEO characteristics and levels of international interdependence
Yeoh and Roth (1999)	The relationship between resources, capabilities and SCA	20 firms in the pharmaceutical industry between 1971 and 1989	R&D and salesforce expenditures affect SCA but effects are influenced by both component and integrative capabilities

issue of corporate strategy within organisations, including the patterns of diversification undertaken (Chatterjee and Wernerfelt 1991; Farjoun 1994) and in particular the relationship between diversification and performance (Hitt and Ireland 1985; Markides and Williamson 1994; Robins and Wiersema 1995). Finally, there is some other empirical work on the fringes of the RBV such as that by Balakrishnan and Fox (1993), which examines the limitations of investment in firm-specific assets. Because such assets are not easily redeployed elsewhere, they do not represent possible collateral for borrowing, with adverse effects on the firm's capital structure (Balakrishnan and Fox 1993).

Research relating to the core perspectives of the RBV has progressed from relatively simple efforts at understanding the importance of resources in terms of overall success (Hall 1992) to more ambitious attempts to extend the scope of the resource-based view beyond the boundaries of the firm (Maijoor and Van Witteloostuijn 1996). In an early study, Hall (1992) surveyed UK chief executives to determine their views on the relative importance of a select list of intangible resources in terms of the overall success of the business. Rankings were elicited for two time periods and three resources; namely, company reputation, product reputation and employee know-how were consistently ranked one, two and three respectively. Furthermore, these resources were seen by respondents as likely to take longest to re-create if the company had to start from scratch, confirming the important link between resource accumulation and competitive importance (Dierickx and Cool 1989). Miller and Shamsie (1996) examined the relative impact on performance in the movie studio business of two broad sets of resources, namely, property-based resources such as long-term contracts with star actors and knowledge-based resources such as creative and technical skills.

Their longitudinal study of performance over the period 1936 to 1955 found that periods of stability rewarded firms with property-based resources but not those with knowledge-based resources, while the opposite was true in periods of uncertainty.

Helfat's (1994) study examined the rent-generating potential of the firm-specific resource, R&D. The study proposed two hypotheses, namely, that the firm-specificity of R&D creates intra-industry differences in R&D applications and that this provides an inherent mechanism by which firms can at least partially appropriate the returns to R&D, which contrasts with the more general view that knowledge produced through R&D tends to diffuse quickly unless given regulatory protection. Examination of R&D expenditures in the US petroleum industry over a seven-year period found support for the former hypothesis, suggesting that R&D investments possess inherent barriers to duplication, though the study does not attempt to correlate this with firm performance.

Similarly, Henderson and Cockburn (1994) also examine the role of R&D as a source of advantage, but their study concentrates on the pharmaceutical industry. They distinguish two types of R&D capability, namely, what they call 'component' competence, which is local knowledge fundamental to solving day-to-day problems, and 'architectural' competence, which is the ability to integrate and use component competences residing both within and outside the firm. The number of patents granted was used as a proxy for competitive advantage and both component and architectural capability were found to influence research productivity, with the latter exhibiting a stronger influence. Yeoh and Roth (1999) adopt a similar approach in a further study of the pharmaceutical industry. They look at R&D expenditures and salesforce expenditures as the key firm resources deployed through either component or integrative (architectural) capabilities to generate sustained competitive advantages which they measure in terms of high-quality products and global market application. They find that R&D expenditure has a positive and indirect effect on competitive advantage, while salesforce expenditures do not affect product quality but have a direct impact on global market application. Component capabilities influence competitive advantage both directly and indirectly through integrative capabilities.

Two studies broadly within the financial services industry have been distinguished by the fact that they adopt perspectives external as well as internal to the firm in examining aspects of the resource-based view. In a study of the US mutual fund industry, Levinthal and Myatt (1994) examine both the organisational and environmental factors responsible for the emergence of resources within the organisation. Their study finds support for their hypothesis that the development of resources is related to (i) the firm's activity in the marketplace, such as its relationships with customers or whether the market is in decline or has demanding customers (Collis 1991; Porter 1990) and (ii) managerial choices about which markets to serve and how to serve them. Less support is apparent for a third influencing variable, namely, organisational factors such as past decisions or what they term 'initial conditions' which cause the firm to focus on a particular capability trajectory. Maijoor and Van Witteloostuijn's (1996) study of the Dutch audit industry goes even further, seeking to extend the resource-based view beyond the level of the firm to that of the strategic group and the industry. In other words, they contend that resources are also rent-producing at the group or industry levels if they cannot be imitated or substituted by firms outside the group or industry. They support this view with an analysis of the Dutch audit industry over a period of 23 years which showed that, by the manipulation of regulatory barriers, one group, namely, large audit firms and their partners, were able to appropriate the rent from the key resource in the audit market, which are the registered accountants (RAs).

A further contribution by Gunther McGrath, MacMillan and Venkataraman (1995), while acknowledging the role of industry in influencing performance, chooses to delve deeper within the firm to study the managerial processes that give rise to competences. They use a narrow definition of competence as the ability of a group initiative reliably and consistently to meet or exceed its objectives. The authors hypothesise that the antecedents of competence and in turn competitive advantage are (i) comprehension, which is the group's understanding of what combinations of resources will enable it to achieve its objectives and (ii) deftness, which is the extent to which the group is operating collectively. The hypotheses were tested on a convenience sample of 160 project initiatives under way in 40 firms in 16 countries. Comprehension and deftness were both found to be positively correlated with competence but the research also revealed a strong correlation between comprehension and deftness, leading the authors to conclude that an interrelated sequence of processes from comprehension through deftness through competence underlies competitive advantage. In contrast, Marcus and Geffen (1998) use a case-based approach to examine the issue of competence acquisition and conclude that both external forces and firm-specific capacities affect the organization's ability to create and acquire new competences.

Three further studies have empirically examined aspects of the resource-based view in the context of international competition. Reviewing the development of the global bearings industry, Collis (1991) illustrates how the superior performance of certain firms is related to their possession of key resources, how structural changes are made to facilitate resource development and how an organisation's heritage constrains its strategic choices. On this basis, Collis (1991) argues that the resource-based view provides a valuable complement to industrial organisation-derived models of competition and advocates its further application in the context of global competition. The contribution by

Roth (1995) is less wide-ranging and explores specifically how the relationship between the international interdependence of the organisation and the characteristics of the CEO interact to influence firm performance. His study found evidence of relationships between the characteristics of the CEO and international interdependence, suggesting that CEOs have an important role in the development and deployment of resources located in different countries. Finally, Mascarenhas, Baveja and Jamil (1998) looked at the dynamics of core competencies in 12 leading multinational companies. The found that competencies could be grouped into three categories, namely, technological know-how, reliable processes and close relationships with external parties, each of which required different approaches in their development.

In summary, the empirical work examining the resource-based view of the firm has been somewhat fragmented and limited in its scope, possibly reflecting a difficulty in examining some of the key concepts (Godfrey and Hill 1995). It has also been quite varied in terms of its hypotheses, methodologies and findings, though some important insights have been generated into the different types of resources that are likely to be a source of competitive advantage. Generally, the studies are viewed by their authors as initial attempts to test the propositions of the RBV (Gunther McGrath, MacMillan and Venkataraman 1995; Maijoor and Van Witteloostuijn 1996) and they have tended to be industry-specific, raising questions about their generalisability. Furthermore, some of the research has sought to expand the resource-based view beyond the boundaries of the firm (Maijoor and Van Witteloostuijn 1996) or has proposed alternative explanations of the antecedents of competitive advantage (Gunther McGrath, MacMillan and Venkataraman 1995). Research work in this direction may be premature given the lack of empirical assessment of the fundamental propositions of the resource-based view to date. Therefore, given the limited and fragmented nature of the empirical work to date, further tests of the resource-based view are necessary to examine the propositions emerging from ongoing conceptual work in the area.

CONCLUSION

The purpose of this chapter as stated in the opening paragraphs is to provide an understanding of the origins, insights and current status of the resource-based view of the firm, which has emerged in recent years as a popular conceptualisation of competitive advantage at the level of the firm. In the early part of the chapter the origins, orientation and development of the resource-based view are discussed. Its underpinnings are in economic models of competition which emphasise firm heterogeneity and which allow for strategic choices in interactions with the environment. This is followed by a detailed discussion of the key assumptions of the RBV. Above-normal profits or rents are assumed to be possible and to accrue to resource scarcity. This focuses attention on the characteristics of key resources, which an examination of the literature suggests can be reduced to market value, appropriability and barriers to duplication. These characteristics explain the persistence of resource heterogeneity central to the attainment of sustained superior returns. However, the process is not automatic, and requires the moderating interventions of managerial choices in the identification, development, protection and subsequent deployment of resources in product markets.

It is argued that though the RBV does not represent the only theory of the firm, it does meet the criteria for a new theory (Conner 1991). Holmstrom and Tirole (1989) specify that any theory of the firm must explain both why firms exist and what determines their size and scope. From the resource-based perspective, firms exist (instead of markets) because of the opportunity to benefit from efficiencies created by asset interdependencies within the firm. Size and scope can be considered a function of resource endowments and the resource-based view 'passes an additional test' in terms of its explanation of performance differentials between firms (Conner 1991). It also meets the requirements specified in Lippman and Rumelt (1982) that a theory must explain both the origins of inter-firm differences and the mechanisms that impede their elimination through competition and entry. Allied to these insights, it was noted that the resource-based view possesses the ability to 'sustain the conversation' within strategic management and between strategic management and branches of economics, making it a reliable foundation on which to build further research (Mahoney and Pandian 1992). In the following chapter, the resource-based view of the firm is used to tackle the overall question examined by this research, namely, how do firms attain a sustainable competitive advantage in a global environment?

4 Sustainable competitive advantage in a global environment

INTRODUCTION

It was noted in Chapter 2 that the global environment presents a challenging arena in which to attain an SCA, and the question of how firms attain such advantages has not been well documented in the extant literature. At the same time, the resource-based view of the firm (RBV) has become popular in the strategic management literature as a theory of competitive advantage. In this chapter, it is proposed to use the RBV as a theoretical lens to examine the question of sustainable competitive advantage in a global environment. The conceptual integration of these two concepts has appeal for two reasons. First, the question of resources has been germane to much of the discussion of competition in international business, particularly apparent in contributions emanating from the economics tradition. This can be seen in the trade theory literature, which was founded on resource asymmetries across countries and the more recent contributions of industrial organisation economics, which emphasise the role of 'firm-specific advantages' in the competitive activities of MNCs. In light of this background, it is desirable to examine the role of resources in a more systematic and comprehensive manner, and this is facilitated by adoption of the resource-based perspective. Second, there is a great deal of intellectual congruence between the international business literature and the resource-based view of the firm. Both have similar backgrounds, rooted in economics, and both have been supplemented by recent contributions from management writers. Such congruence suggests the possibility for shared insights and beneficial exchanges of ideas. The interface of international business and the resource-based view is worthy of examination as a locus for interdisciplinary research.

The purpose of the chapter, therefore, is to extend the resource-based view of the firm to examine the question of sustainable competitive advantage in a global environment. It begins by revisiting the international business literature to review discussion on the nature of the resource pool available to firms operating in global environments. It will be demonstrated that the scope of such a resource pool is greater than that available to purely domestic firms. This is followed by the development and exposition of a resource-based model of SCA in a global environment, demonstrating the links between resources, the location of those resources, strategic orientation and sustained superior performance. A set of ten research hypotheses emerges from the literature review and the conceptual model and these are then outlined. The chapter closes with some concluding remarks on the conceptual issues.

RESOURCES IN A GLOBAL ENVIRONMENT

The previous chapter contends that resources potentially play a critical role in the survival and prosperity of firms. This raises the important question of what resources are typically available to firms operating in a global environment. Such firms may originate in a large domestic market such as the US. They may have production facilities in a number of diverse world locations. They may have downstream sales, marketing and service activities in many world markets. And they may be part of a much larger global conglomerate consisting of different companies, in different businesses, in different regions throughout the world. As a result, they potentially have access to a large and diverse resource pool, elements of which may be located in many different countries. Consequently, discussing resources in the context of firms operating in a global environment necessitates consideration of both country-specific and firm-specific resources. This distinction is quite well established in the international business literature (Dunning 1977; Ghoshal 1987; Kogut 1985b; Roth 1992), though once again inconsistency in the use of terminology does complicate the issue. For example, in his eclectic paradigm, Dunning (1977) uses the term 'ownership advantages' to describe firm-specific advantages (resources). In keeping with the tradition of trade theory, Kogut (1985b) uses the term 'comparative advantages' interchangeably with 'country-specific advantages' and, using the vocabulary of strategic management, he interchanges 'competitive advantages' and 'firm-specific advantages'. For consistency, only the labels 'country-specific resources' (CSRs) and 'firm-specific resources' (FSRs) are employed here. Represented diagramatically, this means that the resource pool available to a firm operating in a global environment looks like that presented in Figure 4.1. It demonstrates that the size of such a pool is potentially vast, particularly in a situation where the firm is widely geographically diversified.

Country-specific resources (CSRs)

The nature and role of country-specific resources was first considered in the work of the early trade theorists. Their analyses focused on basic

Location	Resources	
	Country-specific	Firm-specific
Country of origin		
Host country 1 . . . . Host country *n*		

Figure 4.1 The resource pool of a firm operating in a global environment

factor inputs such as land, labour and capital. In this context, CSRs could be seen as having two clearly definable characteristics. First, they were inherited rather than created, with the result that a country's endowment of CSRs was taken as fixed or static and was not subject to change. Second, CSRs were locationally immobile, meaning that availing of these resources required some form of presence in the country in which they were held (Dunning 1977; Gray 1982). From a competitive viewpoint, the focus of attention was on the basic inputs into the production process and on how endowments of these factors varied from country to country. Attention was also paid to the role of geographic location as a country-specific resource. Geographic nearness to markets was found to influence investment decisions (Davidson 1980), while the role of cultural proximity or psychic distance is said to influence both the location of foreign investment decisions (Johanson and Wiedersheim-Paul 1975; Johanson and Vahlne 1977; O'Grady and Lane 1996) and the nature of these investments (Hennart and Larimo 1998).

In the 1980s, this basic view of the differences between countries was extended to include the dynamic aspects of a country's economic and financial environments. The role of dimensions of a country's market, such as its demographic size, its level of income and its growth potential, was found to influence foreign investment decisions (Davidson 1980). This work was important for two reasons. First, it switched attention from a preoccupation with factor resources to looking at the role of market-based resources where, for example, access to a large foreign market might enable a firm to gain significant economies of scale. Second, it illustrated that resources were not static but subject to change as a nation's economy developed. This issue of change was at the core of the work of writers analysing the financial environments of countries (Feiger 1988; Kogut 1985a). Variations in exchange rates, tax rates and the cost of labour and capital between countries presented opportunities for cost savings and efficiencies for firms in a position to leverage such differentials (Kogut 1985a).

More recent work has broadened the discussion of CSRs still further to include not only inherited resources but also those that are created by a country, which are increasingly being seen as critical to country competitiveness (Choi 1999; Dunning 1998). Again, a range of terminology is used to discuss these created resources including intangible assets (Dunning 1988a), strategic assets (Dunning and Rojec 1993), country capabilities (Kogut 1991) and advanced factors of production (Porter 1990). The common feature of this type of resource is that it is a product of investments made over a long period of time in any given country (Gray 1982). Typical examples of such resources that have been cited in the literature include the nature of the education system (Davidson 1989; Ghoshal 1987; Reich 1991), technological and organisational capabilities (Kogut 1991; Reich 1991), communications and marketing infrastructures (Dunning 1988a; Porter 1990), labour productivity (Lewis *et al.* 1993) and research facilities (Porter 1990). A study by Shan and Hamilton (1991) demonstrated how the success of the US biotechnology industry was a function of a collection of unique, advanced resources, including government support for research in the field, an aggressive entrepreneurial culture supported by favourable capital markets, and a high level of R&D expenditure. Their study also showed that it was a desire to gain access to these unique country-specific resources that was the basis for Japanese cooperative ventures with American firms in this industry. Particular interest has also focused on understanding why countries differ in their stocks of capabilities or advanced factors, which is generally seen as being related to the national economic and institutional arrangements of the country (Kogut 1991; Murtha and Lenway 1994; Porter 1990). Critical influencing variables which have been identified include (i) selection pressures (Kogut 1991) or the demand conditions and firm strategy, structure and rivalry in a country (Porter 1990) and (ii) technological opportunities (Kogut 1991) or the presence of related and supporting industries (Porter 1990).

In summary, the literature on country-specific resources has evolved significantly from the pioneering work of the trade theorists who viewed CSRs as inputs into the production process that were inherited, static and immobile. A variety of other resources in a country's financial and/or product markets have also been identified which are dynamic and enable significant efficiencies to be gained by firms in a position to identify and exploit future trends. The recent attention being paid to a country's stock of advanced and sophisticated resources is also significant in that it has shifted attention from a preoccupation with CSRs leading to cost or efficiency-based advantages to looking at CSRs which might enable firms to gain quality or differentiation advantages (Dunning 1988a; Porter 1990). In conclusion, two salient aspects of CSRs can be identified, namely, that they are external to the firm and that they are imperfectly mobile across national borders. A list of such resources

Table 4.1 Country-specific resources

Country-specific resources	Supporting literature
Basic CSRs Climate; costs of labour and capital; exchange rates; government subsidies and grants; location; natural resources; tariffs and quotas; tax rates	Davidson (1980; 1989), Doz (1986; 1987), Dunning (1977), Feiger (1988), Kogut (1985a), Porter (1980; 1990)
Advanced CSRs Economic, technical and market infrastructures; labour productivity; nature of the education system; organisational capabilities; scientific, technical and market knowledge	Davidson (1989), Dunning (1988a), Ghoshal (1987), Kogut (1991), Lewis *et al.* (1993), Murtha and Lenway (1994), Porter (1990), Reich (1991), Shan and Hamilton (1991)

identified in the literature which have been classified here as those which are either basic or advanced is presented in Table 4.1.

Firm-specific resources (FSRs)

It is argued in Chapter 3 that firm-specific resources can be classed as tangible assets, intangible assets and capabilities. Though these types of distinctions have not been explicitly made in the discourse on international competition, reference to resources comprising each of the three groups of FSRs is commonplace. For example, the building of tangible assets such as world-scale plants where production is centralised and efficiencies maximised has received much attention in the management literature (Gluck 1982; Hout, Porter and Rudden 1982; Porter 1986a). The importance of intangible assets has been given a great deal of attention in the economics literature. For example, patented technology and brand reputation were cited by Kindleberger (1969) as sources of the factor-related and goods-related advantages, respectively, of international competitors. Empirical studies have found, for example, that product differentiation (based on reputation) is the most internationally transferable firm-specific resource (Lall 1980). In general, the changing nature of world economic activity has begun to place a greater premium on the transfer of intangible assets across national boundaries, though this activity is constrained by the presence of immobile clusters of complementary value-adding activities (Dunning 1998). Finally, the role played by the different kinds of capabilities has been highlighted by both economists and management writers. For example, research by Knickerbocker (1973) found that the successful international expansion of US firms was based on a number of specific strengths, including that they (i) conduct extensive R&D, (ii) employ complex, high-technology production methods and (iii) engage in vigorous and sophisticated marketing activities. Empirical work by Kimura (1989) found that technological leadership and complex vertical downstream linkages were among the major influencers of the FDI activity of Japanese semiconductor firms. Capabilities highlighted as being important in the management literature range from design and product development (Peters 1990) to the ability to harness organisational learning (Ghoshal 1987) to planning and administrative systems (Coates 1989) to the flexibility and consensus-building skills of the firm's executives (Fleenor 1993). In short, firms have access to a diverse range of firm-specific resources as well as the country-specific resources outlined above. In addition, these resources may be located in both the firm's country of origin and in any or all of the host countries in which it conducts business.

The geographic location of CSRs and FSRs

It is evident from the literature that, with regard to the location of resources, the major focus of attention has been on the role of the country of origin. For example, the relationship between a country's stock of advanced CSRs and its economic and institutional context was noted above. The relationships between a firm's stock of FSRs and its home country have also been the subject of much interest. Dunning (1981) has argued that firm-specific advantages (resources), though endogenous to particular firms, are not independent of their industrial structure, economic systems and institutional and cultural environments. Thus, for example, much of the international success of Japanese firms has been attributed to the role of their home government and its ministries (Pascale and Athos 1982; van Wolferen 1989), as well as to the ethos of the Japanese population towards work, authority and living standards (Lodge and Vogel 1986). Gray (1982) draws a distinction between 'physical' national characteristics (land, natural resources, labour supply and capital) that influence the stock of country-specific resources and 'social' national characteristics (social structure, tax structure, treatment of R&D and government policy) that influence a country's stock of firm-specific resources. He cites the example of the nineteenth-century German emphasis on scientific education and chemical research (a 'social' national characteristic) as underlying the supremacy of German firms in chemical technology. However, a link between 'physical' national characteristics and firm-specific resources has also been identified by Hood and Young (1979), who contend that the superiority of Japanese firms in product miniaturisation is related to the pressures on physical space in Japan. Recent empirical research by Arora and Gambardella (1997) concluded that domestic market size positively influences the specialisation competencies in firms. Perhaps the most comprehensive treatment of the links between the physical, economic and institutional environment of a country and its stock of CSRs and FSRs is provided by Porter's 'diamond' of national advantage (Porter 1990; 1991). The four central elements of the diamond are factor conditions (which describe a country's stock of CSRs), demand conditions, firm strategy, structure and rivalry, and related and supporting industries, all of which combine to influence the FSRs possessed by firms in a particular country. Both CSRs and FSRs in turn are influenced by government policy and chance (Porter 1990).

But Porter's model has also been subjected to criticism for failing to take account of the role of host countries as well as the country of origin (Cartwright 1993; Hodgetts 1993; Rugman and D'Cruz 1993; Rugman and Verbeke 1993). For example, Rugman and Verbeke (1993) argue that thinking solely in terms of a home-country diamond of advantage is inappropriate, particularly in the context of firms from small nations. In their view, Canadian firms draw on CSRs such as skilled labour in both Canada and the United States. Furthermore, since most Canadian MNCs sell up to 70 per cent of their production in the United States, demand conditions in the latter are relevant to them, as is firm rivalry and the presence of related and supporting industries which in turn influence the stock of FSRs in Canadian firms. Rugman and Verbeke (1993) propose that it is necessary to think in terms of a 'double diamond' approach where conditions in a host country are viewed as being of no less importance than those in the country of origin, while Cartwright (1993) suggests that 'multiple-linked diamonds' are appropriate in the case of New Zealand. These arguments sit easily with prevailing views on the global economy that consider a significant proportion of foreign direct investment to be strategic asset seeking (Dunning 1998; Dunning and Rojec 1993).

In addition, host-country firm-specific resources are embodied in the organisation's international subsidiaries and the nature of these subsidiaries has been the focus of growing research interest in recent years (see, for example, Bartlett and Ghoshal 1986; Birkinshaw and Hood 1998; 2000; Birkinshaw and Morrison 1995; Taggart 1997). For example, Bartlett and Ghoshal (1986) distinguish between subsidiary roles which they variously label as 'implementer', 'contributor' and 'strategic leader', with the latter two types possessing local FSRs which may be important sources of advantage. More generally, Birkinshaw, Hood and Jonsson (1998) find that not only do multinational subsidiaries contribute to firm-specific advantage creation, but they can also drive the process. In summary, a firm operating in a global environment potentially has access to CSRs and FSRs in both its country of origin and in the host countries in which it operates. Widely geographically diversified firms consequently can avail themselves of an extensive range of resources. In the following section, a conceptual model is proposed which delineates the relationships between this global resource pool and the attainment of a sustainable competitive advantage by firms operating in a global environment.

A RESOURCE-BASED MODEL OF SCA IN A GLOBAL ENVIRONMENT

In Figure 3.2, a sequential model demonstrating the relationships between resources, management choice, SCA and superior perform- ance was presented. This model is also suitable for describing the nature of SCA in a global environment. In the latter context, firms can again attain sustainable advantages and economic rents by deploying difficult-to-duplicate resources in ways that create value for global customers. However, this basic model needs extension in a global context. In particular, it is necessary to move beyond simply seeing the firm's resource pool as comprising firm-specific tangible assets, intan- gible assets and capabilities. As argued above, firms operating in a global environment have access to a range of country-specific resources (CSRs) and both these CSRs and the firm-specific resources (FSRs) are located in the country of origin and the host countries in which the firm operates. This resource diversity means that the management role in mediating the process by which resources are converted into sustainable advantages is a particularly complex one. Therefore, a revised and extended model of SCA in a global environ- ment is presented in Figure 4.2.

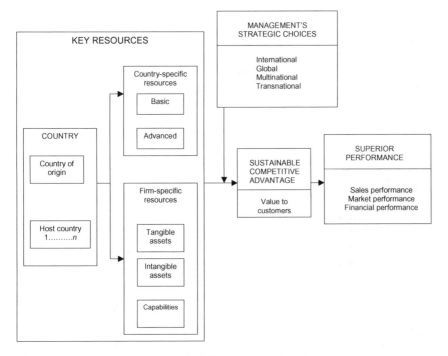

Figure 4.2 A resource-based model of SCA in a global environement

Key resources

The revised model incorporates both country-specific resources (CSRs) and firm-specific resources (FSRs), and also accounts for the range of countries from which these resources might be drawn. The three main types of firm-specific resources were discussed in the previous chapter. Tangible assets are defined as the fixed or current assets of the firm and are characterised by relatively fixed long-run capacity, well-defined property rights and relative ease of competitive duplication. Intangible assets have relatively high capacity, well-defined property rights and are relatively difficult to duplicate due to regulatory restrictions and barriers related to their processes of development. Capabilities, which are described as the 'doing' as opposed to the 'having' within the firm, refer to the skills of individuals as well as the resources created through the multitude of interactions taking place within the firm. Capabilities are characterised by limited capacity in the short run but relatively high levels of capacity in the long run, poorly defined property rights and relatively strong barriers to competitive duplication. Country-specific resources (CSRs) are defined as resources that are external to the firm and imperfectly immobile across national borders. CSRs can also be further divided into two main types, namely, basic CSRs and advanced CSRs, which are distinguished by their relative levels of intangibility and by the processes of their accumulation in a country. Basic CSRs are relatively tangible, as reflected by a country's stock of land or natural resources or its market size. Stocks of basic CSRs are either inherited or fixed, such as a country's climate or are subject to periodic adjustment, such as tariff levels or subsidy levels. Advanced CSRs, such as a country's stock of managerial or technical skills, are less tangible and their development requires sustained and consistent investment over the long run. Finally, the model also accounts for the location of both CSRs and FSRs, which may be dispersed between the firm's country of origin and also any or all of the host countries in which it operates (see Figure 4.2).

Strategic orientation

The basic resource-based model of sustainable competitive advantage outlined in Chapter 3 proposes that management plays a central moderating role in the process by which resources are converted into SCA. Management is charged with a number of responsibilities, including resource identification, resource development and protection and resource deployment in product markets to create value for customers. These tasks remain equally important in the context of firms operating in a global environment. Indeed, it is likely that they are even more challenging, due, for example, to the greater range of resources available to the firm, the greater difficulty in protecting key resources due to the absence of global regulatory framework, the greater difficulty in under-standing the value criteria of diverse sets of customers and the overall increased complexity of the management task.

In the management perspective on international business discussed in Chapter 2, it is evident that these resource-related tasks have not been an explicit topic of interest. Three streams of literature were reviewed, namely, business strategy, organisational structure and managerial processes, and decisions with regard to each of these management tasks have important resource implications. For example, the nature of the firm's organisational structure and its coordination and control processes will affect resource development and protection. The behavioural orien-tation of the firm, which is reflected in its strategy and processes, is likely to affect the task of resource identification. The firm's competitive strategy, whether it emphasises cross-national efficiencies or local responsiveness or both, invariably influences decisions relating to resource deployment. The most integrative scheme available to date, which describes the management of process, structure and strategy in firms trading internationally, is the Bartlett and Ghoshal typology (Bartlett and Ghoshal 1987a; 1989). Their typology identifies four types of firms, each demonstrating a different strategic orientation. First, they describe the 'international' firm which is characterised by an emphasis on the centralisation of decisions in the home country, with the role of foreign subsidiaries being somewhat confined to local adaptation of products developed in the home market. By contrast, the approach of the 'multinational' firm is characterised by decentralisation and by high levels of subsidiary autonomy, with a consequent emphasis on the deve-lopment and deployment of local resources to exploit local opportuni-ties. A third alternative is the 'global' firm, which is a globally scaled organisation seeking to maximise the potential for efficiencies worldwide in a tightly controlled organisation where the key decisions are retained in the home-country headquarters. Finally, there is the 'transnational' firm, which operates as a highly integrated network, where resources are dispersed but jointly developed and shared worldwide through highly coordinated processes. Empirical research by Bartlett and Ghoshal (1989) and Leong and Tan (1993) has identified the presence of each of the four orientations in a sample of firms, implying that each orientation may be found in a global environment. Further research by Luo (1999) has found that the transnational strategy outperforms the other postures in aligning with the market and attaining benefits from both ownership-specific and country-specific advantages. Whichever orientation the firm has will affect its decisions regarding resource identification, develop-ment, protection and deployment. Consequently, the conceptual model of SCA in a global environment adopts the Bartlett and Ghoshal typology as a framework for describing alternative approaches to the moderating role of management illustrated in Figure 3.2.

Sustainable competitive advantage and superior performance

The resource-based view of the firm posits that the deployment of key resources enables the firm to attain a sustainable competitive advantage that in turn leads to levels of performance superior to those achieved by competitors. This proposition also holds in the context of the global environment. Competitive advantage in a global competition is again measured by the firm's ability to deliver relatively more value to its customers than its competitors, and the measurement of the level of advantage will generally necessitate consideration of competitors from a number of countries. Sustained competitive advantage can be expected to lead to superior performance measured by criteria such as sales returns, financial returns and market performance, as discussed in Chapter 3.

In summary, it is asserted that the basic model of the resource-based view of the firm requires some modifications more accurately to describe the nature of sustainable competitive advantage in a global environment. The fundamental logic of the model, which is that key resources effectively deployed by management enable the attainment of SCA and superior performance, still holds. However, the resource pool available to the firm is a more diverse one and the model is extended to incorporate country-specific resources as well as firm-specific resources, and also to illustrate the possible breadth of location of both sets of resources. The management task of converting resources into SCA in a global environment is very challenging; the alternative approaches to this task have been incorporated into the model using the Bartlett and Ghoshal typology.

RESEARCH HYPOTHESES

The model presented in Figure 4.2 suggests a number of causal relationships worthy of exploration. Initially, the RBV suggests that the sustainability of any advantage is a function of the height of the barriers to the competitive duplication of the advantage-generating resource. Barriers to duplication, in turn, are deemed to be a function of the inimitability, immobility and substitutability of the resource. The resource pool of the firm operating in a global environment comprises five different resource groups, namely, tangible assets (TAs), intangible assets (IAs), capabilities (Cs), basic country-specific resources (BCSRs) and advanced country-specific resources (ACSRs). In the following paragraphs, the relative importance of these resource groups as a source of sustainable competitive advantage is examined.

Tangible assets (TAs) are the fixed or current assets of the firm. They include plant, equipment, land, other capital goods and stocks, debtors and bank deposits. Their book value is measurable and this value is reflected in the balance sheet valuation of companies. They are deemed to be relatively transparent, and though they generally have the characteristic of imperfect mobility, they are relatively weak at resisting imitative or substitution efforts by competitors. Firms also possess intangible assets (IAs), which comprise trademarks, patents, copyright, registered designs, contracts, trade secrets, networks, databases, brand reputation and company reputation. The value of intangible assets is relatively difficult to measure and their capacity is relatively high. Intangible assets are relatively difficult to duplicate. Intellectual property is protected within the legal system of property rights, preventing its imitation or mobility without the consent of its owner. Such protection is not as strong in a global environment in the absence of an effective global system of property rights. Substitutability is possible, as reflected, for example, by the efforts of firms to 'invent around' patents. Other intangible assets such as databases, networks and brand and company reputation are even more difficult to duplicate. They are typical of what Dierickx and Cool (1989) term an asset stock, and the inherent specificity and complexity of their accumulation means that they are difficult to imitate or substitute in the short run. Therefore, due to their relatively higher barriers to duplication, it would be expected that intangible assets would be considered by management as a more important source of sustainable competitive advantage in a global environment than tangible assets.

Hypothesis 1: All other things being equal, intangible assets will be perceived to be a more important source of sustainable competitive advantage in a global environment than tangible assets.

Aside from assets, a third category of firm-specific resources is capabilities (Cs). Capabilities comprise the individual skills of a firm's employees as well as resources emerging form the various interactions or routines taking place within an organisation including, for example, those within teams, between workers and managers and between personnel and tangible assets. Capabilities are characterised by poorly defined property rights and a relatively high level of intangibility. Related to their intangibility, capabilities are also relatively difficult to duplicate. The relationship between capabilities and advantage is frequently ambiguous due to the potential tacitness, complexity and specificity of skills, routines and interactions. Because of the relatively high level of these barriers to duplication, it would be expected that management would consider capabilities to be a more important source of sustainable competitive advantage in a global environment than either tangible assets or intangible assets.

Hypothesis 2: All other things being equal, capabilities will be perceived to be a more important source of sustainable competitive advantage in a global environment than either tangible assets or intangible assets.

Country-specific resources (CSRs) comprise basic CSRs and advanced CSRs. Basic CSRs include a country stock of natural resources, its location and climate, its cost of labour and capital and its levels of government subsidies and grants, tariffs, quotas, taxes and exchange rates. Basic CSRs are relatively transparent and tangible. In the cases of natural resources, location and climate they are inherited and fixed. Others such as subsidies and tariffs are not fixed but subject to periodic adjustment by policy makers. Advanced CSRs include economic, technical and market infrastructures, labour productivity, the nature of a country's education system and the country's stock of technical and market knowledge. Advanced CSRs are relatively less transparent and less tangible than basic CSRs. They are not inherited or fixed, but rather the product of sustained investment in the long run. Thus, they are similar to Dierickx and Cool's (1989) concept of asset stocks at the firm level, implying that advanced CSRs cannot be adjusted instantaneously. Like capabilities, advanced CSRs are characterised by relatively high levels of causal ambiguity. For example, it was noted above that the success of the US biotechnology industry was attributed to a combination of advanced CSRs, including government support, an aggressive entrepreneurial culture supported by favourable capital markets and a high level of R&D, though it was difficult to isolate the specific importance of each factor.

In a global environment, firms can gain access to both basic and advanced CSRs. However, it is relatively easy to duplicate a competitor's stock of basic CSRs. For example, it is possible to imitate a competitor's choice of production locations to gain access to similar costs of labour or to benefit from similar tax or exchange rates. In situations where one firm is offered an exclusive deal by a host country, this is a reflection of the political capabilities of that firm (an FSR) rather than any inherent barriers to the duplication of a basic CSR. Even in such cases, competitors have the option of seeking to substitute for such deals through negotiations with third-country governments. Stocks of advanced CSRs are relatively hard to duplicate. They are a product of the institutional and economic environments of a country (Murtha and Lenway 1994; Porter 1990), they do not diffuse easily across national borders (Kogut 1991) and they are causally ambiguous and path-dependent. Firms originating in a given country are likely to have easier access to these advanced CSRs than foreign firms (Kogut 1991; Porter 1990) and their duplication is relatively difficult in the short run. Therefore, because they are more difficult to duplicate, it would be expected that management would consider advanced CSRs to be a more important source of sustainable competitive advantage in a global environment than basic CSRs.

Hypothesis 3: All other things being equal, advanced CSRs will be perceived to be a more important source of sustainable competitive advantage in a global environment than basic CSRs.

Finally, in general terms, it may be contended that resources endogenous to the firm are likely to possess greater barriers to duplication than those that are exogenous due to their lower transparency (Grant 1991a) or higher levels of causal ambiguity (Reed and DeFillippi 1990). In particular, it is possible to suggest that it is easier to duplicate a competitive advantage in a global environment that accrues from, for example, low-cost labour in a foreign production location as the nature of the advantage can be both identified and duplicated by competitors. By contrast, as noted above, firm-specific capabilities are characterised by relatively high barriers to duplication due to their inherent tacitness, specificity and complexity. Therefore, it would be expected that, in general, management would consider firm-specific resources (FSRs) to be a more important source of sustainable competitive advantage in a global environment than country-specific resources (CSRs).

Hypothesis 4: All other things being equal, firm-specific resources (FSRs) will be perceived to be a more important source of sustainable competitive advantage in a global environment than country-specific resources (CSRs).

Key resources and strategic orientation

Management plays a moderating role in the process by which resources are converted into sustainable competitive advantages, and earlier in this chapter it was proposed that the Bartlett and Ghoshal typology captures the alternative approaches that may be found in a global environment. Firms with an 'international' orientation are deemed to be those in which control is maintained by headquarters in the country of origin and where operations in foreign markets are seen as appendages to the domestic corporation (Bartlett and Ghoshal 1989). Consequently, these kinds of firms may be said to be characterised by a somewhat parochial or ethnocentric managerial philosophy (Perlmutter 1969), where the home country is of greatest importance and concern. It is seen as the important source of new developments and products that lead to advantages in domestic and foreign markets. This kind of approach is reflected in the industrial organisation perspective on global competition, where firms are deemed to be able to overcome the inherent costs of doing business abroad due to their ability to leverage idiosyncratic domestic advantages (Hymer 1960; Kindleberger 1969). It might also be typical of firms at an early stage of international development where dependence on the country of origin is high (Johanson and Wiedersheim-Paul 1975). Foreign subsidiaries of international firms are seen as relying on the parent organisation for products that are then adapted to suit local conditions. It follows that, in terms of resource identification, development and deployment, it is expected that the management of international firms would consider home-country resources to be most important. In particular, it is expected that home-country resources that can be embodied in the firm's products and are easily transferable to foreign markets would be highly valued. Therefore,

Hypothesis 5: Intangible assets will be perceived to be a more important source of sustainable competitive advantage in a global environment by management in international firms than by those in multinational, global or transnational firms.

'Multinational' firms are characterised by what is described as a polycentric orientation (Bartlett and Ghoshal 1989; Perlmutter 1969). In other words, foreign subsidiaries are not seen as secondary to operations in the home country, and therefore the firm's structures and processes afford subsidiaries relatively high levels of local autonomy and responsibility. The management of multinational firms is described as having a view of the world that sees foreign markets as potentially very different, requiring relatively high levels of localisation of both products and strategy (Doz 1980; Levitt 1983; Porter 1986a). Though this may not be cost-effective, it is deemed necessary given market differences. In contrast, 'global' firms are characterised by a drive to maximise efficiencies based on a view of the world that sees markets as becoming increasingly homogeneous (Bartlett and Ghoshal 1989; Levitt 1983). This market homogeneity creates opportunities to develop globally standardised or modular products that can be easily and cheaply adapted to local conditions (Porter 1986a). The sale of standardised products creates possibilities for centralised production facilities that may be limited to a number of locations to take advantage of both local factor costs and scale efficiencies (Ohmae 1985). Therefore, though the motive of multinational firms is local responsiveness while that of global firms is worldwide efficiency, it is expected that both will perceive country-specific resources to be important in terms of attaining a sustainable competitive advantage in a global environment.

Hypothesis 6: Country-specific resources will be perceived to be a more important source of sustainable competitive advantage in a global environment by management in multinational and global firms than by those in international and transnational firms.

Hypothesis 7: Basic CSRs will be perceived to be a more important source of sustainable competitive advantage in a global environment by management in global firms than by those in multinational, international and transnational firms.

The 'transnational' is considered to be the most complex of the four strategic orientations, seeking to balance the need for local responsiveness with the desire for global efficiencies while at the same time attempting effectively to transfer resources and learning throughout the firm (Bartlett and Ghoshal 1989). Managing such an organisation calls for a managerial philosophy that is geocentric (Perlmutter 1969) and views foreign markets as being as important as the home market. Firms with a transnational orientation operate on the basis that some resources are best centralised in the home country, some are best centralised in specific world locations and some are best decentralised locally. Overseas subsidiaries are viewed, not as autonomous units or simple extensions of the parent company, but rather as having different roles and activities contributing to the overall organisation. The sub-units of a transnational organisation are seen as highly interdependent, exchanging components, products, resources, people and information, which requires complex communication linkages (Bartlett and Ghoshal 1989). Relational capability has been put forward as a distinctive competence for the transnational firm (Lipparini and Fratocchi 1999). This they describe as the ability to access new knowledge or complementary capabilities and to leverage inter-firm relationships and opportunities as they arise on a global scale. As the transnational requires a complex set of routines and interactions, it would be expected that capabilities would be considered an important source of sustainable competitive advantage in a global environment; hence,

Hypothesis 8: Capabilities will be perceived to be a more important source of sustainable competitive advantage in a global environment by management in transnational firms than by those in multinational, international and global firms.

Finally, the foregoing discussion also highlights the possibility of variations in the perceived importance of both FSRs and CSRs in the firm's country of origin versus those in host countries. It is noted above that the management of international firms perceives the country of origin to be the critical source of innovations and views foreign subsidiaries as something of an appendage to the domestic organisation. In contrast, multinational firms emphasise the importance of differences between countries, necessitating localised decision making and autonomy. Firms with global and transnational orientations adopt a more balanced approach, recognising the importance of resources in the both the country of origin and in host countries. Global firms centralise key decisions and operations in their country of origin but also seek to maximise potential efficiencies through the deployment of resources in host countries. Similarly, transnational firms view foreign operations as contributing to the overall success of the organisation through their access to local CSRs and the effective transfer of FSRs from and between subsidiaries. In summary, international firms perceive operations in the country of origin to be important, multinational firms consider host-country resources to be important, while global and transnational firms view both as equally important; hence,

Hypothesis 9a: Resources located in the country of origin will be perceived to be a more important source of sustainable competitive advantage in a global environment by management in international firms than by those in multinational, global and transnational firms.

Hypothesis 9b: Resources located in host countries will be perceived to be a more important source of sustainable competitive advantage in a global environment by management in multinational firms than by those in international, global and transnational firms.

Hypothesis 9c: Resources located in both the country of origin and host countries will be more likely to be perceived as equally important sources of advantage by management in global and transnational firms than by those in multinational and international firms.

Resources, strategic orientation and superior performance

From the perspective of the resource-based view of the firm, superior performance accrues from the attainment of a competitive advantage. Such advantages are related to the provision of value to customers, and on any given value dimension several firms may have a competitive advantage with the relative size of advantages related to the amounts of value created. The durability or sustainability of such advantages and the resulting superior performance levels are deemed to be a function of how difficult it is for competitors to identify and duplicate the sources of advantage. The more difficult this is to do, the greater the sustainability of superior performance. In other words, the RBV posits that levels of sustained superior performance can be attained by firms in a global environment through the deployment of difficult-to-duplicate resources in ways that create value for customers. We have seen that firms in a global environment have access to five groups of resources, each of which is characterised by varying barriers to duplication. In instances where difficult-to-duplicate resources are identified as being central to the firm's strategic activity, it is expected that levels of sustained superior performance will be observed; hence,

Hypothesis 10: Capabilities and intangible assets will be perceived to be of greater importance by superior performing firms than by inferior performing firms.

CONCLUSION

The aim of this chapter is to provide a conceptual extension to the scope and content of the resource-based view of the firm in order to describe the nature of sustainable competitive advantage in a global environment. It can be seen that the logic of the resource-based view still holds and that sustained superior performance derives from the deployment of difficult-to-duplicate resources in ways that create value for customers. However, some extensions are necessary. The resource pool available to the firm is expanded to incorporate resources that are exogenous to the firm and also to account for the potential dispersion of both CSRs and FSRs across national borders. The Bartlett and Ghoshal typology of strategic orientation is integrated into the model as a frame for the alternative approaches to the moderating role played by management, and a series of ten research hypotheses is proposed.

The global environment is complex and demanding, and attaining levels of sustained superior performance in such an environment is difficult. Simon (1967) notes that the dual task of scholars of management is to conduct research that contributes knowledge to a scientific discipline and to apply that knowledge to the practice of management as a profession. To do this well, Van de Ven (1989) suggests that good theory needs to be developed which provides an intimate understanding of practical problems facing the management profession. The conceptual integration of the literature on international business and the resource-based view of the firm summarised in the model presented in this chapter has sought to respond to these calls. The subsequent chapters describe the empirical examination of the conceptual model and the ten research hypotheses.

5 Competitive advantage in the global automotive components industry

INTRODUCTION

In seeking to draw any conclusions about the determinants of performance differences between firms, it is necessary to isolate possible industry effects by confining the research to one industry (Hirsch 1975; Rouse and Daellenbach 1999). As we are concerned here with competition in a global environment, it is necessary to select an industry that can be classed as global. Several such industries have been identified, including automobiles/motorcycles (Henzler and Rall 1986; Levitt 1983; Porter 1986a), aircraft (Doz 1987; Hout, Porter and Rudden 1982), chemicals (Chakravarthy and Perlmutter 1985; Levitt 1983), pharmaceuticals (Henzler and Rall 1986; Doz 1987) and semiconductors (Kobrin 1991; Levitt 1983; Porter 1986a). These and others, including consumer electronics, electronic instruments and telecommunications, have been the subject of previous research (Roth and Morrison 1990; Roth 1992). For the purposes of this study, the automotive components industry was chosen as the target industry of study. The structure and dynamics of the industry are briefly reviewed below and this is followed by a discussion of the findings of a four-country research study on the industry.

STRUCTURE AND DYNAMICS OF THE INDUSTRY

The fortunes of the automotive components industry are inextricably linked to those of its customers – the automotive original equipment manufacturers (OEMs). Since the late 1980s, global vehicle production has shown little or no growth as the industry experienced recession initially in the United States and followed by Europe and Japan. The impact on the supply business has been significant, with OEMs such as Ford demanding a five-year price freeze from suppliers as part of its Ford 2000 strategy. Commentators continue to be somewhat pessimistic, considering growth prospects to be limited in mature markets and unpredictable in emerging markets (*Financial Times* 1995).

The structure of the industry

The automobile is a complex product consisting of approximately 15,000 components (Cusumano and Takeishi 1991). The most distinguishing feature of the automotive components business is the alternative approaches taken to the organisation of the supply chain by Japanese and Western firms (see Figure 5.1). Automotive OEMs generally deal with primary or 'first-tier' suppliers of major components such as engine parts, electrical parts and so on. These suppliers in turn depend on secondary and tertiary suppliers for the provision of specialist parts or for services such as welding and moulding. Western automotive manufacturers have been more vertically integrated than their Japanese counterparts. Paradoxically, they have also tended to contract directly with a much larger number of external suppliers, a combination that has allowed Japanese car manufacturers to gain a 20–25 per cent cost advantage (Dyer and Ouchi 1993). Though there is evidence of increasing convergence between the two approaches to organising the supply chain (Helper and Sako 1995), the classic Japanese and Western models are illustrated in Figure 5.1.

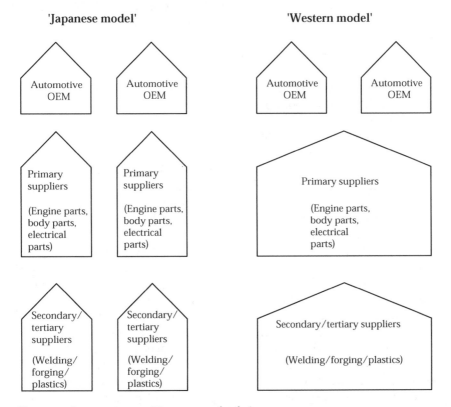

Figure 5.1 Japanese versus Western supply chains

Traditionally the principal difference between the two supply models is to be found in the relationships between the partners in the supply chain (Hyun 1994). In Western countries, parts production tended to be of the stable, high-volume, low-variety type. Competition for business takes place between several suppliers and new business is generally gained at the expense of an existing supplier, with price being the main criterion on which contracts are awarded. The design effort is one-sided, with little collaboration between the OEM and the supplier. Relationships have been generally described as adversarial and distrustful (Bertodo 1991; Cusumano and Takeishi 1991; Dyer and Ouchi 1993; Turnbull, Oliver and Wilkinson 1992). It wasn't untypical for manufacturers even to pay for the suppliers' equipment so that if production faltered, they could remove the machinery and install it in somebody else's factory (*Fortune* 1994). The Japanese model, by contrast, stresses very close collaboration and a high degree of dependency with a limited number of dedicated suppliers. For example, in the case of Nissan suppliers, over 90 per cent of their business is with Nissan (Turnbull, Oliver and Wilkinson 1992). Collaboration takes the form of three types of customised investment, namely, site-specific investments (production plants located close to customers), physical investments (dedicated plant and equipment) and human capital investments (shared design/engineering skills), creating high levels of interdependence (Dyer and Ouchi 1993) and raising the primary supplier to 'co-producer' status (Bertodo 1991). While such collaboration is similar to vertical integration in terms of the benefits of customised investments, the discipline of the market is also retained by the practice of parallel sourcing, whereby OEMs operate a two-vendor policy for parts, encouraging competition between suppliers (Dyer and Ouchi 1993; Richardson 1993).

A second difference is that the Japanese system has a long history of just-in-time (JIT) deliveries of defect-free components. JIT, which was pioneered in the automotive industry (Womack, Jones and Roos 1990), is designed to reduce complexity and costs by eliminating inventories and work in progress to ensure that there are no redundant buffer stocks or quality inspections. Research by Andersen Consulting (1994) demonstrated the impact that JIT has had on the automotive components business. At that stage, almost 40 per cent of what it termed 'world-class' suppliers (i.e. leaders in productivity and quality) were located in Japan. In the case of world-class suppliers of car seats, production on an incoming part took place in 20 minutes, it was delivered to customers on an hourly basis in a journey time which took on average 12 minutes (Andersen Consulting 1994). UK suppliers seeking contracts with Japanese OEMs have been forced to develop their quality systems to gain or maintain 'preferred-supplier status' (Turnbull, Oliver and Wilkinson 1992).

A third major difference concerns the types of parts produced. Japanese 'first-tier' suppliers are most likely to be engaged in the production of complete sub-systems such as braking or transmission systems. Firms in the US and Europe tend to specialise in particular components which are later integrated during the overall production process of the automobile. In summary, the traditional view has been that the Japanese and Western approaches to organising the supply chain are quite different, with the Japanese renowned as the industry leaders. However, there is now evidence of increasing convergence.

The dynamics of the industry

The successful international growth of Japanese automobile manufacturers throughout the 1980s led to the widespread interest in the Japanese model of component sub-supply. During the period from 1965 to 1989, the combined Japanese market share of worldwide passenger car production jumped from 3.6 per cent to 25.5 per cent, due to its quality and cost advantages (Dyer and Ouchi 1993). Several influential studies, most notably Womack, Jones and Roos (1990), advocated imitation of Japanese practices as the most effective response. Indeed, subsequent research points to continuing efficiency and productivity differences between Western and Japanese automotive components firms and advocates rapid imitation of Japanese best practice (Andersen Consulting 1994; Boston Consulting Group 1993; Turnbull, Oliver and Wilkinson 1992; Turnbull *et al.* 1993).

Currently, there is evidence that this advice is being heeded in the industry. Convergence towards the Japanese model can be seen on a number of fronts. There is evidence of increased efforts by major OEMs, particularly in the US, to reduce their levels of vertical integration (Cross and Gordon 1995). Firms in the United States and Europe, which have traditionally tended to manufacture up to 50 per cent of their parts in house, are increasingly looking to reduce these fixed-cost levels and to benefit from the innovations of external specialists. For example, in an 18-month period, GM disposed of its radiator caps, vacuum pumps and 41 other lines of business in its $25 billion per year parts operation to avail of cost savings from non-unionized external parts suppliers (*Fortune* 1994). Car manufacturers are also significantly reducing their overall number of external suppliers. For example, when Ford launched its Tempo model in 1994, it sourced parts from over 700 suppliers, but for its Mercury Mystique model in 1995, this number had fallen to 227 (*Fortune* 1994). In the United Kingdom, the number of direct or 'first-tier' suppliers has fallen from about 1,500 in the 1970s to fewer than 500 in the 1990s (Bertodo 1991). Continued investment in the UK by Japanese OEMs has driven the trend towards fewer, larger and more 'talented' suppliers (Turnbull *et al.* 1993).

There is also evidence that OEMs outside Japan are looking to their suppliers to produce complete sub-systems rather than simply component parts (Turnbull *et al.* 1993). For example, the Mercedes-Benz plant in Tuscaloosa, Alabama operates on the basis of modular assembly, where most of the parts arrive in some twenty modules that are then bolted or welded together. The cockpit comes as a complete unit, with the air conditioner, heater, steering column with airbag and audio system built in (*Fortune* 1994). Allied Signal's purchase of Budd Company's $350 million wheel and brake division is considered to be part of their strategy to become a manufacturer of fully integrated braking systems.

Furthermore, industry associations and policy bodies outside Japan have been at the vanguard of new quality initiatives in the industry. For example, in the UK, 12 British autoparts firms are involved in an initiative launched by the Department of Trade and Industry called 'Learning from Japan', which is aimed at improving supplier quality and productivity levels by studying the operations of the Japanese OEMs in the UK. It would appear that Japanese best practice can be effectively transferred to countries outside of Japan. A study of both US suppliers and Japanese transplants in the United States by Cusumano and Takeishi (1991) found that the Japanese OEMs had been successful in transferring management practices to both groups of suppliers in the US. Furthermore, they found increasing adoption of practices traditionally associated with Japan, indicating a convergence toward the Japanese model. Further evidence of the successful transfer of Japanese best practice has been observed in the UK, Spain and France (Andersen Consulting 1994).

These developments imply that automotive components firms worldwide are competing in an industry which is undergoing a process of restructuring, in which many incumbents are expected to struggle to survive (Key Note 1996; *Tokyo Business Today* 1993). However, it has been argued that this new environment creates opportunities for suppliers, but only if they leave behind their job-shop origins and develop skills in areas such as design, engineering and marketing (*Fortune* 1994). In a study of firms in the UK, the traditional dimensions of quality, price and delivery are now considered to be the basic preconditions for gaining new business by over 60 per cent of 'first-tier' firms (Turnbull *et al.* 1993). In general, the twin abilities of being able to cut costs and to contribute to the research and development efforts of the OEM are considered to be two of the essential ingredients of success (*Financial Times* 1995). A worldwide study of the industry defined the efficiency criterion more precisely as relating to efficiencies in internal processes and in external purchasing/quality activities (Andersen Consulting 1994). In summary, the key success factors in the industry would appear to be:

- efficiencies in internal processes and parts procurement;
- an ability to collaborate and work with buyers and suppliers;
- quality production systems;

- design, engineering and marketing skills;
- large scale and a global presence;
- an ability to develop complete automotive systems rather than mere components.

Reasons for selecting the automotive components industry

The automotive components business was selected as the industry of study because it exhibits many of the key traits that characterise global industries. In Chapter 2, a global task environment or industry is defined as any business arena exhibiting above-average levels of geographic scope, market convergence and cross-national interdependencies. Global industries are characterised by the presence of global customers with universal needs, the presence of global competitors, and pressures for cost reduction, investment intensity and technological intensity (Prahalad and Doz 1987). Evidence of each of these features can be found in the automotive components business. The industry's customer group, automotive OEMs, consists generally of large, globally scaled organisations with predominantly universal needs. Significant levels of global consolidation have taken place in the industry in recent years. For example, Turnbull, Oliver and Wilkinson (1992) noted that of the six remaining vehicle assemblers in the UK in 1992, only two, the Rover Group and Jaguar, were truly indigenous. Since then, both these firms have been acquired by bigger foreign competitors: the Rover Group by BMW AG and Jaguar by Ford Motor Co. Automotive OEMs are also characterised by increasing levels of cooperative activity, particularly joint assembly and R&D. These strategic alliances span the globe in many instances, which has the effect of standardising buyer needs on a global basis. For example, Mitsubishi makes Chrysler-badged cars at its US plant for US sales, supplies engine technology to Porsche, Saab and Volvo in Europe and holds 6.31 per cent of Hyundai in Korea as well as marketing Mercedes-Benz cars in Japan (*JAMA Forum* 1993).

The mature nature of the car industry has resulted in considerable pressures being exerted on automotive components firms to reduce their costs. For example, Ford Motor Co., which buys in up to 70 per cent of its components, has sought a five-year price freeze from its suppliers, asking them to absorb any increase in their costs whether caused by inflation or product improvements and breaking with the industry tradition whereby the OEM automatically paid the supplier a price increase for an improved component. There is also evidence of greater levels of the global sourcing of parts by OEMs. For example, a study by Bertodo (1991) found that in 1980, almost three-quarters of all European parts were sourced either locally or nationally, but by 1990 this figure had dropped to 63 per cent, with the remainder being sourced either regionally or globally. Similarly, an analysis of the Ford Escort model found that its parts were variously sourced from 15 countries spread throughout Europe, North American and Japan (Hibbert 1993).

Recent years have also seen a trend towards the emergence of large, global automotive components suppliers. The international expansion of automotive components manufacturers has generally been driven by the desire to continue to supply present customers as they move to new markets (Carr 1993; Morris 1991). In the case of many Japanese suppliers, their international expansion has been encouraged and facilitated by major OEMs (Cusumano 1985; Smitka 1991) and also by the high value of the yen during much of the 1990s. There are now some very large suppliers with a significant presence in the major regions of the United States, Europe and East Asia. Nippondenso, Toyota's main supplier, generated over 1.3 trillion yen in sales in 1994 and has some 23 production plants outside Japan (*Nikkei Weekly* 1994). The largest components supplier in the United States is GM Automotive Components Group, which makes lights, engine management systems and suspensions and generated $21.2 billion worth of sales in 1993 (*Fortune* 1994). In the mid-1990s, Delphi Automotive Systems ran a promotional campaign stressing that, with its six divisions, 17 technical centres and 190 locations in 31 countries around the globe, it provided one source for all OEMs' component, module and system needs.

High levels of technological and investment intensity can be observed in many sectors of the industry. The production of sophisticated components such as electronic control units, computer chips and safety devices is highly technologically intensive. Even commodity parts such as springs, brackets, bearings and pumps are investment-intensive due to scale requirements. Furthermore, as luxury cars have risen in popularity, the R&D spend incurred by components manufacturers has increased accordingly (Nikko Research Center 1992). In summary, these features and the worldwide convergence of competitive strategy and best practice documented above indicate that the automotive components business is very much a global one.

Finally, the automotive components industry is also a suitable field of study when one looks at the issue of firm size. Conceptual and empirical contributions in the international business literature generally focus on large corporations despite evidence that the top 50 US corporations account for less than one-third of all US trade (Mahini 1990). The resource-based view of the firm does not accord any special significance to firm size and therefore the inclusion of a wide range of firms, in terms of size, is warranted. Because of this, the automotive components sector is a good choice, given that, despite the emergence of some large players, the industry still contains very many small to medium-sized enterprises, particularly at the second- and third-tier levels. Furthermore, as this research focuses on resource-based rather than monopoly-based advantages, it is necessary that the industry selected be characterised by relatively open competition rather than oligopoly or monopoly structures. The automotive components industry is clearly very competitive, with strong price pressure from customers and keen efforts to duplicate best practice by competitors throughout the world.

THE RESEARCH

The above review of the automotive components industry identifies a number of resources likely to be important in the attainment of global competitive advantage. To examine this issue more closely, a research project was drawn up to test explicitly the propositions put forward in the last chapter. As the key variable here is global advantage, it was decided that the research should be carried out in more than one country. Much of the discussion relating to global environments has focused on the growing levels of market convergence and cross-national interdependencies within the 'triad' of North America, Western Europe and Japan (Ohmae 1985). Therefore, data were collected from each leg of the triad, with research being conducted in the United States, Ireland/the United Kingdom and Japan. Details on how the research was conducted are included in the Appendix and the findings are reported below.

THE FINDINGS

The resource pool in a global environment

In Chapter 4, we saw that the resource pool of a firm operating in a global environment comprises firm-specific resources (FSRs) and country-specific resources (CSRs). Building on this distinction, it is proposed that FSRs will be perceived to be a more important source of sustainable competitive advantage in a global environment than CSRs, all other things being equal. These two groupings were further sub-divided. Country-specific resources are made up of basic resources (BCSRs) and advanced resources (ACSRs), while firm-specific resources are classed as being either tangible assets (TAs), intangible assets (IAs) or capabilities (Cs). Similarly, predictions can be made about the relative importance of each of these sub-groupings. As outlined in Chapter 4, intangible assets are likely to be more important than tangible assets, capabilities are likely to be more important than either intangible assets or tangible assets, and finally advanced CSRs are likely to be more important than basic CSRs, all other things being equal.

Summary findings on the global resource pool

The operationalisation of the resource constructs is described in the Appendix. Respondents were asked to rate 16 specific resources in terms of their importance in helping to gain an advantage over competitors. The responses to this question are summarised in Tables 5.1 and 5.2. One of the striking features is the high level of importance that is attributed to almost all of the resources listed. In certain particular cases, importance ratings were extremely high. For example, in the cases of the firm's reputation, design/engineering know-how, expertise of management people and quality control systems, over 95 per cent of all respondents considered these resources to be important or very important in terms of gaining advantage over competitors. Government incentives was the only resource that the majority considered to be unimportant, while just 55 per cent of respondents considered registered designs to be important. Given the generally positive ratings for each resource, some further discrimination of relative importance is provided by the mean score attained on a four-point scale. Viewed in this manner, we see that quality control systems emerges as the most important resource, followed closely by design/engineering know-how and the firm's reputation, with government incentives ranking last, with a mean rating of 2.27 on the four-point scale.

The content validity of these findings was confirmed by a further question that dealt with the relative importance of resources in gaining an advantage over competitors. Respondents were asked to specify, from the list of resources presented, the three most important resources and the three most unimportant resources in terms of gaining advantage. The responses to this question are summarised in Table 5.2. This table documents four sets of rankings for each resource. In the first instance the percentage of respondents considering each resource to be most important is presented. This is followed by a column which reports the percentage of times each resource was afforded a ranking of either first, second or third most important. Negative responses are reported in a similar format in the fourth and fifth columns of Table 5.2. The findings in this table are consistent with those reported in Table 5.1. Again, resources such as design/engineering know-how, quality systems, reputation and the expertise of management are viewed as very important, with an ability to work with customers on design changes/new products also emerging as significant. To the list of less important resources has been added cash in hand/bank, innovative demands of buyers and registered designs.

These findings were first examined in the context of what has been written to date about the automotive components industry. It is noted above that several key success factors in the industry are apparent, including efficiencies in internal processes and parts procurement, an ability to collaborate and work with buyers and suppliers, quality

Table 5.1 Importance of resources in terms of gaining advantage (percentage of all respondents)

Resource	Very important	Important	Unimportant	Very unimportant	Total*	Mean score** (rank)
Quality control systems	68	31	1	0	100	3.67 (1)
Design/engineering know-how	69	27	4	0	100	3.65 (2)
Firm's reputation	62	36	2	0	100	3.60 (3)
Expertise of management people	60	37	3	0	100	3.57 (4)
Ability to work with customers on design changes/new products	63	31	5	0	99	3.55 (5)
Plant & equipment	45	49	5	1	100	3.38 (6)
Access to experienced/skilled workforce	45	43	11	1	100	3.30 (7)
Ability to work with suppliers	38	52	9	1	100	3.27 (8)
Cost reduction demands of buyers	28	56	14	1	99	3.09 (9)
Ability to mobilise multifunctional teams	28	50	17	4	99	3.00 (10)
Cash in hand/bank	20	58	20	2	100	2.96 (11)
Innovative demands of buyers	17	62	19	2	100	2.94 (12)
Process/product patents	30	36	27	8	101	2.90 (13)
Access to labour at low cost	15	61	21	3	100	2.87 (14)
Registered designs	18	37	32	12	99	2.59 (15)
Government incentives	7	33	43	14	97	2.27 (16)

* Totals may not equal 100 due to rounding or the presence of 'don't know' responses.

** Mean score on a 4-point scale, where 4.00 is the maximum importance rating.

(Question: A list of 16 resources is presented below. We would like you to rate how important you believe each of these resources is *in terms of helping you to gain an advantage over your competitors*. A rating of 1 implies that the resource is very unimportant, while a rating of 4 implies that it is very important, in terms of gaining a competitive advantage. (Please *circle* the most appropriate response *for each* of the resources listed.)

Table 5.2 Rankings of resources in terms of importance in gaining advantage

Resource	Percentage ranking resource as most important resources	Percentage appearances in three most important resources	Percentage ranking resource as most unimportant	Percentage appearances in three most unimportant resources
Design/engineering know-how	35.6	53.4	0.4	1.1
Ability to work with customers on design changes/new products	13.5	41.0	0.7	4.2
Expertise of management people	13.1	38.7	0.0	2.3
Quality control systems	6.0	38.7	0.0	0.4
Firm's reputation	10.5	25.2	0.7	5.0
Access to an educated/skilled workforce	6.4	19.9	2.6	8.4
Cost reduction demands of buyers	1.9	12.0	2.2	13.0
Ability to mobilise multifunctional teams	1.1	11.7	9.0	24.9
Ability to work with suppliers	1.5	11.3	6.0	15.3
Plant and equipment	1.9	10.5	0.7	8.8
Process/product patents	1.9	10.2	5.6	32.6
Access to labour at low cost	3.0	9.8	3.7	24.9
Government incentives	0.4	6.0	39.7	64.0
Cash in hand/bank	1.5	5.3	8.2	25.3
Innovative demands of buyers	0.7	3.8	3.7	21.5
Registered designs	0.0	1.5	13.9	42.9

Question: Of the resources listed above, which three do you believe to be most important in terms of helping you to gain an advantage over your competitors? (Please put *number of item* in the appropriate box.)

production systems, design/engineering and marketing skills, large scale/ a global presence and finally an ability to develop complete automotive systems. The issue of quality has received a great deal of attention, particularly when the respective performance of Japanese and Western firms is compared (see, for example, Dyer and Ouchi 1993 and Turnbull, Oliver and Wilkinson 1992). The importance of quality is understandable given the prevalence of just-in-time (JIT) manufacture in the industry for which zero defects are paramount (Turnbull, Oliver and Wilkinson 1992). Several studies document the role of quality and its impact on performance. A study of 56 components makers in the UK by Turnbull *et al.* (1993) found that quality was rated the single most important criterion in winning new business (48 per cent of respondents), ahead of price, the combination of quality and price, the combination of quality/ price/delivery and technological capabilities, in that order. A study in the US by Cross and Gordon (1995) found that quality was considered to be the number one supplier attribute not only by components makers but also by OEMs and agencies (i.e. industry associations and government ministries that interact with the industry), coming out ahead of cost, R&D capability and manufacturing technology. A research study involving 71 firms in nine countries has provided insights into the specific elements of the quality attribute (Andersen Consulting 1994; Oliver *et al.* 1994; Oliver, Delbridge and Lowe 1996). Quality is measured in terms of incoming defects, internal defects and customer complaints, and top-quality systems are characterised by tight discipline and control over internal processes (Andersen Consulting 1994). Rommel, Kempis and Kaas (1994) separated quality into two components, namely, design quality and process quality, and found a direct relationship between quality levels and superior financial performance. Given this kind of focus on quality in the industry, it is not surprising that quality systems are rated the most important resource in terms of gaining a competitive advantage in this study (see Table 5.1).

Research by the Boston Consulting Group (1993) contended that understanding the causes of success or failure required moving beyond the discussion of cost, quality and delivery to what they described as the 'capabilities' that underpinned these attributes. Their study of 56 automotive suppliers in Japan and the United States found that engineering know-how was a critical factor in ensuring that part makers were on the automakers' list of 'potential suppliers'. Several other studies attest the importance of design and engineering know-how (Andersen Consulting 1994; EIU 1996; *Financial Times* 1995). It is deemed to be important given that the speed of new product introductions is becoming a critical factor for automotive manufacturers (EIU 1996). OEMs are also seeking cheaper, lighter and more efficient components. Consequently, the demands for continued investment in R&D are heavy, with tier-one suppliers typically spending in excess of 5 per cent of revenue on this activity (EIU 1996). The findings of this study are consistent with these observations. When respondents were asked to rank which resource was most important in terms of gaining an advantage over competitors, design/engineering know-how clearly emerged as number one (see Table 5.1).

Relationships with buyers and suppliers are perhaps the issues that have received greatest attention in the automotive components literature (see, for example, Bertodo 1991; Cusumano and Takeishi 1991; Dyer 1996; Dyer and Ouchi 1993; Helper and Sako 1995; Hyun 1994; Lewis *et al.* 1993; Turnbull, Oliver and Wilkinson 1992; Richardson 1993). Relationships with customers are seen as critical to (i) the suppliers' ability to deliver quality (Turnbull, Oliver and Wilkinson 1992) and (ii) their ability to gain access to design and engineering competencies (EIU 1996). The importance of supply chain relationships has been well documented. The Andersen Consulting (1994) study reported that a common denominator of world-class plants was their management of the supply chain. Supplier–buyer relationships have been viewed as a particular strength of Japanese parts makers, providing them with a $300–$600 per car cost advantage in the 1980s (*Fortune* 1994). A study of firms in both the United States and Japan identified better performers as those that provide detailed process information to their customers, see customer commitment as long term and expect to engage in joint problem solving (Helper and Sako 1995). Extensive attention has been given to how supply chain relationships can be improved. Cross and Gordon's (1995) study found that all three groups, namely, suppliers, OEMs and agency personnel, rated trust as the most important factor in ensuring long-term supply agreements, ahead of information sharing, concurrent engineering and co-location. Hyun (1994) reported that effective supply chain management requires technical collaboration, multifunctional involvement, a reduction in the number of suppliers, network cooperation and greater levels of multidirectional information flows. These findings supported the earlier work of Bertodo (1991), who proposed that components makers of the 1990s would be characterised by co-producer status, long-term business relationships, multifunctional supplier interfaces and supplier involvement from the concept stage. This study examined both the inward and outward components of the supply chain. Relationships with customers are considered to be very important, reflected in a rating of 3.55 on a four-point scale and ranks as the second most important resource in terms of gaining an advantage over competitors (see Table 5.2). Surprisingly, relationships with suppliers are not afforded a similar level of importance, ranking only ninth in terms of their role in gaining a competitive advantage (see Table 5.2). This is interesting. There is ample evidence that component suppliers have focused on building relationships with their customers – the OEMs – but this process has largely been driven by the auto manufacturers (Dyer and

Ouchi 1993). It would appear that the parts makers have not adopted the practice with regard to their own suppliers. This is surprising given the evidence, which points to the importance of all suppliers in the chain in ensuring that quality standards are met (Turnbull, Oliver and Wilkinson 1992; Lewis *et al.* 1993).

The importance of teams in the building of buyer–supplier relationships and the delivery of quality has been highlighted in the literature. The Boston Consulting Group (1993) study of firms in the US and Japan found that teams were essential in underpinning the 'capabilities-based system', which they viewed as the key feature of successful suppliers. Specialists could synthesise their distinct capabilities and supplement each other's shortcomings (Boston Consulting Group 1993). Rommel, Kempis and Kaas (1994) found that 28 per cent of top-quality companies had workers in self-managing teams whereas there were no such teams in companies with poor quality levels. The Andersen Consulting (1994) study found teams a strong feature of top-performing Japanese plants but not so in the case of firms in Western countries. Just under 60 per cent of UK firms had a team structure, while the figure was as low as 10 per cent in the case of France and zero in Spain. However, the Andersen study concluded that teams were not a prerequisite for success in the industry (Andersen Consulting 1994). Respondents to this study also attach a relatively low level of importance to the ability to mobilise multifunctional teams. It is rated tenth out of the 16 resources and is considered the most important in terms of gaining a competitive advantage by just over 1 per cent of respondents (see Table 5.2).

Finally, much of the commentary in the general press on the automotive components industry suggests that OEMs exert considerable pressure on suppliers for cost savings. Factors such as recession, competition and overcapacity in the OEM sector have forced vehicle manufacturers to squeeze their costs and, given that components account for a very large proportion of expenditure, the supply chain has been hit hardest. This study examined the relative importance of resources derived from the cost reduction demands of buyers as a source of competitive advantage. The findings indicate that they are attributed a relatively low level of importance, rated ninth overall and most important by just under 2 per cent of respondents (see Table 5.2).

In summary, the findings of this study are consistent with much of what has been written about the automotive components industry. The literature is dominated by an emphasis on the issues of design and quality and also on the importance of buyer–supplier relationships. In this study, capabilities such as design/engineering know-how, quality systems and an ability to work with customers emerge as the key resources necessary to gain an advantage over competitors. Somewhat surprisingly, the ability to mobilise multifunctional teams and the ability to work with suppliers are considered to be less important. But in general, the findings suggest that it is the resources specific to the firm that are most critical in ensuring competitive success. This would appear to indicate strong support for the hypotheses made regarding the relative importance of each resource in terms of sustainable competitive advantage. Before examining each of the hypotheses specifically, a confirmatory factor analysis was conducted on the global resource pool. The findings of the factor analysis are discussed in detail in the Appendix, but a five-factor solution supports the resource classification developed in Chapter 4.

Tests of hypotheses on the global resource pool

The resource-based view of the firm suggests that it is those resources that possess the characteristics of value, appropriability and barriers to duplication that are most important in terms of gaining a sustainable competitive advantage. As shown in Tables 5.1 and 5.2, it is primarily firm-specific capabilities such as quality systems, design/engineering know-how and an ability to work with customers that are considered to be of greatest importance. This would appear to indicate support for the predictions of the resource-based view that it is firm-specific capabilities that best meet the criteria necessary for competitive advantage. The four hypotheses concerning the relative importance of the different resource groupings were assessed using paired-sample t-tests and the findings of these tests are reported in Table 5.3. The first proposition is that firm-specific intangible assets will be perceived to be a more important source of sustainable competitive advantage in a global environment than tangible assets. Intangible assets should possess greater barriers to duplication due to the presence of regulatory protection in the case of intellectual property and the complexity and specificity inherent in accumulated assets such as the firm's reputation and its networks. However, in this study tangible assets are rated as being of greater importance than intangible assets, significant at $p = 0.05$ (see Table 5.3). This finding raises two issues. First, it demonstrates that tangible assets may be more important than has been considered to be the case in much of the literature on the resource-based view of the firm. In general, the literature has tended to give a secondary role to tangible assets, suggesting that their relatively high levels of transparency reduced barriers to their duplication (Grant 1991a). Those authors that have emphasised tangible assets have tended to stress the interaction effects between, for example, tangible assets and people or tangible assets and systems (Amit and Schoemaker 1993; Stalk, Evans and Schulman 1992). In this study, the tangible asset plant and equipment was considered to be particularly important, given a rating of 3.38 on the four-point scale and a ranking as the sixth most important of the resources listed. In the factor analysis it loaded with other firm-specific capabilities (see Appendix). This suggests that greater attention

Table 5.3 Relative importance of resources: comparison of means

Resources	Mean (on a 4-point scale)	SD	Differences between means	t-value	df	Sig.
(H1)						
Firm-specific intangible assets	3.0393	0.577	0.1311	3.21	266	p = 0.01
>						
Firm-specific tangible assets	3.1704	0.483				
(H2)						
Firm-specific capabilities	3.4639	0.361				
>						
Firm-specific intangible assets,	3.0393	0.577	0.4246	12.01		
Firm-specific tangible assets	3.1704	0.483	0.2935	10.41	266	p = 0.001
(H3)						
Country-specific capabilities	3.1367	0.479				
>						
Country-specific assets	2.6236	0.602	0.5131	12.81	266	p = 0.001
(H4)						
Firm-specific resources	3.2246	0.349				
>						
Country-specific resources	2.8801	0.435	0.3444	13.20	266	p = 0.001

Note: > = 'are more important than'.

should be given to the role of tangible assets *per se* as well as how these assets interact with other firm-specific resources. Second, it is clear that intellectual property is not considered to be an important source of competitive advantage in the automotive components business. Patents ranked thirteenth and registered designs ranked fifteenth of the 16 resources presented to respondents. This finding raises two further issues. It may be that intellectual property is not important in the auto-motive components business due to the commoditised nature of many of the automobiles components. Its low rating may also be attributable to the fact that the study is examining competitive advantage in a global environment. The absence of an effective global framework for the protection of intellectual property has been the subject of a great deal of both commentary and policy initiatives in recent years. At any rate the low level of importance attributed to intellectual property serves to depress the overall mean importance for intangible assets despite the fact that the firm's reputation is rated as highly important (mean of 3.60 on the four-point scale).

A second hypothesis relating to firm-specific resources is that capabil-ities will be perceived to be more important than either tangible assets or intangible assets. The findings reported in Tables 5.1 and 5.2 suggest that this is so, given the importance being attached to capabilities such as quality systems and design/engineering know-how. This is borne out by the t-tests, which show the mean ratings for capabilities to be significantly greater than those for intangible assets and tangible assets, both significant at $p = 0.001$ (see Table 5.3). Indeed, the mean rating for capabilities is higher than that for all other categories of resources. It is also notable, given that a total of six capabilities is examined in the study, which increases the likelihood of outliers depressing the group average in the same way that intellectual property appeared to depress the average for intangible assets. Not only does this finding support the view, widely expressed within the resource-based literature, that capabilities are important, but it also suggests that there is a variety of specific capabilities within firms that are important. This study examined capabilities at both ends of the supply chain, namely an ability to work with customers and an ability to work with suppliers. The former emerges as very important and the latter as less important. Activities central to the production process such as design/engineering know-how and quality systems emerge from the study as being of critical importance though the ability to mobilise multifunctional teams is viewed as less important. Finally, the expertise of management was also rated very highly by managers responding to the study. Theoretically speaking, this group of capabilities possesses significant barriers to duplication, whether it is the tacitness of managerial expertise (Prahalad and Bettis 1986), the specificity of supply chain relationships or the tacitness and complexity of design/engineering know-how and quality systems. The presence of these barriers means that capabilities represent an important source of competitive advantage.

A particular feature of global competition is that it necessitates consideration of country-specific resources as well as those endogenous to the firm. Two sets of country-specific resources are identified, namely, basic CSRs and advanced CSRs. Basic CSRs are similar to firm-specific tangible assets in that they are transparent and relatively easy to duplicate. Advanced CSRs are less easy to duplicate, given that they are culture-bound and diffuse slowly across borders. Therefore, it is expected that advanced CSRs will be rated higher in terms of gaining a sustainable competitive advantage. Examination of specific elements of each group suggests that this is the case. Almost 20 per cent of respondents consider access to an experienced/skilled workforce to be among the top three most important resources from the list presented (Table 5.2). As noted earlier, both basic CSRs, namely, government incentives and access to labour at low cost, are considered to be relatively unimportant in terms of gaining a competitive advantage. The t-tests of mean differences between both groups confirm that advanced CSRs are more important than basic CSRs as hypothesised, significant at $p = 0.001$ (see Table 5.3). This finding raises important issues for the firm operating internationally. First, it demonstrates the importance of gaining access to advanced CSRs or capabilities that are derived from country conditions in either the firm's home or host countries. A recent line of research, popularised by Porter (1990) and developed by Rugman and D'Cruz (1993) and Dunning (1997; 1998), has elaborated on the connections between countries and the competitiveness of firms in the global environment. It also suggests that firms should try to avail themselves of such advanced CSRs rather than simply seeking access to basic CSRs such as government incentives and low-cost labour. A stock of the latter resources is relatively easy for a competitor to duplicate and consequently does not represent an enduring source of competitive advantage.

Overall, it is proposed that firm-specific resources (FSRs) will be rated as more important than country-specific resources (CSRs), due to the relative barriers to duplication of both groups. CSRs are external to the firm, and in the case of basic CSRs they are transparent and relatively accessible to competitors. Firm-specific resources and, in particular, capabilities are more difficult to identify and to duplicate. The means for tangible assets, intangible assets and capabilities are combined to give an overall mean for FSRs. Likewise the means for basic and advanced CSRs are combined. A t-test of the difference between the two mean figures reveals that FSRs are rated significantly more important ($p = 0.001$). This finding supports the logic of the resource-based view, which emphasises the accumulation of endogenous resources.

In summary, the propositions derived from the literature about the global resource pool are largely supported by the research. Three of the four hypotheses are strongly supported by the statistical tests. These confirm a fundamental proposition of the resource-based view, which is that not all resources are of equal importance in terms of gaining a sustainable competitive advantage. Firm-specific capabilities, as predicted, emerge as the most important resource group. However, the predicted hierarchy of firm-specific resources is not confirmed, as some tangible assets are considered to be very important while some intangible assets are not. This indicates that fully understanding the resource mix within the firm is a difficult task and may be subject to variation attributable to industry conditions. Discernible differences in terms of importance are also evident between the two groups of country-specific resources (CSRs) and, overall, it is concluded that CSRs are less important than resources that are endogenous to the firm. However, as noted in Chapter 3, resources in and of themselves do not confer a competitive advantage. They need to be identified, developed and deployed by management to do so. A further set of hypotheses was developed, delineating the relationship between resources and strategic orientation. The findings concerning this part of the research are examined in the following section.

Resources and strategic orientation

It is proposed in Chapter 4 that each orientation in the Bartlett and Ghoshal typology involves a different approach being taken to the management of the resource pool. Briefly, it is proposed that intangible assets will be perceived as a more important source of competitive advantage by international firms given this group's reliance on their ability to compete internationally using domestically developed advantages which are easily transferable to new markets. It is proposed that country-specific resources will be perceived to be more important by managers in both multinational and global firms, though for quite different reasons. Multinational firms, which emphasise the localisation of strategy due to differences between countries, are likely to be sensitive to country characteristics while global firms seek to maximise efficiencies across world markets, suggesting that they are likely to exploit differences in basic country-specific resources such as government incentives and low labour costs (Kogut 1985a). Finally, given the organisational complexity of the transnational model, it is expected that managers in transnational firms will place a particular emphasis on firm-specific capabilities.

Summary findings on strategic orientation

Strategic orientation was measured using a single-item nominal scale. The scale used category descriptions for each of the four types similar to those used by Leong and Tan (1993). Respondents were asked to choose the statement that most closely described the strategic orientation of their firm and they were asked to select only one statement. The most common strategic orientation in the automotive components industry is the transnational, accounting for almost 30 per cent of the sample. This is very interesting, for three reasons. First, it has been argued that the transnational is a very complex form and that few firms have effectively adopted this orientation (Bartlett and Ghoshal 1990; Ghoshal and Nohria 1993). Second, the transnational is generally associated with very large organisations (Bartlett and Ghoshal 1989; Taylor 1991) and therefore it is surprising to find it prevalent in an industry like this, which is populated by small and medium-sized organisations. Third, previous studies such as those by Leong and Tan (1993) had found only a small proportion of transnationals in their sample, which they had predicted a priori based on the novelty and complexity of the form. Indeed, this finding may serve to support the view attributed to Drucker (1946), which is that the automotive business is the 'industry of industries' and a leader in technological and managerial developments.

Equally surprising, the second largest group (25.5 per cent) classed themselves as multinationals. During the 1980s, in particular, many obituaries were written about the multinational orientation. For example, Levitt (1983) described it as obsolete in a world where markets are converging. Its emphasis on the adaptation and localisation of strategy was deemed to be uncompetitive in an environment where firms could gain efficiencies through standardisation and the integration of activity across borders (Hout, Porter and Rudden 1982; Porter 1986a). However, this study indicates that the multinational form endures even in an industry that can be classed as global. Furthermore, the research records few firms that classify themselves as global – less than 10 per cent of firms in the sample. Though the industry has global characteristics, it appears that most of its incumbents are unwilling or unable to adopt the global form. Finally, a small proportion of firms classed themselves as international (13.9 per cent). Given the small size of many firms in this industry and given that many are likely to serve a small number of customers in large domestic markets such as the United States or Japan, the presence of international firms in the sample was expected, but such a small proportion is surprising.

Tests of hypotheses on resources and strategic orientation

Hypotheses 5 to 8 (Chapter 4) were tested using one-way analysis of variance (ANOVA) and the findings are presented in Table 5.4. The first proposition tested is that intangible assets will be perceived to be more important by international firms than by any of the other three groups. Analysis of the resulting mean values, on the contrary, indicated that both international firms and transnational firms perceive intangible assets to be of relatively equal importance. More importantly, the ANOVA indicated that there are no significant differences between each of the four strategic orientations. This is an interesting finding, which provides support for the industrial organisation perspective on international business. Economists such as Hymer (1960), Caves (1971) and Kindleberger (1969) have argued that to overcome the inherent costs of operating internationally, firms must possess and be able to leverage unique advantages. Intangible assets such as patents or reputation are examples of just such advantages. However, this research indicates that they are of importance to all firms operating in a global environment and not simply those that class themselves as international. Similarly, the internationalisation literature (see Welch and Luostarinen 1988 for a critique) has proposed that firms grow internationally in a step-wise fashion exploiting domestically derived advantages in international markets. But this study indicates that the advantages embodied in intangible assets are essential for firms with orientations other than 'international'.

The second proposition concerns the issue of country-specific resources. In this case, the tests do reveal some significant differences. The research demonstrates that global firms place a greater emphasis on country-specific resources than any of the other three strategic orientations, rating them at 3.08 on the four-point scale (see Table 5.4). A

Table 5.4 An analysis of variance on resources and strategic orientation

Resource	Orientation	Mean (4-point scale)	Source	Sum of squares	d.f.	F ratio	F prob.
H5: IAs (intangible assets)	Total pop.	3.0239					
	Multinational	3.0098					
	Global	2.8077					
	International	3.0721	Between groups	1.6104	3	1.5441	0.2042
	Transnational	3.0855	Within groups	71.2699	205		
H6: CSRs (country-specific resources)	Total pop.	2.8429					
	Multinational	2.7855					
	Global	3.0833					
	International	2.8311	Between groups	1.7788	3	3.3384	0.0203*
	Transnational	2.8184	Within groups	36.4104	205		
H7: BCSRs (basic country-specific resources)	Total pop.	2.5718					
	Multinational	2.5147					
	Global	2.9231					
	International	2.5270	Between groups	3.6703	3	3.7017	0.0126**
	Transnational	2.5256	Within groups	67.7531	205		
H8: Cs (capabilities)	Total pop.	3.4536					
	Multinational	3.4201					
	Global	3.3487					
	International	3.5072	Between groups	0.5855	3	1.4078	0.2416
	Transnational	3.4923	Within groups	28.4210	205		

* Significant at $p \leq 0.05$. A Bonferroni test revealed that global firms are significantly different from multinational and transnational firms.
** Significant at $p \leq 0.05$. A Bonferroni test revealed that global firms are different from each of the other three types.

further hypothesis (H7) examines the particular issue of basic country-specific resources (BCSRs). Again the research demonstrates that global firms rate this group of resources significantly higher than any of the other three groups. In the cases of both H6 and H7, a Bonferroni test is conducted on the ANOVA to determine precisely which groups are significantly different at the $p = 0.05$ level. This test revealed that in the case of H6, global firms differ significantly from multinational firms and transnational firms but not international firms at the 0.05 level, and that multinational firms did not differ from transnational and international firms. In the case of H7, global firms differ significantly from each of the other three groups.

These findings show that global firms attach a high level of importance to country-specific resources. This is in keeping with the literature. In essence, global firms are seen as striving to maximise the opportunity for efficiencies on a worldwide basis. They have been described as firms that exploit arbitrage opportunities created by differences in the costs of production, exchange rates and tax levels between countries (Kogut 1984; 1985a). Furthermore, the exploitation of such opportunities may require that the firm's value chain is globally configured, with different elements located wherever it is most appropriate to do so (Henzler and Rall 1986; Gluck 1982; Porter 1986a, b). This study supports the view that global firms seek to exploit country differences and gain access to country-specific resources. This is particularly true in the case of basic CSRs such as government incentives and low labour costs. Contrary to expectations, multinational firms do not attach a great deal of importance to CSRs. This is a surprising finding. The literature views multinational firms as being polycentric in their orientation (Perlmutter 1969) and therefore very sensitive to the differences between countries. While the research does not exactly reject this view, it does suggest that multinational firms do not attach any particular significance to the role of CSRs in gaining a sustainable competitive advantage. Indeed, multinational firms give the lowest mean importance ratings to both CSRs and basic CSRs (see Table 5.4), though in the latter case, differences were marginal from international and transnational firms.

Finally, it is proposed that capabilities will be perceived to be a more important source of sustainable competitive advantage by managers in transnational firms than by any of the other three groups. This contention is based on the acknowledged complexity of the transnational form (Bartlett and Ghoshal 1989). Transnational firms are those that seek to balance three conflicting goals, namely, the desire to transfer learning between organisational sub-units, the desire to maximise efficiencies, and the need for local responsiveness. Effectively doing so requires a complex and interdependent organisational form involving flows of resources, people and information (Bartlett and Ghoshal 1989), which places a great deal of importance on the organisation's internal processes or, more generally, its firm-specific capabilities. However, as shown in Table 5.4, transnational firms do not consider capabilities to be significantly more important than the other three types. High levels of importance were attributed to capabilities by all the groups, with international firms and transnational firms rating them as being of above-average importance. This finding suggests that even though the transnational may be a more complex strategic orientation, this does not imply that effective capabilities are any less important in the cases of other strategic orientations. The analysis of H2 found that capabilities are perceived to be more important than any of the other resource groups available to the firm competing internationally, and H8 indicates that this is true irrespective of the strategic orientation of the organisation.

The findings reported above would appear to indicate that, with some exceptions, the Bartlett and Ghoshal typology is not a good taxonomy for understanding the management of resources in a global environment. The research shows that global firms attribute significant levels of importance to country-specific resources, generally, and to basic CSRs in particular. However, no significant differences were found in the cases of firm-specific resources such as intangible assets and capabilities. These types of resources, it would appear, are considered to be important irrespective of the overall strategic orientation of the firm. One possible counter-argument to the view that the Bartlett and Ghoshal typology is weak in terms of understanding resources in a global environment is that difficulties are caused by the classification of resources into broad groups such as tangible assets and capabilities. This line of reasoning might proceed as follows: even though international firms, for example, may not perceive firm-specific intangible assets (IAs) to be more important than the other three groups, they may perceive particular IAs such as patents to be significantly more important. However, this is unlikely given the findings of the factor analysis presented in the Appendix, which shows that most of the resources listed group around the a priori categories. In addition, it must also be recognised that the Bartlett and Ghoshal typology does not focus explicitly on the question of resource deployment in a global environment. However, its discussion of issues such as orientation, strategy, structure and process has clear resource implications from which the hypotheses are derived. The Bartlett and Ghoshal typology and related literature also have implications regarding the geographic source of these resources, a question to which we now turn.

Tests of hypotheses on resource location and strategic orientation

Firms operating in a global environment potentially have access to resources located in both their home country and in any or all of the host countries in which they operate. These resources may be specific to the firm, for example, in its international subsidiaries, or they may be country-specific. A review of the literature on the four strategic orientations suggests that they ascribe different levels of importance to resources located in their countries of origin and to those in the host countries in which they operate. For example, international firms are described as ethnocentric in their orientation and reliant on advantages that have been developed in their home countries. In contrast, multinational firms are described as having a polycentric orientation and, due to their attributed higher levels of sensitivity to country differences and local needs, it is expected that they would perceive host-country resources to be relatively more important than global, international and transnational firms. Global firms seek to leverage domestically derived advantages in world markets but also pursue worldwide efficiencies through the exploitation of local resources, while transnational firms are deemed to attribute high levels of importance to both home- and host-country resources. Therefore it is proposed that both global and transnational firms will be more likely to perceive resources located in both their countries of origin and host countries as being of equal importance compared with multinational and international firms.

The construct 'resource location' was operationalised using a nominal scale and tested using chi-square analysis. The findings, shown in Table 5.5, reveal no significant differences between the strategic orientations in terms of the perceived importance of resource location. In line with the a priori predictions, a higher proportion of international firms consider home-country resources to be most important compared with the other three groups. However, a slightly higher proportion of the global/transnational group than the multinational group consider host-country resources to be most important (see H9b), while a slightly larger proportion of multinational firms than global/transnational firms consider home- and host-country resources to be of equal importance, a view which runs counter to Hypothesis 9c. In each case, these differences were not statistically significant at the $p = 0.05$ level.

The findings reported in Table 5.5 provide some interesting insights. Only slightly more than 10 per cent of all respondents consider host-country resources to be most important in terms of gaining an advantage over competitors (see row totals, Table 5.5). This is a surprising finding and particularly so in the case of firms with a multinational orientation which are reputed to emphasise local country differences. It implies that host-country resources, in the main, are not seen as being of any more importance in terms of SCA than resources located in the firm's country of origin. This is emphasised by the importance attributed to home-country resources by over 40 per cent of the sample. This finding supports much of what has been written in the literature about the role of domestically derived advantages in international competition. But it also runs counter to the arguments implicit in the internationalisation

Table 5.5 Importance of resource location by strategic orientation

Number Row % Col %	Multinational	International	Global/ transnational	Row total
Home country is most	25	17	39	81
important	30.9	21.0	48.1	41.5
	39.7	50.0	39.8	
Host country is most	6	3	11	20
important	30.0	15.0	55.0	10.3
	9.5	8.8	11.2	
Both are equally important	32	14	48	94
	34.0	14.9	51.1	48.2
	50.8	41.2	49.0	
Column	63	34	98	195
total	32.3	17.4	50.3	100.0

Chi-square	Value	d.f.	Significance
Pearson	1.34870	4	0.85306
Likelihood ratio	1.33257	4	0.85583
Mantel–Haenszel test for linear association	0.00080	1	0.97743

Minimum expected frequency   3.487
Cells with expected frequency < 5   1 OF 9   (11.1%)
Number of missing observations: 72

literature (Welch and Luostarinen 1988) that home-country resources are important in the early stages of international development and that host-country resources become relatively more important as the firm becomes an experienced international competitor. This study indicates that domestically derived advantages are of importance irrespective of the strategic orientation of the firm and provides further confirmation of H5, which revealed that intangible assets (which embody domestically derived advantages) are considered important by all firms irrespective of their strategic orientation.

It is also noteworthy that almost half of the respondents (48 per cent – see row totals) consider home- and host-country resources to be of equal importance. This indicates that they consider it necessary to be able to utilise resources in both their countries of origin and in their host countries to gain an SCA in a global environment. This represents a formidable challenge. Managers must be able to develop the skills to identify potential resources located in other countries. They must also put in place the kinds of organisational processes which ensure that these resources are developed, nurtured and deployed in ways which enable the firm to gain advantages. And the findings suggest that this view is shared by managers, irrespective of the strategic orientation of their firms.

In summary, the overall purpose of this section was to examine a series of hypotheses regarding the relationship between the firm's resource pool and its strategic orientation. In the main, the hypotheses derived from the literature are not supported by the research. With some notable exceptions, managers in firms with different strategic orientations do not have markedly different views on the relative importance of the five resource groups or on the location of these resources. This relative consistency of opinion raises the question of what separates successful firms from their less successful counterparts. We now turn to this issue.

The impact of resources on performance

A review of recent commentaries on the automotive components industry suggests that it is a difficult industry in which to earn high levels of profit or economic rent. Its fortunes are very closely tied to those of its customers, the automobile manufacturers. When the automotive business is in recession, the components business is also adversely affected. Throughout the early 1990s, worldwide recession reduced the demand for new cars and trucks, leading to overcapacity in the industry and a reduction in new vehicle production (*Nikkei Weekly* 1995). This was accompanied by efforts within the OEM sector to reduce costs and there was increased evidence of automakers pursing value-for-money strategies. Given that parts represent the largest proportion of the automakers' costs, it was inevitable that severe downward pressure would be put on the cost of incoming parts. In Japan, many parts makers responded to these developments by seeking to reduce their own costs through locating production outside of Japan. For example, Matsushita Battery Industrial Co. moved its low-end battery production operations to Poland to avail of low labour costs, while the transfer of production by the Showa Group to its American subsidiary, American Showa Inc., enabled it to announce record sales and net profits through December 1996 (*Nikkei Weekly* 1996).

An analysis of performance figures in the industry confirms this gloomy picture. For example, in the United Kingdom, overall sales of motor vehicle parts rose between 1988 and 1990, fell in 1991 and rose again in 1992 (*Business Ratio Plus* 1994). The UK market also showed an improving profitability position in the early 1990s but return on capital in the business was generally low at 9.6 per cent in 1992/93. Average return on sales in the industry has also been low at approximately 6 per cent (EIU 1996). Another notable trend in the UK is the reduction in stock-to-sales levels as suppliers move towards more just-in-time systems. Credit periods to clients for the industry tend to be 50 days and the average borrowing ratio in 1992/93 was at 127.9 per cent, indicating that many suppliers are highly indebted (*Business Ratio Plus* 1994).

Perhaps the most accepted model for analysing industry profitability is the Porter five-forces model (Porter 1980). Examining the automotive components industry through the lens of the Porter framework helps to illustrate the key drivers of profitability in the industry. The most important determinant is the bargaining power of buyers. The OEM group is more concentrated than its suppliers, parts represent a significant portion of its purchases and many of the components are relatively standard and undifferentiated. One commentator described suppliers as mushrooms in a metaphor suggesting that they have, for years, 'been kept in the dark and covered with manure' by OEMs who draw up parts specifications, circulate them to different bidders and ask for detailed price quotes (*Fortune* 1994). It is interesting that some parts makers have responded to this power imbalance by attempting to forward integrate into vehicle manufacturing. For example, Toyo Koki Co. Ltd, which is partly owned by Mitsubishi Motors and NHK Spring Co., has begun producing recreational vehicles (RVs) in Japan (Masayoshi 1993). Competition between parts makers is accentuated by the large number of small and medium-sized suppliers (though consolidation is increasing) in an industry with slow growth, overcapacity and few bases for product differentiation. So despite the fact that there are barriers to entry in terms of economies of scale and distribution relationships, little threat of substitutes and low bargaining power of suppliers, profitability is low due to the strength of the other two forces. Therefore, it is interesting to try to understand the characteristics of highly profitable firms in this low-profit industry. Before examining this issue in greater depth, summary findings are provided for each of the performance indicators used in this study.

Summary findings on performance

The 'performance' construct was operationalised using four measures, namely, overall sales growth, world market share, return on total assets (ROTA) and return on total sales (ROS). Measures were taken at three time intervals, 1990, 1992 and 1994, in order to assess the sustainability of superior performance. Overall findings for each performance measure are reported in Table 5.6. There are two notable features in this table. First it indicates a gradual improvement on all four performance measures over the five-year period being examined. This suggests that the industry is staging a recovery from the period of recession in the early 1990s. The proportion of very poor performers, that is, firms with ROTAs and ROSs of less than 5 per cent, is steadily falling, while the proportion attaining returns above 15 per cent is on the increase. Second, the table suggests that many of the firms in the sample are performing very well. On average over the five years, almost one-fifth of the sample

Table 5.6 Overall profitability levels in the sample*

Performance measure		1994	1992	1990
Annual sales growth				
Less than 10%		43.4	49.4	49.8
Between 10% and 40%		46.4	42.3	39.3
Greater than 40%		8.6	3.7	4.5
Missing		1.5	4.4	6.3
	Total	100.0	100.0	100.0
World market share				
Less than 1%		37.8	39.3	42.7
Between 1% and 5%		25.5	25.5	24.7
Between 6% and 10%		13.1	10.1	9.0
Greater than 10%		15.7	15.0	12.7
Missing		7.9	9.4	10.8
	Total	100.0	100.0	100.0
Return on total assets (ROTA)				
Less than 5%		29.2	32.2	34.1
Between 5% and 10%		24.3	23.6	24.3
Between 11% and 15%		16.1	15.7	15.4
Greater than 15%		24.7	21.0	17.6
Missing		5.6	7.4	8.6
	Total	100.0	100.0	100.0
Return on sales (ROS)				
Less than 5%		36.0	38.2	42.3
Between 5% and 10%		31.8	31.8	31.1
Between 11% and 15%		15.0	11.2	9.4
Greater than 15%		12.4	11.6	9.7
Missing		4.9	7.3	7.4
	Total	100.0	100.0	100.0

* Percentages represent the proportion of the total sample selecting a given option. 'Missing' row also includes firms not doing business during 1990 and/or 1992.

reported ROTA levels of greater than 15 per cent. The proportion is somewhat lower for the return on total sales measure (see Table 5.6). Against this, it is also apparent that a high proportion of respondents are performing poorly on all dimensions, with, for example, almost 50 per cent of the sample attaining sales growth levels of less than 10 per cent.

As the focus of this research is the question of sustained superior performance, we are interested in firms that perform consistently well or consistently poorly over the five-year period under consideration. It is important to distinguish these consistent performers from firms which, for example, might have attained an ROTA of greater than 15 per cent in 1990, dropped back to between 5 per cent and 10 per cent in 1992 and rose again to greater than 15 per cent in 1994. Therefore, firms in the sample are distinguished on the basis of both the consistency and the level of their performance over the period under observation. The findings indicate that on measures such as profitability and market share, the majority of the sample has performed at a consistent level. It is interesting that, in particular, almost three-quarters of the sample reported the same market share position over the five years, indicating that share gains and indeed losses are difficult to achieve in this type of time frame.

Tests of hypotheses on performance

The overall quality of performance for each respondent is calculated taking into account the consistency of that performance (see Appendix). In the cases of ROS and ROTA, top, poor and average performers are selected as follows. Top performers are firms attaining a performance level that has not fallen below 11 per cent over the five-year period. Given the insights provided by the published performance data shown earlier, this is deemed to be a conservative cut-off point. Poor performers are firms attaining less than 5 per cent returns for each of the three years. Two-group discriminant analysis is conducted to separate top-performing from poorly performing firms. The procedure of selecting out the central cluster allows a starker comparison of differences between high and low performers (Rouse and Daellenbach 1999). In this case we are interested in simultaneously considering the effect of the five broad groups of resources, namely firm-specific tangible assets (TAs), firm-specific intangible assets (IAs), firm-specific capabilities (Cs), basic country-specific resources (BCSRs) and advanced country-specific resources (ACSRs). The discriminant equation reads as follows:

$$Y = v1X1 + v2X2 + v3X3 + v4X4 + v5X5$$

where

   Y = Index score for each case
   v = Arbitrary weights
   X1 = TAs
   X2 = IAs
   X3 = Cs
   X4 = BCSRs
   X5 = ACSRs

The results of a discriminant analysis using the profitability measures as the dependent variable are presented in Table 5.7. In the case of return on sales, top-performing firms reported higher mean ratings for capabilities, intangible assets and tangible assets, with lower mean ratings for both basic and advanced country-specific resources. Significance tests demonstrate that the groups are significantly different with respect to the mean importance attached to capabilities and that the differences with respect to intangible assets, basic CSRs and advanced CSRs lie just outside the

Table 5.7 Findings of the discriminant analysis on performance (profitability)

A. *Perceived importance of resources by return on total sales*

	ACSR	BCSR	FSC	FSIA	FSTA
Top performers	3.07092^1	2.56383	3.51418	3.19858	3.27660
Poor performers	3.23775	2.75735	3.35147	3.00980	3.12500
Significance	$p = 0.10$	$p = 0.10$	$p = 0.05$	$p = 0.10$	
Standardised discrim. function coefficients	−0.62676	−0.54205	0.51614	0.26683	0.47204

Classification results and canonical discriminant function

Percentage of 'grouped' cases correctly classified	Eigenvalue	Canonical corr.	Wilks's lambda	Chi-square	df	Sig.
66.96%	0.1864	0.3963	0.842907	18.885	5	0.0020

B. *Perceived importance of resources by return on total assets*

	ACSR	BCSR	FSC	FSIA	FSTA
Top performers	3.13655^1	2.46386	3.50602	3.05622	3.20482
Poor performers	3.27011	2.81897	3.36839	3.11494	3.14655
Significance		$p = 0.001$	$p = 0.05$		
Standardised discrim. function coefficients	−0.33056	−0.82174	0.61998	0.26802	0.40516

Classification results and canonical discriminant function

Percentage of 'grouped' cases correctly classified	Eigenvalue	Canonical corr.	Wilks's lambda	Chi-square	df	Sig.
65.96%	0.1972	0.4059	0.835377	24.569	5	0.0002

[1] Mean score on a 4-point scale where 4.00 is the maximum importance rating.

$p = 0.05$ level. The standardised canonical discriminant function coefficients for each variable indicate that both basic and advanced CSRs as well as capabilities are important in discriminating between the two groups. However, the coefficients of the former two groups of resources are preceded by a minus sign, indicating that high levels of perceived importance on these variables is negatively associated with superior performance. The strongest indicator of top performance, therefore, is capabilities, which is very much in keeping with the hypothesis. In terms of the quality of the discriminant analysis, over two-thirds of 'grouped' cases are correctly classified. The canonical correlation value of 0.3963 shows that the percentage of the total variance attributable to differences between the groups is almost 40 per cent, which is a moderate figure. The observed significance of 0.0020 indicates that differences between the groups are statistically significant at the $p = 0.01$ level.

The results for return on total assets (ROTA) are similar to those for the return on sales (ROS) measure. Top-performing firms give higher mean ratings to capabilities and tangible assets but not to intangible assets or basic and advanced CSRs. The top-performing group differs significantly from the poor-performing group in terms of its mean rating for capabilities (significant at $p = 0.05$) and for basic country-specific resources (significant at $p = 0.001$). A high level of perceived importance for basic country-specific resources strongly reduces the firm's chances of being in the top-performing group. Overall, the two groups are significantly different at $p = 0.001$. As is the case with the ROS measures, the discriminant function is a moderately good one. Variation between the groups accounts for over 40 per cent of the total variance and two-thirds of the cases are correctly classified.

When performance is measured in terms of world market share, some very interesting patterns emerge (see Table 5.8). Overall, the two groups are significantly different at the $p = 0.05$ level. Again, top-performing firms give higher mean ratings to capabilities and intangible assets but

Table 5.8 Findings of the discriminant analysis on performance (market share and sales growth)

A. Perceived importance of resources by world market share

	ACSR	BCSR	FSC	FSIA	FSTA
Top performers	3.21186[1]	2.61017	3.49492	3.19774	3.16102
Poor performers	3.15278	2.64583	3.42222	2.90278	3.17188
Significance				$p = 0.01$	
Standardised discrim. function coefficients	0.07863	−0.26239	0.17605	0.98767	−0.35346

Classification results and canonical discriminant function

Percentage of 'grouped' cases correctly classified	Eigenvalue	Canonical corr.	Wilks's lambda	Chi-square	df	Sig.
56.13%	0.0846	0.2793	0.921985	12.225	5	0.0318

B. Perceived importance of resources by sales growth

	ACSR	BCSR	FSC	FSIA	FSTA
Top performers	3.05882[1]	2.50000	3.46078	3.31373	3.29412
Poor performers	3.19722	2.64167	3.30889	3.04444	3.05833
Significance					
Standardised discrim. function coefficients	−0.71708	−0.49882	0.13112	0.48846	0.69329

Classification results and canonical discriminant function

Percentage of 'grouped' cases correctly classified	Eigenvalue	Canonical corr.	Wilks's lambda	Chi-square	df	Sig.
71.43%	0.1626	0.3740	0.860105	10.926	5	0.0529

[1] Mean score on a 4-point scale where 4.00 is the maximum importance rating.

also to advanced country-specific resources and lower mean ratings to basic country-specific resources and tangible assets. The mean ratings of the two groups differ significantly only in the case of intangible assets (significant at $p = 0.01$) and this variable has clearly the highest standardised coefficient. This suggests that intangible assets are positively associated with monopoly power. This finding is consistent with the monopoly rights given to firms possessing patents and registered designs, as these resources are protected by regulatory barriers to duplication. But it would also appear to suggest that the firm's reputation can represent a quasi-monopoly generating resource. Reputation is an example of an accumulated asset (Dierickx and Cool 1989) and is protected by complexity and specificity, which makes it difficult to duplicate in the short run. However, in this case the discriminant function is quite weak with an eigenvalue of 0.0846 and its correct classification of only 56 per cent of cases is little better than chance.

Finally, the findings of the discriminant analysis using average sales growth as the dependent variable are reported in Table 5.8. In this case the differences between the two groups are not statistically significant, slightly above the $p \leq 0.05$ level at $p = 0.0529$. This is to be expected since sales growth is a function of market demand whereas share and profitability are affected by competition, which is the issue of central interest here. However, again several notable patterns emerge. Top-performing firms give higher mean ratings to the three firm-specific resources, while poor-performing firms attribute more importance to country-specific resources. Firm-specific tangible assets attained the highest standardised coefficient, indicating that it is the variable which discriminates most between the two groups, closely followed by advanced CSRs which have a negative effect, and intangible assets which have a positive effect. The discriminant function is quite good, correctly classifying over 70 per cent of cases.

Overall, the findings strongly support the hypothesis that capabilities and intangible assets will be perceived to be more important by top-performing firms than by poorly performing firms. It is clear from the analysis that top-performing and poorly performing firms in a global environment differ significantly in terms of their resources perceptions. Top-performing firms attach greater levels of importance to difficult-to-duplicate resources such as capabilities and intangible assets. Poor-performing firms attribute more importance to country-specfic resources such as gaining access to low-cost labour. As predicted in Chapter 4, country-specific resources are easier to duplicate than firm-specific resources and are therefore less likely to be important as a source of sustainable competitive advantage in a global environment. The research confirms the central thesis of the resource-based view that not all resources are of equal importance in terms of gaining advantage and that those resources that are most difficult to duplicate are likely to be of most significance.

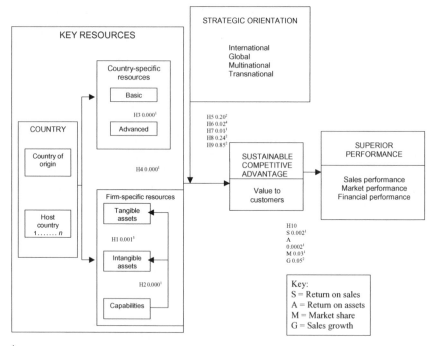

[1] Indicates that the hypothesis was supported.
[2] Indicates that the hypothesis was not supported.
[3] Indicates that the hypothesis was not supported.
[4] Indicates support for one part of the predicted relationship.

Figure 5.2 Test measures for the relationships in the conceptual model

CONCLUSION

The purpose of this chapter is to report the main findings of an analysis of data collected from the sample of automotive components firms in Ireland, the United Kingdom, the United States and Japan. These data are used to test the ten hypotheses developed in Chapter 4. The findings show that the hypotheses relating to the firm's resource pool in a global environment are largely supported by the research. However, hypotheses relating to the important link between resources and strategy are much less well supported. The analysis reported in the previous section shows that a final hypothesis relating to the link between resources and performance is supported by the research. These findings with respect to the ten hypotheses are summarised below and a revised conceptual model showing the relevant test statistics obtained in this study is presented in Figure 5.2. The implications of these findings for research and practice are discussed in the following chapter.

H1: All other things being equal, intangible assets will be perceived to be a more important source of sustainable competitive advantage in a global environment than tangible assets. *Not supported by the research.*

H2: All other things being equal, capabilities will be perceived to be a more important source of sustainable competitive advantage in a global environment than either tangible assets or intangible assets. *Supported by the research.*

H3: All other things being equal, advanced CSRs will be perceived to be a more important source of sustainable competitive advantage in a global environment than basic CSRs. *Supported by the research.*

H4: All other things being equal, firm-specific resources (FSRs) will be perceived to be a more important source of sustainable competitive advantage in a global environment than country-specific resources (CSRs). *Supported by the research.*

H5: Intangible assets will be perceived to be a more important source of sustainable competitive advantage in a global environment by management in international firms than by those in multinational, global and transnational firms. *Not supported by the research.*

H6: Country-specific resources will be perceived to be a more important source of sustainable competitive advantage in a global environment by management in multinational and global firms than by those in international and transnational firms. *Not supported by the research.*

H7: Basic CSRs will be perceived to be a more important source of sustainable competitive advantage in a global environment by management in global firms than by those in multinational, international and transnational firms. *Supported by the research.*

H8: Capabilities will be perceived to be a more important source of sustainable competitive advantage in a global environment by management in transnational firms than by those in multinational, international and global firms. *Not supported by the research.*

H9a: Resources located in the country of origin will be perceived to be a more important source of sustainable competitive advantage in a global environment by management in international firms than by those in multinational, global and transnational firms. *Not supported by the research.*

H9b: Resources located in host countries will be perceived to be a more important source of sustainable competitive advantage in a global environment by management in multinational firms than by those in international, global and transnational firms. *Not supported by the research.*

H9c: Resources located in both the country of origin and in host countries will be more likely to be perceived to be of equal importance by management in both global and transnational firms than by those in multinational and international firms. *Not supported by the research.*

H10: Capabilities and intangible assets will be perceived to be of greater importance by superior performing firms than by inferior performing firms. *Supported by the research.*

6 Conclusions

INTRODUCTION

Firm heterogeneity is a controversial question. In the main, economists have downplayed discretionary firm differences given their concerns with broader aggregates such as the industry and the economy (Nelson 1991). A notable exception is the work of the evolutionary economists (Schumpeter 1934; Nelson and Winter 1982), who adopt a view of economic change based on the diverse innovative activities of firms in an uncertain environment. Sociologists have been concerned with the persistence of heterogeneity, particularly in situations where organisational recipes for success are relatively well known (Carroll 1993). Barriers to imitating successful moves include, for example, structural inertia in the organisation and expectations concerning future environmental changes (Hannan and Freeman 1984; Carroll 1993). Firm heterogeneity is central to the study of strategic management which, by its nature and its audience, is firmly grounded in practice (Rumelt, Schendel and Teece 1991). Strategy, structure, process and performance differences between firms are widely documented in its extensive case-based research. In a global environment, where the geographic scope of business is increasing, where markets in different countries are converging and where cross-national interdependencies are increasing, firm heterogeneity is an important question. Firms competing in the same industry and for the same customers are likely to have diverse national origins and to have originated in very different cultural and institutional environments. We saw in Chapter 4 that country of origin affects a firm's resource configuration and the stock of firm-specific and country-specific resources that it deploys in its product markets. Empirical analysis has also demonstrated that firms from different countries may have different organisational arrangements and may play the competitive game by different rules. For example, it is noted in Chapter 5 that the supply chain of Japanese firms in the automotive components industry was initially very different from that which was popular in Western countries and also in Chapter 1 we saw how dramatically successful

Japanese automotive OEMs have been compared to their counterparts in the United States.

Furthermore, it is noted in Chapter 2 that the global environment is characterised by high levels of complexity, rapid change, high volatility and high levels of perceived uncertainty. In this scenario, the question of performance heterogeneity at the firm level is an important one, of relevance to both managers and researchers. This book seeks to contribute to our understanding of how firms attain a sustainable competitive advantage leading to superior performance. In doing so, it integrates perspectives from strategic management and international business. Organisational success and failure are at the heart of strategic management and it has been suggested that while the origins of the field lie in practice and codification, its advancement increasingly depends upon building theory that helps to explain this heterogeneity (Rumelt, Schendel and Teece 1991). In the process, this book has drawn insights from the neighbouring disciplines of organisation theory and economics to provide an integrated conceptual argument.

SUSTAINABLE COMPETITIVE ADVANTAGE IN A GLOBAL ENVIRONMENT

The relationship between the firm as an entity and its environment has always been a controversial one and there are many strands of literature that bring their own unique perspectives to this question. Some, such as Bain/Mason industrial organisation economics and organisational ecology, do not concern themselves with firm-level issues but adopt the more aggregated positions of the industry and the population (of organisations) respectively. But they are also characterised by a determinism that has influenced a great deal of thinking in strategic management (Bourgeois 1984). For example, Porter (1980) took the basic ideas of the Bain/Mason structure–conduct–performance paradigm and, switching it to the level of the firm, described how the presence of a range of industry conditions interfered with free competition, allowing for the persistence of abnormal returns. He modified this analysis in a later book (Porter 1985) to argue that sustainable competitive advantage can be attained by adopting positions of either cost leadership or differentiation contingent on the structural conditions prevailing in the industry. This is generally described as a positioning-based approach to strategy (Porter 1996) and concurs with contingency theorists who advocate that there are neither universal principles of organisation nor that each organisation is unique, but rather that cognisance needs to be taken of the particular external conditions faced by a given firm. Excessive determinism in the strategy literature has been criticised for failing to acknowledge the way in which organisational actors make strategic choices, which determines how an organisation finds itself within a particular context in the first place (Bourgeois 1984; Child 1972). Sociologists writing within the fields of resource dependency and human ecology recognise the role of choice and highlight the equifinality of the interactions between the firm and its environment. Similarly, the resource-based view of the firm provides an alternative view of performance heterogeneity rooted in the strategic choices firms make concerning both the development and deployment of their resource pools. In a global environment where the resource configurations of firms differ, the relationship between resources and performance heterogeneity becomes an important matter for investigation.

The international business literature is distinguished by its recognition of the challenges posed by changes in the international business environment, including the emergence of global industries (Levitt 1983; Ohmae 1985). Organisational responses to these changes in terms of business strategy, organisational structure and managerial processes are documented in a broad range of empirical and conceptual research. But there is little consensus emerging from this literature on the determinants of performance heterogeneity in a global environment. Strategic management research, generally, has been criticised for being *ad hoc* in its approach (Teece 1984) and much of the evidence of superior performance in international business is anecdotal (Doz 1987). Commentaries on trends in particular industries and on the strategies employed by particular firms are pervasive. For example, Hamel and Prahalad (1985) describe how Japanese television manufacturers built up a large US volume base by first selling private-label TV sets at low cost and then investing in new process technologies to generate advantages of scale and quality. Koepfler (1989) describes how System Software Associates, Inc. (SSA), based in the US, recognised that the business operations of potential clients were similar worldwide and built a $62 billion company by marketing an integrated application software system for use on IBM mid-range computers. Similarly, an analysis of the chocolate industry by Yip and Coundouriotis (1991) found the presence of some strong drivers of globalisation and that firms such as M&M Mars and Jacobs Suchard could operate with just a few dedicated factories located around the world. Countless other such case studies are available in the literature, but this kind of inductive reasoning fails to provide a coherent explanation of the determinants of superior performance. There are too many extraneous variables that may account for success or failures and it is difficult to gauge the impact of the particular characteristics of the firm or of the conditions faced by firms in any given industry.

An alternative approach has been to frame the management task in terms of the conflicting pressures for the maximisation of integration and efficiencies across countries with the need for responsiveness to the local conditions faced by subsidiaries. This has resulted in the prevalence of a contingency-based approach to strategy and performance in the literature. Some industries are viewed as being predominantly global in nature, with similar demand characteristics across countries implying that attempting to maximise efficiencies and pursue low-cost strategies is most desirable (Porter 1986a; Yip 1989). Others mandate strategic adaptation and the pursuit of differentiation strategies across countries in order to cope with the persistence of cross-cultural differences (Douglas and Wind 1987; Porter 1986a). And some other industries are perceived as requiring multifocal (Prahalad and Doz 1987) or trans-national (Bartlett and Ghoshal 1989) approaches due to the presence of pressures for both integration and responsiveness. Environmental conditions have been commonly summarised in 2 × 2 matrices which use integration and responsiveness (or similar concepts) as the discriminating variables and advocate the matching of strategy, structure and process with the particular conditions being faced (Henzler and Rall 1986; Porter 1986a; Yip 1989). Consequently, descriptions of strategy in the international business literature have been strongly deterministic in their orientation. The distinctive nature of the different environments faced by firms has driven much of the analysis and descriptions of strategy have been strongly positioning-based, advocating efficiency (low cost), responsiveness (differentiation) or both.

Leaving aside the cautionary comments made earlier, adopting a deterministic view of strategy in international business is not necessarily a weak approach. The strategic management literature regularly invokes managers to properly understand and respond to the particular set of environmental conditions that their firms may face. What is more troubling is the lack of empirical validation of the central tenets of this contingency approach. This is vividly illustrated in a line of research conducted in the US on what are classed as global industries (Morrison and Roth 1992; 1993; Morrison, Ricks and Roth 1991; Roth 1992; Roth and Morrison 1990). The approach adopted in each of these studies is relatively similar. A variety of global industries are identified through a review of the literature, substantiated by, for example, the existence of at least one global competitor and a high level of intra-industry trade. Samples of business units are selected from the different industries. Perceived conditions in the industries are measured using either Prahalad and Doz's (1987) integration–responsiveness framework (e.g. Roth and Morrison 1990) or Porter's (1986a) coordination–configuration framework (e.g. Roth 1992). Cluster analysis is then used to identify groups of firms who perceive different environmental pressures in the industry and consequently use different business-level strategies measured by parameters such as marketing differentiation, cost control, product specialisation and others. In each case, a number of different clusters of firms is found to exist in a global industry. For example, Roth's (1992) study found five types, which he labelled as 'concentrated hub', 'local innovator', 'technical innovator', 'regional federation' and 'primary global'. Furthermore, he found no significant differences between each of the five types on four performance measures, namely, five-year sales growth, earnings per share, five-year earnings growth and five-year income growth. Similarly, few performance differences were observed between clusters in both other studies by these authors (see, for example Roth and Morrison 1990; Morrison and Roth 1992; 1993) and in a replication of the Roth and Morrison (1990) study in a single industry, namely, construction equipment by Johnson (1995). An alternative approach adopted by Carpano, Chrisman and Roth (1994) matched combinations of strategy based on segmentation and geographic scope with whether the firm was operating in a global (favouring integration) or multidomestic (favouring responsiveness) industry. Here again some of the hypothesised performance relationships in both types of industry are not supported. These empirical findings raise doubts about the merits of the contingency perspective as a theory of performance heterogeneity in a global environment. The research has shown that very different types of firms have been found to be operating in global industries with equal levels of effectiveness. Predictions that firms emphasising global efficiencies or adopting low-cost positions will prevail in global industries have not been borne out. At a functional level, a similar picture has emerged. Research in the marketing literature has shown that the standardisation of marketing activity has not resulted in superior levels of performance in a global industry (see, for example, Samiee and Roth 1992 and Shoham 1995 for a review). In summary, empirical research has not produced convincing support for the view that positioning-based strategies lead to superior performance.

It was against this background of the relative dominance of a deterministic approach and weak anecdotal and empirical support that the resource-based perspective (RBV) was adopted. It proposes that sustainable competitive advantage in a global environment can be explained by the presence of resource asymmetries between firms and the deployment of these resources in product markets. The RBV has emerged in the strategic management literature as an alternative to the industry-based explanations of performance heterogeneity at the firm level. In this research, it is extended to the context of a global environment with promising results. Conceptually, the RBV is broadened to take account of exogenous country-specific resources available to the firm as well as the geographic breadth of those resources. Several key differences in the perceived importance of elements of the resource pool are observed in the empirical research. More critically, resource perceptions are positively related to sustained superior performance in a global environment. The RBV proposes that Ricardian rents can accrue to firms in competitive industries where resources are limited or quasi-limited in supply. Resources such as capabilities have these characteristics because they are both difficult to understand due to causal ambiguity and difficult to duplicate in the short run. This research showed that firms perceiving capabilities to be the most important source of competitive advantage attained high levels of profitability measured by return on total assets (ROTA) and return on total sales (ROS), which were used as proxy measures for the concept of rent.

In moving away from a focus on positioning strategies which match with environmental conditions, this book shares some of the strands of the economic paradigm of international business, particularly the industrial organisation perspective, trade theory and the eclectic paradigm. The early industrial organisation literature was concerned with what advantages enabled MNCs to overcome the costs of doing business internationally and enabled them to compete effectively with local competitors in different countries. In what essentially concurs with the resource-based view, IO economists argue that MNCs deploy idiosyncratic advantages, which are derived from their countries of origin (Hymer 1960). Typical of the advantages of the MNC that are cited in this literature include resources such as knowledge and information (Caves 1971), entrepreneurial skills (Graham 1978), ownership of a brand name (Kindleberger 1969) and extensive R&D (Knickerbocker 1973). Similarly, trade theory and the eclectic paradigm highlight the potential importance of country-specific resources. Home-country-specific resources may be a source of advantage for an MNC while immobile host-country resources may result in the MNC building foreign production facilities (Dunning 1997). The resource-based view of the firm supports and extends this economic literature in three ways. First, it provides a broad comprehensive framework for understanding the relative importance of all the resources available to the firm operating in a global environment. The economic literature only distinguishes firm-specific and country-specific resources, while in the model presented in Chapter 4 of this book both of these groups are included and important sub-divisions within the groups are noted. Second, the findings of the empirical research demonstrate that some resources are more important than others in terms of gaining a competitive advantage in a global environment, with difficult-to-duplicate endogenous resources such as capabilities emerging as the most important. Finally, the economic paradigm has, to a large extent, focused on competition between MNCs and host firms in the countries in which they do business. However, it is clear from the management literature that competition *between* MNCs is also intense and is a particular feature of global industries. A resource-based model of sustainable competitive advantage applies as easily to competition between MNCs as it does to that between host firms and MNCs.

The findings of the research reported here beg the question of whether the industry matters in terms of firm-level performance in a global environment. In the strategic management literature, the weight of the empirical evidence reviewed in Chapter 3 suggests that firm-specific variables explain a greater proportion of performance differences than industry dimensions, though dissenting voices continue to emerge (McGahan and Porter 1997). This study examined the firm side of the equation only and found a positive relationship between firm differences and performance in a low-profit, global industry. However, adopting a balanced view suggests that both elements are important (Aharoni 1993a). For example, metaphorically speaking, Foss (1996a) describes both as blades of a scissors of competitive advantage. Recent research has begun to advocate consideration of both organisation and competition as the most effective way forward in understanding firm actions and performance (Henderson and Mitchell 1997). But it is noteworthy that while the resource-based view is strongly firm-oriented, it does not ignore industry. A core proposition is that the resources deployed by the firm should create value for customers (Barney 1991; Coyne 1986). Some authors go further, suggesting that the resource-based view acts as a bridge between firm-based and industry-based perspectives on advantage (Amit and Schoemaker 1993; Collis and Montgomery 1995). At a theoretical level, the RBV and Bain/Mason IO, which underlies the industry perspective, have been considered similar in that both recognise that the firm's environment constrains strategy (Conner 1991). Empirical research has shown that the resource-based view can be applied at the level of the strategic group and the industry as well as the firm (Maijoor and Van Witteloostuijn 1996). In summary, while its emphasis is on firm asymmetries, the RBV does not ignore industry. But its orientation is strongly voluntaristic and it proposes that a firm possesses the ability to influence its own destiny by the resource choices that it makes in any given set of industry and competitive conditions. The research reported here provides support for the view that sustained superior performance can be attained by firms in a low-profit, global environment and that the attainment of such returns is related to their resource choices.

In summary, the global environment is a relatively new and distinctly competitive business scenario. It is characterised by high levels of change, volatility and uncertainty, but this can also be said of other task environments. What distinguishes global environments is the geographic scope of customers, competitors and factors of production. High levels of international interdependency mean that events and decisions made in one country can affect the entire organisation. This book has shown that the pool of resources available to the firm is spread across country boundaries and throughout its international subsidiaries. Understanding the advantage-creating dimensions of this resource pool can enable the firm to ensure its long-term survival and prosperity.

LIMITATIONS

All studies of this type have limitations that should be borne in mind when considering their findings. For example, the results reported here are confined to one industry – automotive components. Some previous research on global industries has focused on single industry units (Johnson 1995), though, in the main, scholars have examined several industries simultaneously (see, for example, Morrison and Roth 1992 and Roth 1992). As this study was concerned specifically with examining the impact of resources on performance, it was necessary to isolate possible industry effects (Hirsch 1975). The automotive components industry was selected because it exhibits many of the features of a global industry, such as the presence of global customers with universal needs, pressures for cost reduction and high levels of technological intensity. However, the model presented in Chapter 4 is applicable to any global industry and the same relationships between resources, strategic orientation, SCA and superior performance can be expected to exist. Consequently, the findings presented here are generalisable to other global industries, though additional empirical work to test the resource-based model of competitive advantage would be desirable.

This study is cross-sectional, which is important given its concern with the question of sustainable competitive advantage. However, account was taken of the durability of performance differences by asking managers to report details of performance for three intervals over a five-year period. Though this approach creates the possibility of inaccuracies in the recall of data, it is hoped that the problem was minimised by the fact that managers simply had to select points on an ordinal scale rather than recall precise details. Nevertheless, a longitudinal approach appears to be a desirable method for examining sustainable competitive advantage, and its adoption should be considered for future empirical work in the area (Rouse and Daellenbach 1999). Some existing empirical contributions use a quasi-longitudinal approach in their analyses of published historical data (Levinthal and Myatt 1994; Maijoor and Van Witteloostuijn 1996; Makadok and Walker 2000).

Alternative approaches are generally available for the operationalisation of research constructs and choices have to be made. In this study, the operationalisation of the constructs, key resources and sustainable competitive advantage, are particularly noteworthy. Both can be measured using a one-stage or a two-stage procedure and, in this study, the former was adopted in both cases. Key resources can be measured by either asking respondents to assess the relative importance of a given set of resources (the one-stage approach) or by examining both the perceived importance of resources and whether the firm believes that it possesses them. The former was considered to be the more parsimonious approach. It was also considered to be reliable, given the established relationship between managerial cognition and strategic action (Clapham and Schwenk 1991; Gioia and Chittepeddi 1991; Weick 1979). Scanning the strategic context or 'sensemaking' activities by managers influence actions undertaken and consequent performance levels (Thomas, Clark and Gioia 1993). It follows that resources that are perceived to be important by managers are also expected be the ones that are developed and deployed in the marketplace. However, it is recognised that this may not be true in all cases and that forces such as structural inertia and path-dependencies may prevent some resource development. Consequently, future studies may prefer to adopt the two-stage approach to resource measurement.

Similarly, sustainable competitive advantage can be operationalised in different ways. The approach adopted in this study was that SCA was combined with resource perceptions and managers were asked to rate resources in terms of their importance in gaining an advantage over competitors. In this case, the actual type of competitive advantage was not specified. Competitive advantage is defined in Chapter 2 as the relative superior provision of value to customers over that provided by competitors. A more complex approach to its measurement would be first to ask managers to specify what they perceive to be the value dimensions in the industry and then follow this with questions relating to relative performance *vis à vis* competitors in these dimensions. Both approaches rely on managerial perceptions of competitive advantage. As this research was concerned with resource-generated advantages, it was considered to be important to link resources with advantage in the minds of managers. Respondents specified whether they perceived any particular resource to be important in generating competitive advantage, and the presence or absence of superior performance levels was used as an indication of the actual attainment of that advantage.

A number of issues relating to sampling and fieldwork are also worthy of note. First, the sample contained a mix of first-tier and second-tier suppliers, which varied across the four countries under study. For example, given that Ireland has no automotive assembly operations, it has a relatively small proportion of first-tier suppliers. In contrast, the JAPIA directory from which the Japanese sample was drawn contains only the names of first-tier suppliers. Although first- and second-tier suppliers operate at different stages of the component production chain, it is recognised that competitive pressures in the industry generally are very much a function of the fortunes of the OEM sector. Therefore, it is expected that both types of suppliers face similar pressures, though possible differences between them need to be taken into account when considering the findings.

Finally, there was a high level of item non-response (22 per cent) with respect to the question of strategic orientation. There are a number of possible explanations for this. As this question was placed on the front cover of the questionnaire, it may simply have been missed, which seems to support Dillman's (1978) view that no questions should appear on the front cover of a mail questionnaire. He also suggests that the opening question should be 'easy to answer' and 'applicable to everyone'. While it was hoped that the question on strategic orientation fitted these dimensions, this may not in fact have been the case, and it is possible that some respondents did not find that any of the Bartlett and Ghoshal types accurately described their organisation. However, this is unlikely for two reasons. First, a previous test of the typology by Leong and Tan (1993) used a similar self-typing approach without reporting any difficulties. Second, there were no notes on returned questionnaires to suggest that respondents had difficulty with this question. Nevertheless, this high level of item non-response needs to be taken into account when considering the findings of the study. In particular, it may help to explain the absence of significant relationships between the firm's strategic orientation and its resource pool, which are documented in Chapter 5.

IMPLICATIONS FOR MANAGERS AND POLICY MAKERS

The findings of this study have implications for managers both within and outside the automotive components industry. The operational validity (or actionability) of a theory concerns the ability of practitioners to implement actions by manipulating its independent variables (Thomas and Tymon 1982). The RBV is a strongly normative theory in its proposition that sustainable competitive advantage and superior performance can be gained by the deployment of difficult-to-duplicate resources in ways that create value for customers. But while this logic is simple, its implementation is not easy and skills in doing so are themselves sources of SCA (Castanias and Helfat 1991). For example, identifying which of a firm's resources are important in gaining a competitive advantage can be a problem. Advantage-creating resources vary from industry to industry and over time as the bases of competitive advantage shift (Prahalad and Hamel 1990). But this research indicates that managers should answer three important questions about their firm's resource pool, namely, (i) what resources are important in creating value for customers? (ii) what are the barriers that prevent the duplication of these resources by competitors? and (iii) can the firm appropriate the value created by these resources? Finding answers to these questions has important implications. It means that managers should think of their firm's competitive strategy as a process of deploying its resources to create value for customers. They must think about the development and retention of these key resources. And they must think about the development and/or acquisition of the resources that the firm needs both now and in the future in order to ensure its survival and success.

This study has shown that firm-specific capabilities are the most difficult set of resources for a competitor to duplicate. Advantages built on these resources are the most sustainable. In particular, in the context of competition in a global environment, endogenous capabilities are far superior to, for example, availing of low-cost labour or government incentives in terms of gaining advantage. The research has also indicated that SCA is often due to the interaction effects of a number of resources such as the combined result of the integration of tangible assets and capabilities. The inverse is also true, namely that advantages accruing from, for example, individual personnel within the firm can be risky. In industries such as advertising, consulting and fund management, advantages can disappear due to the ease of mobility of human resources. A case in point in the automotive business concerned the hiring by Volkswagen in Germany of a purchasing executive and a number of members of his staff from GM. As noted in Chapter 5, the cost of incoming parts is an important determinant of the profitability of an OEM; therefore the purchasing department is a key resource. GM subsequently sued Volkswagen, accusing their former executive and his team of stealing some of their trade secrets. Furthermore, human resources can appropriate much of the value that they create, as evidenced by, for example, the escalating salaries being paid to top athletes in the sports business.

The findings also suggest that it is the resources that accumulate over time within the firm that provide the most enduring advantages. Resource development is the product of ongoing decision making by managers, which sets the firm on a path trajectory that may be positive or negative with respect to the market. These resource decisions are characterised by high levels of specificity. They are impossible to duplicate and can only be matched by another firm that has made exactly the same set of decisions in the same circumstances. This suggests that resource decisions should be guided by market trends. Doing so places the firm on a positive path trajectory and implies that market orientation is a key advantage-creating resource (Hunt and Morgan 1995). However, such resource bets are made under conditions of uncertainty and a capacity to change direction remains important.

The findings also further our understanding of sustainable competitive advantage in the global automotive components industry. An extensive literature exists which has documented management practices in the industry, particularly those of Japanese components suppliers. It might be expected, therefore, that the sources of competitive advantage in this industry are well known. The literature has highlighted the importance of quality systems, design/engineering know-how and supply chain relationships. This study confirmed the importance of these firm-specific capabilities and explained why they are sources of advantage. However, it also indicated that not all firms in the industry understand the importance of these resources and that these perceptions of relative resource importance are related to performance levels. Though the sources of advantage are well documented, some firms seem to have a better understanding of the prerequisites of success than others. Furthermore, the study shows that successful components suppliers not only realise the importance of excellence in the aforementioned capabilities, but also understand the role of other difficult-to-duplicate resources. In particular, successful firms place a premium on building their reputation, which was found to be highly correlated with superior profitability. This again illustrates the beneficial outcomes accruing to investments in an accumulated resource.

The resource-based view of the firm is concerned with competition at the level of the firm, but its logic and insights should also be considered by policy makers. Competition at the level of the country has occupied the minds of economists since Adam Smith (1776), and the subsequent work of trade theorists has explained relative country competitiveness in terms of asymmetries in factor endowments. The work of Porter (1990) brought a distinctly strategic management flavour to the debate on country competitiveness. His basic proposition is that competition takes place at the level of the firm, not the level of the country, and that a country's relative competitiveness is a function of the competitive advantages of its firms. Particular countries succeed in certain industries because of the relative global superiority of their firms, whether they are, for example, German chemical companies or Italian footwear firms.

Porter's (1990) work went on to explain the role of the firm's home country in generating internationally competitive firms which he framed in terms of the familiar diamond of factor conditions, demand conditions, firm strategy, structure and rivalry and the presence of related and supporting industries. The role of government in this framework is to contribute to the upgrading of the competitive advantages of its country's firms by its actions relating to each element of the diamond. In effect, the policy role becomes one of constantly striving to improve a country's resource pool and, in particular, to build its stock of 'advanced factors of production' which Porter sees as most significant in attaining competitive advantages. His analysis of the role of resources at a national level implicitly endorses the resource-based approach to strategy (Grant 1991b), which is ironic given the importance that he has placed on industry dimensions in his analysis of firm-level competitive advantage (see, for example, Porter 1980).

Accepting the view that country competitiveness is a function of the competitive advantages of its firms also has important policy implications relating to the controversial question of the national origin of a country's firms (Reich 1990). The increasing levels of foreign direct investment (FDI) documented in Chapter 1 mean that a higher proportion of the wealth of many countries is accounted for by foreign firms. This is particularly true in the case of Ireland, whose recent rapid growth rates have become the subject of much attention (*Economist* 1997b). A policy of openness to trade has resulted in many MNCs setting up operations in Ireland; foreign-owned firms account for approximately 30 per cent of the economy and 40 per cent of exports (*Economist* 1997b). Foreign investment is mobile and the market for it competitive. From a policy viewpoint, what becomes important is how to attract inward FDI and the resource-based view of the firm is helpful in understanding how countries can succeed in this competitive market. For example, Ireland's success is seen as a function of many factors such as 10 per cent tax rates in the manufacturing and internationally traded services sectors, English as the spoken language, and a well-educated workforce. The RBV enables us to understand the relative importance of these kinds of resources. As is the case at the level of the firm, harder-to-duplicate resources are advantageous. For example, low labour costs are not a basis upon which to build sustainable advantages in the market for FDI. Low-cost labour used to be a competitive strength in Ireland, but political events can easily undermine such advantages. Britain's decision to opt out of the Social Charter, which is an important element of the European integration effort, improved its cost position relative to other European countries. Firms like Digital in Galway, Ireland, and Hoover in Dijon, France, moved production to the UK to avail of these cost advantages combined with a large local market. The fall of communism meant that the countries of Central Europe became attractive locations for production in labour-intensive industries due to their very low costs. Consequently, one of Ireland's automotive components firms, Packard Electric, which is part of the GM group, relocated its production of cable harnesses to the Czech Republic in 1995. Instead, Ireland's current competitiveness in the market for FDI is related to some less imitable factors such as a tradition of foreign, particularly US, firms locating here (a positive path dependency), a sustained high level of investment in third-level education (an advanced CSR) and its industrial development body, the IDA, which possesses a high level of accumulated capability in attracting inward investment.

The logic of the RBV is helpful in explaining country competitiveness generated by both indigenous and foreign-owned firms. Countries can generate sustained success through the possession of difficult-to-duplicate national resources. As is the case at the level of the firm, a country's success is rarely due to just one resource but rather the interaction of a number of resources, as the example of Ireland demonstrates. The macro-level also suggests an interesting avenue for further research related to the speed of imitation of advantage-creating resources. Some country-specific resources, as noted in Chapter 4, are related to cultural and institutional environments and diffuse very slowly across borders (Kogut 1991; Murtha and Lenway 1994). But even the duplication of transparent resources such as tax levels and government incentives is often irregular, suggesting that the problem of structural inertia is greater at a national level. More generally, the insights of the RBV on the nature of resources and their role in generating national advantages are worthy of further investigation.

RESEARCH DIRECTIONS

Several research issues emerged over the course of the study. These range from reflections on the approach adopted to thoughts on the future directions of research employing a resource-based perspective. These implications for researchers are discussed in the following paragraphs.

The benefits of an interdisciplinary approach

As noted in Chapter 1, calls for an interdisciplinary approach to international business research have become increasingly frequent in recent years. The primary reason for this trend would appear to be the inherent multidisciplinarity of the international business literature (Dymsza 1984a). In a field of study influenced by so many of the social sciences and business sub-disciplines, an approach that integrates one or more of these perspectives has an appealing logic. But it appears, to an extent, that an interdisciplinary approach is simply seen as a good thing and its potential benefits are not always well spelled out. Some exceptions are Daniels (1991), who highlighted that it may result in research that is of increased relevance to practitioners, and Dunning (1989), who noted the potential synergies that could be gained during the research process.

This study adopted an interdisciplinary approach on a number of levels. It took cognisance of both the economic and management perspectives in international business research. The benefits of this exercise were twofold. First, it enabled the identification of several parallel themes and insights that have been labelled differently and, in the main, discussed separately. It highlights the need for management researchers, particularly, to examine some of the insights from the economic literature that has preceded much of management research (Kogut 1989). For example, Hymer's seminal thesis in 1960 (Hymer 1960) documented the growing homogenisation of consumer markets throughout the world, which became the subject of intense debate in the management literature during the 1980s (see, for example, Boddewyn, Soehl and Picard 1986; Douglas and Wind 1987; Levitt 1983; Robinson 1986). Second, reviewing the two streams of literature has helped to highlight the weaknesses of both. For example, the economic literature has generally been more concerned with explaining why MNCs exist rather than how they might be more effectively managed (Porter 1986a). This is particularly true of internalisation theorists, who focus on explaining why the hierarchical form of the MNC is favoured ahead of the market mechanism. As management questions have been raised, these theorists have argued that they can be comfortably accommodated within internalisation theory, whether it be by 'bringing management back in' (Buckley 1993) or by describing the transnational in terms of the interplay of location-bound and non-location-bound advantages (Rugman and Verbeke 1992), though this does appear to overstretch the elasticity of the transaction cost concept.

On another level, this study integrated perspectives from strategic management and international business. The benefits that were realised at this level concern our understanding of sustainable competitive advantage in a global environment. The extant management literature has adopted a deterministic, positioning-based approach to competitive advantage. It highlights that firms face the conflicting pressures of maximising efficiencies accruing from cross-border integration while also responding to the differences between countries. Alternative strategic and structural arrangements that have been proposed have been framed by the need to manage this conflict. However, the early work of authors in strategic management such as Selznick (1957) and the more recent emergence of the resource-based view of the firm have highlighted that firm-specific variables also contribute significantly to our understanding of competitive advantage. This suggests the need to revisit economic concepts in international business, particularly the work of industrial organisation economists, who stress the importance of firm-specific advantages in international competition. In the context of inadequate empirical support for the positioning-based approach, the integration of perspectives from strategic management has highlighted the potential of an alternative explanation of performance differences based on firm-specific characteristics. Empirical verification of a resource-based model of sustainable competitive advantage in a global environment marks a step in the integration of strategic management and international business.

This study also incorporated perspectives from organisation theory and organisational economics. The benefits of integrating these strands of literature are that they play an important role in the clarification of key constructs. Both the concepts of SCA and the global environment are discussed regularly in the literature but are inadequately defined. Understanding the characteristics and role of the environment has been a central concern of organisation theorists. Separation of the general and task environment (Bourgeois 1980a) is important as it enables a distinction to be made between the process of globalisation and the presence of global industries. Organisation theory also provides a rich foundation for debates at the determinism/voluntarism interface, such as those concerning competitive advantage. The rigour of economic reasoning also helps to clarify the concept of advantage. For example, Kay (1993) defines its key features as being relativism (to a context or a competitor) and value in the marketplace.

In summary, an interdisciplinary approach has many benefits, including the integration of complementary perspectives, the addition of richness to debates and recommendations and the clarification of important constructs. It strengthens research aimed at understanding broad questions of relevance to practitioners (Daniels 1991), of which attaining levels of sustained superior performance is one. As Simon (1967) notes, it is the task of scholars to conduct research that helps to advance the practice of management as a profession. In attempting this difficult task, a broad approach is desirable, as each new perspective has the potential to contribute an important piece to the overall puzzle.

The resource-based view in international business research

As noted earlier in the book, applying the RBV to the international context has much appeal due to the pre-eminence of resources in core theories of international business such as trade theory and the industrial organisation paradigm. A review of recent literature in the field highlights some attention to resource-related questions without specifically adopting the logic and language of the resource-based view of the firm. For example, Rugman (1987) identifies mineral resource rights, vertical integration, cheap energy inputs, marketing skills, brand-name products and customised production as the firm-specific advantages of successful Canadian multinationals. More generally, Hamel and Prahalad (1988) identify factor cost differences, global scale and global distribution as sources of competitive advantage that enable firms to build a global presence, defend domestic dominance and overcome national fragmentation. In the early 1990s, the resource-based view of the firm was used by Tallman (1991) in his analysis of market entry by automotive manufacturers, by Collis (1991) in his analysis of global competition in the bearings industry and to a lesser extent by Aharoni (1993b) in his discussion of competitive advantage in different types of international industries. Recent years have seen the emergence of models of the multinational firm based on the logic of the resource-based view of the firm, including those of this author (Fahy 1994; 1998a; Fahy *et al.* 2000) and those of Geringer, Li and Tallman (1994), Hooley *et al.* (1996), Tallman and Fladmoe-Lindquist (1994; 1997) and Tsang (1997).

This research highlights the bilateral benefits of a resource-based analysis of international business as predicted by Ghoshal and Westney (1992). Extending the RBV to the global context requires some extensions to the basic model, as discussed in Chapter 4. Most notably, it focuses attention on the nature of the resource pool, particularly its potential scope in a global context. It also raises awareness of the role of countries in the resource endowments of firms (Porter 1990; 1991). This latter issue, in particular, has been largely ignored in the strategic management literature. Equally, international business research has benefited from the application of the resource-based view. The RBV provides a comprehensive model for examining resource-related questions and offers an alternative explanation of sustained superior performance to the dominant positioning-based approach.

Resource-based perspectives can easily be extended into other areas of international business research. For example, Wright and Ricks (1994) identify international alliances and coalitions as a core area for further research in the field. Some contributions have already adopted a resource-based approach to research on the cooperative activities of firms (see, for example, Combs and Ketchen 1999; Lorenzoni and Lipparini 1999). As noted earlier, Tallman (1991) has used the resource-based framework to examine international market entry and this has continued in some more recent work (see Tallman and Fladmoe-Lindquist 1997). Wright and Ricks (1994) also identify international entrepreneurship and the internationalisation of small businesses as another key research direction. The resource-based view of the firm does not attach any special importance to firm size and applies easily to large as well as small firms. These represent some current and potential future applications of the resource-based view in international business research, though its main focus is likely to remain as a theory of sustainable competitive advantage.

The future of the resource-based view

The RBV is still a relatively new theory of the firm and additional insights and perspectives continue to emerge. Conceptual and empirical issues which should be considered in future work are discussed in the following paragraphs.

Conceptual issues

The RBV has attracted the interest of a substantial number of scholars in the field of strategic management, as evidenced by the range of contributions described in Chapter 3. Its popularity is further confirmed by the award of the 1994 *SMJ* best-paper prize to Birger Wernerfelt, who first coined the phrase 'resource-based view' in 1984 (Zajac 1995). Reflecting on its development, Wernerfelt (1995) suggested that the RBV is here to stay because it is a truism that firms have different resource endowments, a fact that he considers will lead authors to drop the compulsion to note that an argument is 'resource-based'. A portent for its future is to be found in an emerging debate in the marketing literature. The RBV framework has been adopted by marketing writers in their analysis of competition and the role of marketing assets, though is has been accompanied by an unhelpful re-labelling as the 'comparative advantage theory of competition' (Hunt and Morgan 1995). Its application in marketing has attracted some strong criticism (Deligonul and Cavusgil 1997), though this appears to have been motivated as much by a reaction to the sweeping claim of Hunt and Morgan (1995) that their contribution is a new and integrated theory that replaces the neoclassical theory of perfect competition rather than any difficulty with its content *per se*. Deligonul and Cavusgil (1997) argue that Hunt and Morgan's theory is grounded in the same exchange paradigm as the neoclassical theory and therefore cannot challenge, let alone replace, it. In their critique, Deligonul and Cavusgil (1997) use some strong language, describing aspects of Hunt and Morgan's (1995) article as 'a folk narrative', 'not at all epistemologically novel' and 'like a snake swallowing its tail'. Hunt and Morgan (1997) counter that their theory, now re-labelled again as the 'resource-advantage theory of competition' does not replace the neoclassical theory but is rather a general theory of competition.

As we saw in Chapter 2, during the review of the economic paradigm of international business, claims of a general theory tend to go unresolved (McClain 1983). A more constructive criticism of the Hunt and Morgan approach is provided by Dickson (1996), who argues that it does not fully embrace the dynamic disequilibrium paradigm. Building on his theory of competitive rationality (Dickson 1992), Dickson notes that heterogeneity in supply and demand is a virtuous cycle with no clear beginning or end as firms respond to changing demand by experimenting with new ways of serving customers. He criticises Hunt and Morgan's (1995) matrix of competition for being static whereas leading multinational firms are constantly striving to move from one competitive advantage to another (Mascarenhas, Baveja and Jamil 1998). The resource-based model of competitive advantage presented in Chapter 3 has a dynamic element whereby management is charged with the responsibility of rebuilding resources as they are used up and also with developing new resources. As Dickson (1996) notes, these resource-building decisions set the firm on a path dependency, which may be positive or negative. He cites the example of Netscape's decision to give away over 10 million copies of its Navigator software which, in effect, created a standard for commercial Internet use as an example of a positive supply and demand path dependency. This issue of path dependencies has also recently begun to receive more attention in the strategy literature (Teece, Pisano and Shuen 1997). It is noted that historical decisions may have many consequences, resulting, for example, in a firm with the best products losing out in the marketplace because it has locked into inferior technologies. The importance of path dependencies is emphasised in conditions where 'increasing returns to adoption' exist, that is, where technologies and the products embodying those technologies become more attractive the more they are adopted (Teece, Pisano and Shuen 1997). As the resource-based model is based on the deployment of resources to create value for customers, it must take account of the diversity of both market demand and resource supply. The implications of dynamic disequilibrium need to be more fully explored in the future development of the model.

The concept of dynamism highlights the links between the resource-based view of the firm and the Schumpeterian/evolutionary theory of economic change (Nelson and Winter 1982; Schumpeter 1934), which is also described as the neo-Austrian perspective on competition (Hill and Deeds 1996). Evolutionary economists propose that firms compete primarily through a struggle to improve and innovate (Barney 1986c). These efforts are characterised by a poor understanding of the causal structure of the firm's technologies, and organisational routines are developed and bettered through repetition and practice (Nelson and Winter 1982). This learning-by-doing means that the current capability of a firm is extremely difficult to copy even when best practice is observed. In the literature on the resource-based view of the firm, this proposition is central to Dierickx and Cool's (1989) treatment of accumulated asset stocks. It also suggests that further integration of the RBV and the evolutionary economics literature will help to increase our understanding of how the firm's resource pool is developed and also provides a potential explanation for firm failure based on the inability to change trajectory due to historical choices made. This latter point is considered to complement the population ecologist's concept of structural inertia (Barney and Ouchi 1986), so incorporating the work of these sociologists may also further enrich the analysis.

Another emerging line of research which is based on evolutionary economics and the resource-based view of the firm has sought to develop an alternative to transactions cost theory and its explanation of the firm as existing to keep in check transaction costs arising from the self-interested motivations of individuals. Kogut and Zander (1992) propose that what firms do better than markets is the sharing and transfer of the knowledge of groups and individuals within the organisation, with the result that its boundaries can be explained without appealing to the notion of opportunism. Firms are viewed as social communities in which individual and social expertise is transformed into economically useful products and services by the application of higher-order organising principles such as cultures, languages and codes. Firms exist because they provide a social community of voluntaristic action structured by organising principles that are not reducible to individuals (Kogut and Zander 1992). This 'knowledge-based' view of the firm is supported by Conner and Prahalad (1996), while Foss (1996b, c) has defended the need to retain the transaction cost framework. This is an interesting debate because it has also been extended to the international business arena (Kogut and Zander 1993), where the transaction cost approach has been used extensively to explain the existence of the MNC. Again Kogut and Zander (1993) argue that MNCs arise not out of the failure of markets, but out of their superior efficiency as an organisational vehicle for the transfer of knowledge across borders. Inevitably, this proposed new theory has provoked debate (see, for example, Kogut and Zander 1995; Lowe 1995; McFetridge 1995). These contributions indicate the emergence of another research stream that examines the nature of a very important firm-specific capability, namely, organisational knowledge in both a domestic and international context.

In summary, an abundance of conceptual work is continuing on themes closely related to the resource-based view of the firm, including, for example, the recent alignment of perspectives from the RBV with those from the order-of-entry literature (Lieberman and Montgomery 1998; Schoenecker and Cooper 1998) and the application of RBV perspectives to the question of new product development (Verona 1999). Perhaps the most noticeable feature of the emerging literature has been the broadening of the theoretical base of the RBV evident in the contributions of authors like Hunt and Morgan (1995) and Kogut and Zander (1992), who incorporate perspectives from neoclassical and evolutionary economics respectively. Even more ambitious contributions have been the recent articles by Oliver (1997) and Rindova and Fombrun (1999), who describe a view of sustainable competitive advantage that combines both institutional theory and the resource-based view of the firm. Given the links between a firm's resource endowments and its institutional context highlighted at several points throughout this book and by the work of authors such as Porter (1990; 1991) and Tallman and Fladmoe-Lindquist (1997), this appears to be a further, very promising, research direction. Nevertheless, new developments of the resource-based view will also require attention to a number of empirical questions.

Empirical issues

As noted in Chapter 3, an increasing amount of empirical work is taking place within the parameters of the RBV, though the methods of data collection are uncertain and in need of further development (Hoskisson *et al.* 1999). Future empirical research should seek to provide a better understanding of some of the core elements of the basic model presented in Chapter 3. In particular, there is a need to illuminate the role played by management in the process by which resources are converted into positions of advantage. In contrast to the view put forward by Hill and Deeds (1996), resources in and of themselves are not sufficient to explain persistent differences in firm profitability. The management literature highlights that executives play a role in the process of converting resources into something of value to customers (Williams 1992). This involves resource identification, development, protection and deployment (Amit and Schoemaker 1993), and managerial skill in these activities is in itself a source of sustainable competitive advantage (Castanias and Helfat 1991). It is important that future research finds suitable ways of operationalising this management role. Given this study's concern with competition in a global environment, the Bartlett and Ghoshal (1989) typology was used but was found to be very weak in helping to understand the role of management. This may be explained by the tendency in both the strategic management and international business literature for typologies of strategy to exhibit greater levels of industry fit rather than resource fit. For example, the Bartlett and Ghoshal typology takes explicit account of industry pressures for integration and responsiveness (Bartlett and Ghoshal 1989; Ghoshal and Nohria 1993), while Porter's (1985) generic strategies of cost leadership and differentiation are related to his earlier work on the structural features of industries (Porter 1980). It is necessary to review available typologies of strategy to find out whether and how they incorporate the management of resources by the firm. It may even be necessary to develop a 'resource-based' typology of strategy. Whatever approach is adopted, the role of management in the process by which resources are used to gain advantages remains an important research question.

Similarly, the empirical examination of the firm's resource pool poses problems. For example, resources fall within the realm of what Godfrey and Hill (1995) describe as 'unobservables' in strategic management research. Their critique relates particularly to firm-specific capabilities that are characterised by high levels of tacitness and causal ambiguity. A research difficulty is created because the less observable the resource and the less easy it is to understand, the greater the likelihood that it is also an important source of sustainable competitive advantage. Taking this thinking to its logical conclusion implies that the 'best' resource can never be identified and, as Collis (1994) notes, the strategy field will never find the ultimate source of SCA. Trying to find out which capability is superior leads one into the arena of meta-capabilities and the problem of infinite regress (Collis 1994). From a research point of view, the impossibility of identifying all sources of advantage must be taken as a given. This study adopted an approach used in some previous studies (Aaker 1989; Hall 1992) and presented respondents with a given resource set. There is merit in examining the relative importance of those resources that can be identified and also in understanding their role in performance heterogeneity at the firm level. However, Rouse and Daellenbach (1999) advocate research approaches that take the researcher into the organisation, such as high-intrusion ethnographic methods like participant observation that they feel enable a high level of sense-making and richer desciptive and analytical possibilities for the data. The use of inductive, case-based methods that focus on a single or a few firms is also favoured by Hoskisson *et al.* (1999).

Finally, one unexpected finding of this study was that tangible assets were perceived to be a more important source of competitive advantage than intangible assets. This is surprising given that the literature suggests that intangible assets possess greater barriers to duplication and are therefore likely to be a more important source of advantage. This finding suggests three possible research directions. First, it may be worthwhile to examine if it is unique to the automotive components industry. Many of the products used in car production are relatively basic, commodity-type products such as bearings, rubber hoses and cable harnesses, and this may explain why, for example, intellectual property is not considered to be a very important resource. Second, it suggests that the proposed ease of duplication of some tangible assets is worthy of re-examination. For example, Grant (1991a) has argued that tangible assets are relatively transparent and therefore easy to copy. The findings of this study suggest that this is not the case as far as a firm's plant and equipment is concerned; this factor was rated the sixth most important resource of the 16 presented to managers (see Table 5.1). Despite the extensive documentation of production and operations management practices in this industry, plant and equipment does not appear to be a resource that is easy to duplicate. Plant and equipment, in general, is often the result of sustained investment and may be protected by economic deterrents such as economies of scale (Collis and Montgomery 1995; Rumelt 1987). Consequently, it may be a resource that is more difficult to duplicate than has heretofore been considered to be the case. A third research direction suggested by the high level of importance attributed to plant and equipment is an exploration of the relationship between tangible assets and capabilities. Links between these two groups of resources have been highlighted by some researchers (see, for example, Amit and Schoemaker 1993 and Stalk, Evans and Schulman 1992). A factor analysis of the resource pool showed that plant and equipment loaded with capabilities such as design/engineering know-how, the expertise of management, quality systems, relationships with customers and the ability to mobilise multifunctional teams. This reflects the kind of interaction effects described by Amit and Schoemaker (1993) and suggests that tangible assets may combine with capabilities to provide an important source of advantage. Examining the extent of this interaction would increase our understanding of the nature of the firm's resource pool.

In summary, the prospects for further research in the area of the resource-based view of the firm are positive, with many of its core propositions in need of further clarification and empirical verification, and with a number of interesting conceptual debates beginning to emerge. Finally, it is worth noting the effectiveness of the total design method (Dillman 1978), which was used to collect the data used in this study. Conducting accurate cross-cultural research is difficult due to a plethora of methodological, sampling and measurement problems. The mail survey technique is an attractive vehicle for collecting data but is renowned for its low response rates, particularly where the source and target countries differ (Jobber and Saunders 1988). This study adopted the total design method (TDM) in the construction and implementation of the research instrument, generating a very satisfactory response rate averaging just over 50 per cent across four countries. The highest response (74 per cent) was in the source country – Ireland – while the lowest at 38 per cent in both Japan and the

US compared very favourably with the norm for mail surveys (Hart 1987). The TDM did not overcome the problem of source-country effects but greatly reduced its significance by generating satisfactory returns in all countries (Fahy 1998b). It suggests that the TDM may be an effective approach for the design of commercial studies and its adoption should be considered for future cross-cultural research.

CONCLUSION

The title of the 1996 annual meeting of the Academy of International Business was 'IB as an Integrating Discipline: Duality as a Way of Life' and the call for papers for this meeting advocated the desirability of moving beyond duality in analysis. The concept of business strategy in international business research has been dominated by the duality of reconciling the need for cross-border integration and efficiencies with requirements for adaptation and local responsiveness. While this effectively describes the nature of the challenges facing international managers, it has resulted in the dominance of a deterministic, positioning-based approach to understanding performance heterogeneity which, to date, has not been empirically validated. This book took a different approach, integrating perspectives from strategic management, economics and organisation theory to propose a resource-based model of sustainable competitive advantage in a global environment. In doing so, it sought to contribute to the stock of knowledge in a number of ways. First, it has examined two very germane but poorly defined concepts, namely, sustainable competitive advantage and the global environment. It has provided a clarification of what these concepts mean and examined them in unison. Second, it has shown that, in a global environment, the basic resource-based model requires important conceptual extensions to describe fully the nature of the resource pool available to firms. Endogenous resources remain important and are central to the attainment of advantages, but firms also have access to a range of country-specific resources located in the potentially wide range of countries in which they conduct business. Third, this model was tested in a global industry across four countries using a methodology that shows some promise in cross-cultural research. Finally, the study proposed an explanation for the presence of sustainable competitive advantage in a global environment based on the deployment of difficult-to-duplicate resources by firms in ways that create value for customers. The findings mark an important step in improving our understanding of the nature of global sustainable competitive advatange (GSCA). More work remains to be done in examining and clarifying specific elements of the model, but the resource-based view of the firm holds some promise for further illuminating these important questions.

7 Appendix
Research Design

Good research design reflects the important relationship between theory and method (Morgan and Smircich 1980). The theoretical basis of the research is the resource-based view of the firm, which has a strongly economic orientation, and the research design ought to reflect these theoretical origins. Its ontological assumptions are that the world is a real, external and objective phenomenon but also that it is an evolving process, creating opportunities for those with the appropriate ability to mould and exploit relationships in accordance with their interests. The design sought to reflect both the rationality of classical economics as well as to incorporate the voluntarism and choice inherent in the RBV. From an epistemological perspective, this implies a positivist stance with an emphasis on the empirical analysis of concrete relationships in an external social world (Burrell and Morgan 1979). The design was classically positivist, testing theoretically grounded hypotheses via a cross-sectional study of a representative sample (Easterby-Smith, Thorpe and Lowe 1991). But, given that the assumption of total objectivity is relaxed in the resource-based view, this positivist approach is supplemented with some additional research, including depth interviews and historical analysis.

EXPLORATORY RESEARCH

The research began with some initial exploratory investigation of the major issues involved. This phase of the research included consultation with industry experts and a series of in-depth interviews with management personnel in a number of leading Japanese automotive components firms. Discussions were held with personnel in two industrial development agencies, namely, the Irish Industrial Development Authority (IDA) and the Japanese External Trade Organisation (JETRO), as well as the Japanese Automotive Parts Industries Association (JAPIA). These discussions were designed to glean information on the major trends and developments in the industry and also to gain further understanding of the differences and similarities between Japanese and Western perspectives on competitive strategy in the industry.

The second stage of the exploratory research was a series of in-depth interviews, conducted on site with the management personnel in four Japanese automotive components firms, namely, Topy Industries (wheels), Calsonic Corporation (radiator and exhaust systems), Kinugawa Rubber Company (engine parts) and NSK (bearings). The purpose of the interviews was to explore the views of Japanese managers on the relationships between the major variables under consideration in the study. The interviews were unstructured and conducted in English, except for the case of NSK, which was conducted through an interpreter. The most notable points emerging from this series of discussions were the following:

1   Automotive components suppliers tend to expand globally in response to a desire to follow customers rather than to avail themselves of country-specific resources such as low labour costs or government incentives.
2   Most R&D activity remained located in, and controlled from, Japan.
3   Overseas subsidiaries were primarily staffed by local personnel, with very few Japanese employed, and executives considered a localised strategy to be critical due to trade conflict and local content issues as well as the unique local physical conditions which affected automobile design.
4   Components suppliers reported that they were experiencing severe downward price pressure from original equipment manufacturers (OEMs) due to the strength of the yen and the overall recession in the industry.
5   Intellectual property, such as patents and designs, were considered to be relatively unimportant in this industry.
6   Among the factors considered to be critical for success in the industry were engineering and technical capabilities, the ability of top management to make sound and timely decisions, the excellence of quality control systems and relationships with buyers.

This phase of the research indicated some initial support for the broad hypothesis that firm-specific resources would be a more important source of sustainable competitive advantage than country-specific resources. It was also helpful in illuminating the broad conditions facing the industry, which need to be taken into account when interpreting the results from the quantitative phase of the study. Finally, it helped to inform the questionnaire design phase of the research.

QUESTIONNAIRE DESIGN

Conducting cross-cultural research presents a variety of difficulties, including, for example, methodological problems, sampling problems and measurement problems, which have been the subject of much attention in the literature (see, for example, Douglas and Craig 1983; Nassif *et al.* 1991; Peterson 1993; Singh 1995). Therefore, great care needs to be taken in the design and conduct of the research to ensure the reliability and validity of the findings. The mail survey technique was chosen as it is considered to be a valuable tool for gathering cross-cultural data due to its potential for wide coverage at low cost (Glazer 1966; Green and White 1976; Douglas and Shoemaker 1981).

However, a well-documented weakness of the mail survey is its susceptibility to low response rates, giving rise to problems of non-response error (Yu and Cooper 1983). This study adopted the approach of Dillman (1978), a social scientist, who provides arguably the most comprehensive approach, combining both a theoretical foundation and an operational scheme that can be effectively applied in management research. Known as the total design method (TDM), it asserts that survey response can be explained in terms of the theory of social exchange, which means that the actions of individuals are motivated by the return these actions are expected to bring. Adopting this view implies that survey response is a function of (i) minimising the prospect's costs of responding, (ii) maximising the rewards for doing so, and (iii) establishing trust that those rewards will be delivered. The appeal of the TDM is that it provides the researcher with a comprehensive set of theoretically based and empirically tested guidelines for survey design, questionnaire construction and questionnaire implementation. Refined over the course of 50 studies, the method predicts that response rates can consistently reach 75 per cent (Dillman 1978).

A number of management researchers in the United States have experimented with the method. Walker, Kirchmann and Conant (1987) argued that the method was of limited value to management research because one of its key tenets, namely, an appeal emphasising social usefulness, was, they felt, somewhat less appropriate in a commercial context. Nevertheless, they conducted two surveys using variations of the total design method on commercial populations and achieved response rates of 65.3 per cent and 36.9 per cent. Similarly, a study by Paxson (1992) compared response rates for a TDM and a non-TDM approach to the study of commercial enterprises, with the TDM method yielding a superior response rate of 59 per cent versus 18 per cent for the non-TDM method.

Incorporating the social exchange perspective into the research design requires that the three objectives of maximising reward, minimising cost and establishing trust are met. A series of steps for doing so are outlined by Dillman (1978), each of which was followed in this study (see Table A.1). The cover letter plays an important role in maximising reward through its tone and content. The questionnaire is also an important tool in maximising reward, but has a key role to play in minimising the cost of

Table 7.1 Research design: incorporating social exchange

Research objectives	Instructions	Procedure in this study
Maximise reward	(a) Show positive regard	Respondents told that they were part of a carefully selected sample and that the research could not be completed without their help Also, real signatures were used on all correspondence
	(b) Give verbal appreciation	Verbal appreciation was given on the cover letter and the questionnaire
	(c) Use a consulting approach	A consulting tone was adopted on the cover letter
	(d) Support respondent values	The cover letter explained that the research dealt with an issue of high relevance to the respondent group
	(e) Offer tangible rewards	(See section on establishing trust below)
	(f) Make questionnaire interesting	Every effort was made to ensure that the questionnaire was as interesting as possible
Minimise cost of responding	(a) Make the task appear brief	A small four-page questionnaire in booklet form was used. The cover letter noted that little time was necessary to complete the questionnaire
	(b) Reduce physical and mental effort required	All questions involved selecting from a range of responses, reducing the mental effort required
	(c) Eliminate chances for embarrassment or any implication of subordination	Every effort was made to eliminate chances of embarrassment and implications of subordination
	(d) Eliminate direct monetary cost	Stamped addressed/international business reply return envelopes were provided, eliminating any direct monetary costs
Establishing trust	(a) Provide token of appreciation in advance	A plastic laminated Celtic Art design bookmark was enclosed with each questionnaire
	(b) Identify with a known organisation that has legitimacy	The logo of the source university appeared prominently on the cover letter and the questionnaire

Source: Reprinted from *Industrial Marketing Management*, Vol. 27, No. 6, J. Fahy, 'Improving response rates in cross-cultural mail surveys', 459–467, 1998. Reproduced with permission from Elsevier Science.

responding (see Table 7.1). Trust was established through the inclusion of a token of appreciation with the mailing as well as the prominent identification of the source university on the front cover of the questionnaire.

Questionnaire construction is a critical activity due to the interviewer's limited opportunity to influence the respondent in a mail survey. Dillman (1978) proposes a detailed set of rules for constructing mail questionnaires, summarised in Table 7.2. In terms of questionnaire format used in this study, the most significant variation from the TDM was the inclusion of questions on the front and back pages of the booklet. This was necessary in order to keep the questionnaire to a maximum of four pages in length, conveying a sense that it could be completed quickly. Page sizes were reduced to 90 per cent rather than 79 per cent for ease of legibility and to give an impression of spaciousness. Overall, it is felt that the objective implicit in the TDM, which is that a questionnaire should be 'attractive, well-organised ...and look[s] easy to complete' (Dillman 1978: 121), was achieved. The same questionnaire was used in Ireland, the United Kingdom and the United States. The questionnaire was translated into the Japanese language for distribution in Japan but no other changes to its format and style were necessary.

OPERATIONAL DEFINITION OF RESEARCH CONSTRUCTS

The key research constructs in this study are: (i) the resource pool of the firm in a global environment; (ii) strategic orientation in a global environment; (iii) sustainable competitive advantage in a global environment; and (iv) sustained superior performance in a global environment.

Key resources in a global environment

The resource pool in a global environment comprises five categories of resources, namely, basic country-specific resources (BCSRs), advanced country-specific resources (ACSRs), firm-specific tangible assets (TAs), firm-specific intangible assets (IAs) and firm-specific capabilities (Cs). These resources may reside in both the country of origin of the firm as well as in the host countries in which it operates. The five groups were operationalised in a list of 16 specific resources. Where possible, only resources which are consistently identified in the literature as belonging to one of the five groups were used to ensure content and discriminant validity (Venkatraman and Grant 1986). Therefore, 'access to labour at low cost' and 'government incentives (e.g. subsidies and/or corporate tax reductions)' were selected as the two basic country-specific resources. Three ACSRs were listed, namely, 'access to an educated and/or skilled workforce', 'the innovative demands of buyers' and 'the cost reduction demands of buyers'. For firm-specific resources, 'your plant and equipment' and 'your cash in hand/bank' represented tangible assets, while 'your firm's reputation', 'your registered designs' and 'your process/

Table 7.2 Procedure for questionnaire construction

Content	Instructions	Procedure in this study
Format and printing	The questionnaire is printed as a booklet. No questions are permitted on the front or back pages. Pages are reduced to 79 per cent of their original size. The questionnaire booklet is reproduced on white or off-white paper	A four-page booklet format was used. Questions were included on the front and back covers. Pages were reduced to 90 per cent of their original size and printed on off-white paper
Order of questions	Most important questions are located at the start of the questionnaire. Group questions of similar content together. Ensure a logical flow. Objectionable questions should be positioned after less objectionable ones	This study followed all four ordering principles
The first question	Should be related to the survey topic, easy to answer, neutral, applicable to everyone, interesting to everyone	The first question sought to meet all these criteria
Formulating the pages	Use lower case for questions, upper case for answers. Identify answer categories on left with numbers. Establish a vertical flow. Provide directions for how to answer. Make questions fit each page. Transitions used for a new line of inquiry, at start of new pages and to break up monotony	Lower case used for questions and upper case for most answers. Answer categories were identified on the left with numbers. Clear directions for answering were provided for each question in lower case in parentheses. Vertical flow used and questions made to fit the page. Transitions used to meet the criteria specified
The front cover	Contains a study title, a graphic illustration, any needed directions and the name and address of the study sponsor	Included title, graphic illustration, assurances of confidentiality and gratitude and the opening question. Contained source university logo
The back cover	Consists of an invitation to make additional comments and plenty of white space	The back cover included six classification questions, a statement of gratitude and a return address
Pre-test	Pre-test the questionnaire using three groups, namely, colleagues, potential 'users' and a sample of the population	The questionnaire was pre-tested as instructed on all three interest groups

Source: As for Table 7.1.

product patents' represented intangible assets. Finally, six capabilities were listed, namely, 'your design and/or engineering know-how', 'your ability to work with suppliers', 'expertise of your management people', 'your quality control systems', 'your ability to work with customers on design changes and new products' and 'your ability to mobilise multi-functional teams'. The 16 resources were not grouped in any systematic way but appeared in random order in the questionnaire. The list of resources was not rotated, but presented in the same order in all questionnaires. Respondents were asked to rate each resource in terms of its importance in gaining an advantage over competitors on a four-point Likert scale ranging from very unimportant to very important.

The location of resources was represented using a nominal scale where respondents were asked to select one of three options. The expression 'where your firm is headquartered' was used as a proxy for country of origin due to the occasional difficulty in identifying this because of international mergers and acquisitions. The expression 'in other countries in which we operate' was used to define host countries. Respondents were then asked to select whether resources in the country of origin or host countries were most important in terms of gaining an advantage over competitors or whether each was equally important.

Strategic orientation in a global environment

Alternative approaches for measuring a construct such as business strategy have been proposed in the strategic management literature (see, for example, Snow and Hambrick 1980). This study adopted a self-typing approach, given the limitations imposed by the mail survey technique. The advantages of self-typing are that the top manager's perceptions and opinions largely determine the organisation's strategic orientation; it also enables the generation of large databases for hypothesis testing (Snow and Hambrick 1980). To enable valid self-typing, care must be taken with the operationalisation of the construct. Operationalising strategy as a research construct has been widely discussed (see, for example, Ginsberg 1984; 1988; Ginsberg and Venkatraman 1985; Hambrick 1980; Harrigan 1983; Snow and Hambrick 1980; Venkatraman and Grant 1986). Alternative approaches at the business level include the measurement of parts of the strategy, multivariate measurement of strategy and typologies of strategy (Hambrick 1980). This study adopted the typology approach, which is favoured because of its comprehensiveness and integrative nature (Hambrick 1980). Furthermore, the strategic typology is deemed to be useful as a predictor or moderator variable (Hambrick 1980), which is precisely the role ascribed to strategic orientation in the resource-based view of the firm.

The Bartlett and Ghoshal (1989) typology is the most complete and integrative scheme for describing strategic orientation in a global environment. This typology was operationalised on a nominal scale using written descriptions of the four categories. This approach has been used in previous studies, including tests of the Miles and Snow (1978) typology by Snow and Hrebiniak (1980) and of the Glueck (1976) typology by Hitt, Ireland and Palia (1982) and Hitt, Ireland and Stadter (1982), though its limitations as a measure of complex constructs have been noted by Jacoby (1978) and Venkatraman and Grant (1986). A previous empirical test of the Bartlett and Ghoshal typology by Leong and Tan (1993) also used the self-typing approach, incorporating a nominal scale of single-item measures. This study adopted similar category descriptions to those used by Leong and Tan (1993). The expression 'seeking to build a strong presence in each of the countries in which it operates through a sensitivity and a responsiveness to the needs of local customers' was used to describe a 'multinational' firm. Similarly, 'seeking to build cost advantages through the location of activities in low-cost regions, the rationalisation of manufacturing and the standardisation of products', 'seeking to exploit the firm's innovations and skills in foreign markets' and 'seeking to maintain a balance between the needs to be both efficient across countries as well as responsive to the needs of local customers' were used to describe 'global', 'international' and 'transnational' firms respectively. The expressions were not rotated but presented in the same order in all questionnaires.

Sustainable competitive advantage in a global environment

Competitive advantage is a concept that measures the relative provision of value for customers by different firms. Alternative approaches were considered for the operationalisation of the SCA construct. A possible, two-stage, approach was to ask respondents to define what were the value dimension(s) in the industry and then to rate how their firm compared with competing firms on this/these dimension(s). It was rejected due to potential for inconsistency in both the definitions of value as well as the range of competing firms to be considered. As the research is concerned with the attainment of SCA deriving from resource deployment, the SCA construct was operationalised in conjunction with statements relating to resources. Respondents were asked to consider the relative importance of resources in terms of 'gain[ing] an advantage over your competitors'.

Sustained superior performance in a global environment

Like the strategic orientation construct discussed above, the operationalisation of performance has been the focus of a great deal of attention in the strategic management literature. It has been argued that new strategies and competitive realities mandate a move away from a sole reliance on financial-based measures to other variables such as quality, manufacturing effectiveness, market share, innovation and customer satisfaction (Eccles 1991; Kaplan and Norton 1992). Similarly, Chakravarthy (1986) and Doyle (1994) advocate the measurement of a range of variables that match the minimum expectations of all key stakeholders. Eccles (1991) notes that the central question regarding performance measurement is whether or not the measures are appropriate given a chosen strategy. The essence of the resource-based view of strategy is that resources are deployed to attain sustainable competitive advantage from which economic rents are earned. Therefore, the measurement of profitability is necessary as it is a suitable proxy for the attainment of rents. This study used two measures of profitability, namely, return on total assets (ROTA – used as a proxy for return on investment – ROI) and return on sales (ROS), both of which are appropriate given that they measure past performance (Doyle 1994). In addition to these financial indicators, measures of both sales growth and market share were also obtained, enabling the assessment from primary data of both the financial and operational domains of organisational effectiveness (Venkatraman and Ramanujam 1986), similar to the approaches used by Bourgeois (1980b) and Gupta and Govindarajan (1984). These four measures were strongest in explaining performance variations in a factor analysis conducted by Woo and Willard (1983) of 14 different operationalisations of performance using the PIMS database. Their study concluded that ROI and ROS, in particular, were important measures of performance.

Due to the sensitivity of the data being collected, respondents were provided with ordinal scales for each performance measure and invited to check the most appropriate boxes. For the measure 'annual sales growth over the preceding year', three scale points were presented, namely, 'less than 10 per cent', '10 per cent–40 per cent' and 'greater than 40 per cent'. The market share measure used was 'world market share', which was chosen to overcome the problem of market definition and was deemed appropriate given that the study concerned performance in a global environment. Four scale points were presented, namely, 'less than 1 per cent', '1 per cent–5 per cent', '6 per cent–10 per cent' and 'greater than 10 per cent'. 'Return on total assets (ROTA)' was defined as the ratio of profit before interest and taxes over fixed plus current assets, while 'return on sales (ROS)' was similarly defined as the ratio of profit before interest and taxes over total sales. The 'before interest and taxes' measure of profits was chosen to overcome the problems caused by international variations in interest and tax levels. The same four scale points, namely, 'less than 5 per cent', '5 per cent–10 per cent', '11 per cent–15 per cent' and 'greater than 15 per cent' were used for both the ROTA and ROS measures. Of particular interest from a resource-based perspective is the sustainability of superior performance, which means that the superior performance resists erosion. As any measures of the future sustainability would be speculative, performance measures were obtained for three intervals over the five years preceding the study, namely, '1990', '1992' and '1994'.

SAMPLING

The sampling unit of the population was the top manager within these firms. This individual was variously described as managing director, chief executive officer (CEO) or president. The firm's top manager was deemed to be the key informant, given the likelihood that this individual would have the broadest view of the firm's resource pool in a global environment and given that the top manager's perceptions and opinions largely determine the firm's strategic orientation (Snow and Hambrick 1980). Using one informant who was willing to furnish their perceptions has been seen as adequate in overcoming the variance among managers' perceptions within firms and the lack of external confirmation of these perceptions (Leong and Tan 1993). It is the same procedure as used in a previous empirical test of the resource-based view of the firm by Hall (1992).

The next step was to identify the sampling frame and to try to eliminate the possibility of non-coverage error. Lists of automotive components firms were obtained for each of the four countries. In the case of Ireland, the Irish Trade Board's directory of automotive components firms was used as the sampling frame. This directory is distributed to buyers in the industry through the Trade Board's network of offices worldwide. Each entry contained the firm's name, address, telephone numbers, contact names, ownership, products, age, number of employees and customers. In the case of the United Kingdom, the IMS directory of European automotive suppliers was used. The IMS directory contains over 4,000 entries and is compiled from annual reports, company press releases, questionnaires and telephone interviews. Information provided with each entry was variable but potentially included the firm's name, address, telephone numbers, contact names, product lines, number and location of plants, number of employees, customers and some financial information. The Automotive Parts and Accessories Association in the United States was contacted in connection with the development of the sampling frame for that country. This association recommended the ASIA/MEMA/APPA (Automotive Service Industry Association/Motor & Equipment Manufacturers' Association/Automotive Parts and Accessories Association) annual trade show directory as the most comprehensive listing of US automotive components firms. Entries in the directory included each firm's name, address and telephone numbers, as well as information on products and contact names. Finally, in the case of Japan, the Japan Auto Parts Industries Association (JAPIA) directory of manufacturers was used as the sampling frame. Information provided on each firm included name, address and telephone numbers, age, number of employees, product lines and capital in Japanese yen. A Japanese-language version of the directory was used in the mailing process.

The four directories selected were deemed to be the most comprehensive available for each country. Their scope and level of detail on each entry were variable. The Trade Board directory used in the case of Ireland is comprehensive and detailed. The IMS directory used for the UK is less comprehensive, due to its European-wide scope and levels of detail on each entry were variable. The trade show directory used for the US may not be fully comprehensive due to the absence of some firms from the annual show and the level of detail on each firm was more limited than in the case of Ireland and the UK. The JAPIA directory is detailed and comprehensive but membership of the association is generally limited to first-tier suppliers. In contrast, Ireland has few first-tier suppliers, while the listings for the UK contained a mix of both first- and second-tier suppliers.

The remaining steps involve determining the sample size, selecting the sampling procedure and selecting the sample. Regarding sample size, Ireland was a unique case given its relatively small population of automotive components firms. Therefore it was decided to survey all firms listed in the Irish Trade Board directory. A sample size of 200 firms for each of the other three countries was deemed to be sufficient to meet the study objectives and data analysis requirements of the research. Samples were selected using a simple random sampling procedure in order to minimise the problem of sampling error. This involved using a table of random numbers to identify sampling units.

FIELDWORK

Dillman's (1978) instructions regarding the implementation of mail surveys focuses primarily on the design of the cover letter and the follow-up process (see Table 7.3). Central to the process is the need for an overall sense of personsalisation in the study, which can be achieved not only through the use of names and real signatures but also by postage rates used, timing of mailings/follow-ups and the tone of follow-up letters.

The cover letter for this study was limited to one page, emphasised the usefulness of the study, noted the importance of the target for the successful completion of the study, assured confidentiality and informed the respondent of the enclosure of a bookmark as a token of appreciation

Table 7.3 Implementing mail surveys

Implementation steps	Instructions	Procedure in this study
The cover letter	One page maximum, designed carefully, dated, contains real signature	Cover letter was one page. Followed four-paragraph, TDM design emphasising usefulness, importance of target, confidentiality and gratitude. Dated on day of posting and contained real signature
Prepare the envelope	Use business envelopes with individually typed addresses	This procedure was followed
Add postage	Use first-class mail rates	Regular mail and airmail rates used
Identify the questionnaire	Use a prominently displayed serial numbering system	The serial number was clearly presented in top left-hand corner of the questionnaire and explained in the cover letter
Prepare return envelopes	Use pre-printed business reply envelopes	Stamped addressed envelopes used in source country. International business reply envelopes used elsewhere
Assemble mail-out package	Questionnaire folded in three parts, return envelope enclosed, cover letter folded over both	This procedure was followed in this study
Select mail-out date	Tuesdays where possible	Mail-outs timed to try to ensure targets received materials in mid-week
Follow-up procedures	One week – postcard reminder. Three weeks – letter and replacement questionnaire. Seven weeks – letter and replacement questionnaire	Postcard reminder sent after one week. Letter and replacement questionnaire sent after three weeks. No further mailings. Both postcard reminder and follow-up mailing followed detailed TDM instructions

Source: As for Table 7.1.

for the completion of the questionnaire. The only significant deviation from the TDM was the decision not to offer respondents a copy of the results, as previous research (Jobber, Mirza and Wee 1991) has indicated that it does not significantly increase response rates in commercial studies and may indeed cause some non-response where executives believe that sensitive information might be released to possible competitors.

The international researcher is faced with the choice of conducting the study from a domestic base or collaborating with colleagues in other countries. The former entails the additional risk that response rates will be further depressed when the source country is different from that of the respondent (Jobber and Saunders 1988). In this study a combination of both methods was used. For the two Western countries, the United Kingdom and the United States, the research was conducted from the source country – Ireland. Stamped addressed envelopes are considered to have a positive effect on response rates (Jobber 1986). For convenience this approach was used in Ireland, though an international business reply envelope, as recommended in the TDM, was used for respondents from the United Kingdom and the United States. However, in the case of Japan, questionnaires were distributed from, and returned to, a partner Japanese university using stamped addressed envelopes. Each questionnaire was identified with a serial number located in the top left-hand corner removing anonymity. The final important deviation from the TDM concerned the follow-up procedures that were used (see Table 7.3), which involved two rather than three stages. Due to resource constraints, there were no follow-up mailings in the case of Japan.

DATA PROCESSING

Overall response rates were very satisfactory (see Table 7.4) despite the fact that many of the questions in the study could be considered highly sensitive and likely to lead to low response rates (Jobber and Saunders 1988). In the source country, Ireland, a total of 42 responses was received, giving an overall response rate of 74 per cent, reaching the level claimed by Dillman (1978). Final returns for the United Kingdom were 111, or 51 per cent. Returns from the United States were somewhat lower at 38 per cent, perhaps supporting the view that commercial populations in this country are over-researched (Petry and Quackenbusch 1974; Yu and Cooper 1983), though this figure is still very satisfactory for mail surveys seeking sensitive information and not providing anonymity (Hart 1987). A similar response rate of 38 per cent from Japan was very satisfactory, given possible cultural barriers and also that there was only one mailing in that country.

The overall quality of returns was very high. Particularly satisfying was the low level of incomplete questionnaires, suggesting that the questionnaire had met one of its key design objectives – that of being easy to complete. In addition, item non-response was not a major factor despite the sensitivity of much of the data. The only important exception related

Table 7.4 Response rates

Country	Population/ sample	Returned unopened	Total responses	Refusals	Not applicable*	Incomplete	Total usable responses
Ireland	57	0	42 (74%)	0	4	0	38 (67%)
United Kingdom	200	10	101 (51%)	7	5	0	89 (45%)
United States	200	1	75 (38%)	3	2	0	69 (35%)
Japan	200	0	76 (38%)	1	3	1	71 (36%)
Total							267

* Companies reporting that they were no longer operating in the automotive components industry.

to the question on strategic orientation, which was placed on the front cover of the questionnaire and was unanswered in 15 per cent of returns. This would appear to support Dillman's (1978) view that no questions should appear on the front cover of the questionnaire. In only one case was the serial number identifying the respondent removed.

Tests of non-response bias were conducted for each of the four countries. Data were collected from respondents on the firm's age, product range and size, which were compared with published data on non-responding firms where such information was available. Open questions were asked regarding the firm's age and product range, which were subsequently coded. Five age categories were developed which broadly coincided with some significant events influencing the industry, such as world wars and the oil crisis. Seven product categories were developed along traditionally important industry lines, namely, (i) engine parts, (ii) electrical parts, (iii) drive, transmission and steering parts, (iv) suspension and brake parts, (v) body parts, (vi) accessories and (vii) others. Firm size was measured in terms of numbers of employees using a nominal scale.

In the case of the United Kingdom sample, information was available on the product range and size of non-responding firms. A chi-square test revealed no significant differences between respondents and non-respondents. In the case of the United States, information was only available on the product range variable, which again was not statistically significantly different from that of respondents. Information on all three variables was available for Japanese firms. The chi-square test revealed no significant differences in relation to firm age and product range, though a difference (significant at $p = 0.05$) was observed in relation to size with both small firms (fewer than 100 employees) and large firms (more than 2,000 employees) under-represented in the sample. Similarly in the case of Ireland, no differences were observed with respect to age and product range, though the responding group did contain a higher proportion of firms with more than 100 employees (significant at $p = 0.05$).

A factor analysis was then conducted for two reasons. First, it is clear from the review of the automotive components literature that there is a great deal of interaction between the different resource elements. For example, good relationships in the supply chain are seen to underpin quality systems, while the use of multifunctional teams is posited to enhance relationships with customers. A factor analysis enables a closer examination of the interaction between the different resources. Second, it performs a confirmatory role in assessing whether the a priori classification of the 16 resources into five groups is indeed a valid one.

The results of the factor analysis are shown in Table 7.5. The table reveals that five factors have an eigenvalue of greater than one, suggesting that a five-factor solution is most appropriate. In addition, over 56 per cent of the total variance is attributable to these five factors. A varimax rotation of the factors shows that a number of variables load heavily on

Table 7.5 Confirmatory factor analysis

*Factor extraction initial statistics**

Factor	Eigenvalue	%. of variance	Cum. %
1	3.19445	20.0	20.0
2	1.63442	10.2	30.2
3	1.53566	9.6	39.8
4	1.40297	8.8	48.5
5	1.20941	7.6	56.1
6	0.99351	6.2	62.3
7	0.90654	5.7	68.0
8	0.81484	5.1	73.1
9	0.74596	4.7	77.7
10	0.67873	4.2	82.0
11	0.61827	3.9	85.8
12	0.57531	3.6	89.4
13	0.47926	3.0	92.4
14	0.45553	2.8	95.3
15	0.40162	2.5	97.8
16	0.35353	2.2	100.0

Varimax rotation of factors

	Factor 1	Factor 2	Factor 3	Factor 4	Factor 5
KNOWHOW**	0.64611	0.15353	0.22157	−0.16861	−0.06778
QUALSYS	0.55188	0.03187	−0.03475	0.18161	0.22576
RELCUST	0.51391	0.03803	0.41937	−0.28344	0.29834
MANAGMT	0.46131	−0.06260	0.28915	0.42389	−0.31369
TEAMS	0.58292	0.08504	0.01680	−0.02156	0.12612
SUPPLIER	0.15162	0.19927	0.66617	0.14469	0.13974
REPUTAT	0.02427	0.03777	0.67559	0.21961	−0.01880
DESIGNS	−0.08957	0.75211	0.32913	0.03061	0.09321
PATENTS	0.18392	0.83890	−0.07101	0.06238	−0.05404
CASH	0.11774	0.19923	0.21727	0.58346	0.05488
PLANT	0.69565	−0.11198	−0.06259	0.27919	0.01469
LABCOST	−0.08805	0.03559	−0.16052	0.68236	0.35022
GOVINC	0.08171	−0.03745	0.18824	0.68495	0.07415
LABSKIL	0.41798	0.33831	−0.46252	0.18542	0.07624
COSTBUY	0.13989	−0.21229	0.12057	0.15390	0.80045
INNOVBUY	0.16093	0.26537	0.02518	0.16003	0.66347

*Bartlett test of sphericity = 594.26990, Significance = 0.00000

**Key: CASH (cash in hand/at bank), COSTBUY (the cost reduction demands of buyers), DESIGNS (registered designs), GOVINC (government incentives), INNOVBUY (the innovative demands of buyers), KNOWHOW (design/engineering know-how), LABCOST (access to labour at low cost), LABSKIL (access to an educated/skilled workforce), MANAGMT (expertise of management people), PATENTS (process/product patents), PLANT (plant and equipment), QUALSYS (quality control systems), RELCUST (ability to work with customers), REPUTAT (firm's reputation), SUPPLIER (ability to work with suppliers), TEAMS (ability to mobilise multifunctional teams).

factor 1. However, five of these variables had been classed a priori as firm-specific capabilities (Cs), namely, design/engineering know-how (KNOWHOW), the expertise of management (MANAGMT), quality systems (QUALSYS), an ability to work with customers on design changes and new products (RELCUST) and the ability to mobilise multifunctional teams (TEAMS). Closely related to these variables are plant and equipment (PLANT) and access to an educated/skilled work-force (LABSKIL). Overall, factor 1 would appear to describe variables that are firm-specific. In the main, they relate to firm-specific capabilities and it is interesting that plant and equipment, which is generally classed as a tangible asset, is closely associated with capabilities in the minds of managers. This indicates support for some existing literature that notes the close relationship between tangible assets and capabilities (see, for example, Stalk, Evans and Schulman 1992). Loading heavily on factor 2 are cash in hand/at bank (CASH), government incentives (GOVINC), access to labour at low cost (LABCOST) and to some extent the exper-tise of management (MANAGMT). Leaving aside the last variable, the issue of finance could be said to be the primary issue underlying factor 2. Factor 3 is also a little unclear, involving a mix of firm-specific intangible assets and firm-specific capabilities, including the ability to work with suppliers (SUPPLIER), the ability to work with customers on design changes and new products (RELCUST) and the firm's reputation (REPUTAT). However, it is possible to suggest that the ability to network is a key theme underlying this factor, given that both ends of the supply chain are represented. Clear patterns emerge with respect to factors 4 and 5, which emphasise intellectual property and the influence of OEMs respectively (see Table 7.5).

Finally, as the focus of the research was on sustainable advantage, it was necessary to distinguish consistently good and poor performers. We will use the example of return on total sales (ROS) to demonstrate how top, poor and average performers are classified. Respondents were asked to select one of four performance points, namely, less than 5 per cent, 5 to 10 per cent, 11 to 15 per cent and greater than 15 per cent for each of the three time intervals. Each performance point was given a score of 1 to 4 in ascending order. Therefore, a score of 3 implies that the firm had attained ROS levels of less than 5 per cent for each of the three time intervals. Sixty-eight firms in the sample reported this level of perform-ance. On the other hand, the very top performers were those firms attaining returns of greater than 15 per cent for each of the three intervals (that is, those scoring 12 points). Twenty-two firms in the sample attained this level of performance. All other firms in the sample scored somewhere between 3 and 12 points. In the cases of ROS, ROTA and market share, top and poor performers are selected as follows. 'Top performers' are firms attaining a performance score of greater than or equal to 9, that is, firms whose performance levels have not fallen below

Table 7.6 Quality of performance in the sample

Performance group	ROS Freq.	%	ROTA Freq.	%	Mkt share Freq.	%	Sales Freq.	%
Top performers	47	17.6	83	31.1	59	22.1	17	6.4
Average performers	132	49.4	103	38.6	83	31.1	173	64.8
Poor performers	68	25.5	58	21.7	96	36.0	60	22.5
Missing	20	7.5	23	8.6	29	10.9	17	6.4
		100.0		100.0		100.0		100.0

11 per cent over the five-year period. 'Poor performers' are firms attaining less than 5 per cent returns for each of the three years (that is, firms scoring 3 points). In the case of average sales growth over the preceding year, top performers are in the range of 7 to 9 points, while poor performers scored 3 points. A summary of the three performance groups for the four measures is presented in Table A.6.

Bibliography

Aaker, D. A. (1989) 'Managing assets and skills: The key to a sustainable competitive advantage', *California Management Review* 31, 2: 91–106.

Aaker, D. A. (1998) *Strategic Market Management*, 5th edition, New York: John Wiley & Sons.

Agthe, K. E. (1990) 'Managing the mixed marriage', *Business Horizons* 33, 1: 37–43.

Aharoni, Y. (1966) *The Foreign Direct Investment Decision Process*, Boston, MA: Harvard Graduate School of Business Administration.

Aharoni, Y. (1993a) 'In search for the unique: Can firm-specific advantages be evaluated?', *Journal of Management Studies* 30, 1: 31–49.

Aharoni, Y. (1993b) 'From Adam Smith to Schumpeterian global firms', in A. M. Rugman and A. Verbeke (eds) *Research in Global Strategic Management*, Greenwich, CT: JAI Press Inc., 17–39.

Aldrich, H. (1979) *Organisations and Environments*, Englewood Cliffs, NJ: Prentice-Hall.

Aldrich, H. and Pfeffer, J. (1976) 'Environments of organisations', *Annual Review of Sociology* 2: 79–105.

Aliber, R. Z. (1993) *The Multinational Paradigm*, Cambridge, MA: MIT Press.

Amit, R. and Schoemaker, P. J. (1993) 'Strategic assets and organisational rent', *Strategic Management Journal* 14, 1: 33–46.

Andersen Consulting (1994) *World Manufacturing Competitiveness Study: The Second Lean Enterprise Report*, London: Andersen Consulting & Co.

Andrews, K. R. (1971) *The Concept of Corporate Strategy*, New York: Dow Jones–Irwin.

Ansoff, I. (1965) *Corporate Strategy*, New York: McGraw-Hill.

Arora, A. and Gambardella, A. (1997) 'Domestic markets and international competitiveness: Generic and product-specific competencies in the engineering sector', *Strategic Management Journal* 18: 53–74.

Arpan, J. S., Flowers, E. B. and Ricks, D. A. (1981) 'Foreign direct investment in the United States: The state of knowledge in research', *Journal of International Business Studies* 12, 1: 137–154.

Astley, W. G. and Van de Ven, A. H. (1983) 'Central perspectives and debates in organisation theory', *Administrative Science Quarterly* 28, 2: 245–273.

Baden-Fuller, C. W. and Stopford, J. M. (1991) 'Globalisation frustrated: The case of white goods', *Strategic Management Journal* 12, 7: 493–507.

Baden-Fuller, C. W. (1992) *Rejuvenating the Mature Business*, London: Routledge.

Baghai, M., Coley, S. C. and White, D. (1999) 'Turning capabilities into advantages', *McKinsey Quarterly* 1, 101–109.

Bain, J. S. (1968) *Industrial Organization*, 2nd edition, New York: Wiley.

Balakrishnan, S. and Fox, I. (1993) 'Asset specificity, firm heterogeneity and capital structure', *Strategic Management Journal* 14, 1: 3–16.

Baliga, B. R. and Jaeger, A. M. (1984) 'Multinational corporations: Control systems and delegation issues', *Journal of International Business Studies* 15, 2: 24–40.

Barney, J. B. (1986a) 'Strategic factor markets: Expectations, luck and business strategy', *Management Science* 32, 10: 1231–1241.

Barney, J. B. (1986b) 'Organisational culture: Can it be a source of sustained competitive advantage?', *Academy of Management Review* 11, 3: 656–665.

Barney, J. B. (1986c) 'Types of competition and the theory of strategy: Toward an integrating framework', *Academy of Management Review* 11, 4: 791–800.

Barney, J. B. (1989) 'Asset stocks and sustained competitive advantage: A comment', *Management Science* 35, 12: 1511–1513.

Barney, J. B. (1991) 'Firm resources and sustained competitive advantage', *Journal of Management* 17, 1: 99–120.

Barney, J. B. (1996) 'The resource-based theory of the firm', *Organisation Science* 7, 5: 469.

Barney, J. B. and Ouchi, W. G. (1986) *Organisational Economics*, London: Jossey-Bass Publishers.

Bartlett, C. A. (1983) 'MNCs: Get off the reorganisation merry-go-round', *Harvard Business Review* 61, 2: 138–146.

Bartlett, C. A. (1986) 'Building and managing the transnational: The new organisational challenge', in M. E. Porter (ed.) *Competition in Global Industries*, Boston, MA: Harvard Business School Press, 367–404.

Bartlett, C. A., Doz, Y. L. and Hedlund, G. (1990) 'Introduction: The changing agenda for researchers and practitioners', in C. A. Bartlett, Y. Doz and G. Hedlund (eds) *Managing the Global Firm*, London: Routledge.

Bartlett, C. A. and Ghoshal, S. (1986) 'Tap your subsidiaries for global reach', *Harvard Business Review* 68:6. 171–182.

Bartlett, C. A. and Ghoshal, S. (1987a) 'Managing across borders: New strategic requirements', *Sloan Management Review* 28, 4: 7–17.

Bartlett, C. A. and Ghoshal, S. (1987b) 'Managing across borders: New organisational responses', *Sloan Management Review* 29, 1: 43–53.

Bartlett, C. A. and Ghoshal, S. (1989) *Managing Across Borders: The Transnational Solution*, Cambridge, MA: Harvard Business School Press.

Bartlett, C. A. and Ghoshal, S. (1990) 'Matrix management: Not a structure, a frame of mind', *Harvard Business Review* 68, 4: 138–145.

Bartlett, C. A. and Ghoshal, S. (1991) 'Global strategic management: Impact on the new frontiers of strategy research', *Strategic Management Journal* 12: 5–16.

Bartlett, C. A. and Ghoshal, S. (1992) *Transnational Management: Text, Cases and Readings in Cross–Border Management*, Homewood, IL: Irwin.

Baumol, W. J., Panzer, J. and Willig, R. (1982) *Contestable Markets and the Theory of Industry Structure*, New York: Harcourt, Brace Jovanovich.

Beer, M. and Davis, S. M. (1976) 'Creating a global organisation: Failures along the way', *Columbia Journal of World Business* 72–84.

Bertodo, R. (1991) 'The role of suppliers in implementing a strategic vision', *Long Range Planning* 24, 3: 40–48.

Bettis, R. A. (1991) 'Strategic management and the straitjacket: An editorial essay', *Organisation Science* 2, 3: 315–319.

Bettis, R. A. and Hall, W. K. (1981) 'Strategic portfolio management in the multibusiness firm', *California Management Review* 24, 1: 23–38.

Bharadwaj, S. P., Varadarajan, P. R. and Fahy, J. (1993) 'Sustainable competitive advantage in service industries: A conceptual model and research propositions', *Journal of Marketing* 57, 4: 83–99.

Bhide, A. (1986) 'Hustle as strategy', *Harvard Business Review* 64, 5: 59–65.

Birkinshaw, J. M. and Hood, N. (1998) 'Multinational subsidiary evolution: Capability and charter change in foreign-owned subsidiary companies', *Academy of Management Review* 23, 4: 773–795.

Birkinshaw, J. M. and Hood, N. (2000) 'Characteristics of foreign subsidiaries in industry clusters', *Journal of International Business Studies* 31, 1: 141–154.

Birkinshaw, J. M., Hood, N. and Jonsson, S. (1998) 'Building firm-specific advantages in multinational corporations: The role of subsidiary initiative', *Strategic Management Journal* 19, 3: 221–241.

Birkinshaw, J. M. and Morrison A. J. (1995) 'Configurations of strategy and structure in subsidiaries of multinational corporations', *Journal of International Business Studies* 26, 4: 729–753.

Birkinshaw, J. M., Morrison A. J. and Hulland, J. (1995) 'Structural and competitive determinants of a global integration strategy', *Strategic Management Journal* 16, 8: 637–655.

Black, J. A. and Boal, K. B. (1994) 'Strategic resources: Traits, configurations and paths to sustainable competitive advantage', *Strategic Management Journal* 15: 131–148.

Boddewyn, J. J., Soehl, R. and Picard, J. (1986) 'Standardisation in international marketing: Is Ted Levitt in fact right?', *Business Horizons* 29, 6: 69–75.

Boston Consulting Group (1993) *Context of US–Japan Automotive Issues and Competitiveness of Automobile-Parts Suppliers.*

Bourgeois, L. J. (1980a) 'Strategy and environment: A conceptual integration', *Academy of Management Review* 5, 1: 25–39.

Bourgeois, L. J. (1980b) 'Performance and consensus', *Strategic Management Journal* 1, 3: 227–248.

Bourgeois, L. J. (1984) 'Strategic management and determinism', *Academy of Management Review* 9: 4, 586–596.

Boxall, P. and Steeneveld, M. (1999) 'Human resource strategy and competitive advantage: A longitudinal study of engineering corporations', *Journal of Management Studies* 36, 4: 443–464.

Brouthers, L. E., Brouthers, K. D. and Werner, S. (1999) 'Is Dunning's electic framework descriptive or normative?', *Journal of International Business Studies* 30, 4: 831–844.

Brown, W. R. (1976) 'Islands of conscious power: MNCs in the theory of the firm', *MSU Business Topics* 24: 34–75.

Brush, T. H. and Artz, K. W. (1999) 'Toward a contingent resource-based theory: The impact of information asymmetry on the value of capabilities in veterinary medicine', *Strategic Management Journal* 20, 3: 223–250.

Buckley, P. J. (1983) 'New theories of international business: Some unresolved issues', in M. Casson (ed.) *The Growth of International Business*, London: Allen and Unwin, 34–50.

Buckley, P. J. (1988) 'The limits of explanation: Testing the internalisation theory of the multinational enterprise', *Journal of International Business Studies* 19, 2: 181–193.

Buckley, P. J. (1990) 'Problems and developments in the core theory of international business', *Journal of International Business Studies* 21, 4: 657–665.

Buckley, P. J. (1991) 'The frontiers of international business research', *Management International Review* 31: 7–22.

Buckley, P. J. (1993) 'The role of management in internalisation theory', *Management International Review* 33, 3: 197–207.

Buckley, P. J. and Casson, M. (1976) *The Future of the Multinational Enterprise*, London: Macmillan Press.

Burrell, G. and Morgan, G. (1979) *Sociological Paradigms and Organisational Analysis: Elements of the Sociology of Corporate Life*, London: Heinemann.

Business Ratio Plus (1994) 'Motor component and accessory manufacturers', Hampton: ICC Group Publications.

Buzzell, R. D. and Gale, B. T. (1987) *The PIMS Principles: Linking Strategy to Performance*, New York: The Free Press.

Calvet, A. L. (1981) 'A synthesis of foreign direct investment theories and theories of the multinational firm', *Journal of International Business Studies* 12, 1: 43–60.

Capron, L. and Hulland, J. (1999) 'Redeployment of brands, salesforces, and general marketing management expertise following horizontal acquisitions: A resource-based view', *Journal of Marketing* 63, 2: 41–54.

Carpano, C., Chrisman, J. J. and Roth, R. (1994) 'International strategy and environment: An assessment of the performance relationship', *Journal of International Business Studies* 25, 3: 639–656.

Carr, C. (1993) 'Global, national and resource-based strategies: An examination of strategic choice and performance in the vehicle components industry', *Strategic Management Journal* 14, 7: 551–568.

Carroll, G. R. (1993) 'A sociological view on why firms differ', *Strategic Management Journal* 14, 5: 237–249.

Cartwright, W. R. (1993) 'Multiple linked "diamonds" and the international competitiveness of export-dependent industries: The New Zealand experience', *Management International Review* 33, 2: 55–70.

Casson, M. (1979) *Alternatives to the Multinational Enterprise*, London: Macmillan Press.

Casson, M. (1985) 'Multinational monopolies and international cartels', in P. J. Buckley and M. Casson (eds) *The Economic Theory of the Multinational Enterprise*, London: Macmillan Press, 60–97.

Casson, M. (1987) *The Firm and the Market*, Oxford: Basil Blackwell.

Casson, M. (1991) 'Internalisation theory and beyond', in *Recent Research on the Multinational Enterprise*, Cheltenham: Edward Elgar Publishing, 4–27.

Castanias, R. P. and Helfat, C. E. (1991) 'Managerial resources and rents', *Journal of Management* 17, 1: 155–171.

Caves, R. E. (1971) 'International corporations: The industrial economics of foreign investment', *Economica*, 38: 1–27.

Caves, R. E. (1974) 'Industrial organisation', in J. H. Dunning (ed.) *Economic Analysis and the Multinational Enterprise*, London: Allen & Unwin, 115–146.

Chakravarthy, B. S. (1986) 'Measuring strategic performance', *Strategic Management Journal* 7, 5: 437–458.

Chakravarthy, B. S. and Lorange, P. (1984) 'Managing strategic adaptation: Options in administrative systems design', *Interfaces* 14, 1: 34–46.

Chakravarthy, B. S. and Perlmutter, H. V. (1985) 'Strategic planning for a global business', *Columbia Journal of World Business*, 20, 2: 3–10.

Chamberlin, E. H. (1933) *The Theory of Monopolistic Competition*, Cambridge, MA: Harvard University Press.

Chandler, A. D. (1962) *Strategy and Structure: Chapters in the History of American Industrial Enterprise*, Cambridge, MA: MIT Press.

Chandy, P. R. and Williams, T. G. (1994) 'The impact of journals and authors on international business research: A citational analysis of JIBS articles', *Journal of International Business Studies* 25, 4: 715–728.

Chatterjee, S. and Wernerfelt, B. (1991) 'The link between resources and type of diversification: Theory and evidence', *Strategic Management Journal* 12, 1: 33–48.

Child, J. (1972) 'Organisation structure, environment and performance – the role of strategic choice', *Sociology* 6: 1–22.

Choi, C. J. (1999) 'Global competitiveness and national attractiveness', *International Studies of Management and Organisation* 29, 1: 3–13.

Chrisman, J. J., Hofer, C. W. and Boulton, W. R. (1988) 'Toward a system for classifying business strategies', *Academy of Management Review* 13, 3: 413–428.

Clapham, S. E. and Schwenk, C. R. (1991) 'Self-serving attributions, managerial cognition, and company performance', *Strategic Management Journal* 12, 3: 219–229.

Coase, R. H. (1937) 'The nature of the firm', *Economica*, 4: 386–405.

Coates, N. (1989) 'Strategic issues in corporate planning in United States and United Kingdom-based multinationals', in A. R. Negandhi and A. Savara (eds) *International Strategic Management*, Lexington, MA: Lexington Books, 127–140.

Collis, D. J. (1991) 'A resource-based analysis of global competition: The case of the bearings industry', *Strategic Management Journal* 12: 49–68.

Collis, D. J. (1994) 'How valuable are organisational capabilities?', *Strategic Management Journal* 15: 143–152.

Collis, D. J. and Montgomery, C. A. (1995) 'Competing on resources: Strategy in the 1990s', *Harvard Business Review* 73, 4: 118–128.

Combs, J. G. and Ketchen, D. J. (1999) 'Explaining interfirm cooperation and performance: Toward a reconciliation of predictions from the resource-based view and organizational economics', *Strategic Management Journal* 20, 9: 867–888.

Conner, K. R. (1991) 'A historical comparison of resource-based theory and five schools of thought within industrial organisation economics: Do we have a new theory of the firm?', *Journal of Management* 17, 1: 121–154.

Conner, K. R. and Prahalad. C. K. (1996) 'A resource-based theory of the firm: Knowledge versus opportunism', *Organisation Science* 7, 5: 477–501.

Cool, K. and Schendel, D. (1988) 'Performance differences among strategic group members', *Strategic Management Journal* 9, 3: 207–233.

Coyne, K. P. (1986) 'Sustainable competitive advantage – What it is and what it isn't', *Business Horizons* 29, 1: 54–61.

Craig, C. S. and Douglas, S. P. (2000) 'Configural advantage in global markets', *Journal of International Marketing* 8, 1: 6–26.

Cross, B. and Gordon, J. (1995) 'Partnership strategies for market success', *Business Quarterly* 60, 1: 91–96.

Cubbin, J. (1988) 'Is it better to be a weak firm in a strong industry or a strong firm in a weak industry?', London: London Business School, Centre for Business Strategy, No. 49.

Cummings, S. (1993) 'The first strategists', *Long Range Planning* 26, 3: 133–135.

Cusumano, M. A. (1985) *The Japanese Automobile Industry: Technology and Management at Nissan and Toyota*, Cambridge, MA: Harvard University Press.

Cusumano, M. A. and Takeishi, A. (1991) 'Supplier relations and management: A survey of Japanese, Japanese-transplant and U.S. auto plants', *Strategic Management Journal* 12, 8: 563–588.

Czinkota, M. R., Rivoli, P. and Ronkainen, I. A. (1989) *International Business*, Chicago, IL: The Dryden Press.

Daft, R. L. and Lewin, A. Y. (1990) 'Can organisation studies break out of the normal science straitjacket? An editorial essay', *Organisation Science* 1: 1–9.

Daniels, J. D. (1991) 'Relevance in international business research: A need for more linkages', *Journal of International Business Studies* 22, 2: 177–186.

Daniels, J. D., Pitts, R. A. and Tretter, M. J. (1984) 'Strategy and structure of US multinationals: An exploratory study', *Academy of Management Journal* 27, 2: 292–307.

Daniels, J. D., Pitts, R. A. and Tretter, M. J. (1985) 'Organising for dual strategies of product diversity and international expansion', *Strategic Management Journal* 6, 3: 223–237.

Davidson, W. H. (1980) 'The location of foreign direct investment activity: Country characteristics and experience effects', *Journal of International Business Studies* 12, 3: 9–22.

Davidson, W. H. (1989) 'Ecostructures and international competitiveness', in A. R. Negandhi and A. Savara (eds) *International Strategic Management*, Lexington, MA: Lexington Books, 3–27.

Day, G. S. (1994) 'The capabilities of market-driven organisations', *Journal of Marketing* 58, 4: 37–52.

Day, G. S. and Wensley, R. (1988) 'Assessing advantage: A framework for diagnosing competitive superiority', *Journal of Marketing* 52, 2: 1–20.

de Vasconcellos E Sa, J. A. and Hambrick, D. C. (1989) 'Key success factors: Test of a general theory in the mature industrial-product sector', *Strategic Management Journal* 10, 4: 367–382.

Deligonul, Z. S. and Cavusgil, S. T. (1997) 'Does the comparative advantage theory of competition really replace the neoclassical theory of perfect competition?', *Journal of Marketing* 61, 4: 65–73.

DeNero, H. (1990) 'Creating the "hyphenated" corporation', *McKinsey Quarterly* 4: 153–174.

Dicken, P. (1992) *Global Shift: The Internationalisation of Economic Activity*, 2nd edition, London: Paul Chapman Publishing, 1–5.

Dickson, P. R. (1992) 'Toward a general theory of competitive rationality', *Journal of Marketing* 56, 1: 69–83.

Dickson, P. R. (1996) 'The statics and mechanics of competition: A comment on Hunt and Morgan's comparative advantage theory', *Journal of Marketing* 60, 4: 102–106.

Dierickx, I. and Cool, K. (1989) 'Asset stock accumulation and sustainability of competitive advantage', *Management Science* 35, 12: 1504–1511.

Dill, W. R. (1958) 'Environment as an influence on managerial autonomy', *Administrative Science Quarterly* 2, 2: 409–433.

Dillman, D. A. (1978) *Mail and Telephone Surveys: The Total Design Method*, New York: John Wiley & Sons.

Douglas S. P. and Craig, C. S. (1983) *International Marketing Research*, Englewood Cliffs, NJ: Prentice-Hall.

Douglas S. P. and Craig, C. S. (1989) 'Evolution of global marketing strategy: Scale, scope and synergy', *Columbia Journal of World Business* 47–59.

Douglas, S. P. and Rhee, D. K. (1989) 'Examining generic competitive strategy types in U.S. and European markets', *Journal of International Business Studies* 20, 3: 437–463.

Douglas, S. P. and Shoemaker, R. (1981) 'Item non-response in cross-national attitude surveys', *European Research* 9, 3: 124–132.

Douglas, S. P. and Wind, Y. (1987) 'The myth of globalisation', *Columbia Journal of World Business* 22, 4: 19–29.

Doyle, P. (1994) 'Setting business objectives and measuring performance', *European Management Journal* 12, 2: 123–132.

Doyle, P., Saunders, J. A. and Wong, V. (1992) 'A comparative study of British, U.S. and Japanese marketing strategies', *Journal of International Business Studies* 53, 3: 157–163.

Doz, Y. L. (1976), 'National policies and multinational management', unpublished doctoral dissertation, Graduate School of Business Administration, Harvard University.

Doz, Y. L. (1980) 'Strategic management in multinational companies', *Sloan Management Review* 21, 2: 27–46.

Doz, Y. L. (1986) *Strategic Management in Multinational Companies*, Oxford: Pergamon Press.

Doz, Y. L. (1987) 'International industries: Fragmentation versus globalisation', in B. K. Guile and H. Brooks (eds) *Technology and the Global Industry*, Washington, DC: National Academy Press, 96–118.

Doz, Y. L., Bartlett, C. A. and Prahalad, C. K. (1981) 'Global competitive pressures and host country demands: Managing tensions in MNCs', *California Management Review* 23, 3: 63–74.

Doz, Y. L. and Hamel, G. (1990) 'Control, change and flexibility: The dilemma of transnational collaboration', in C. A. Bartlett, Y. Doz and G. Hedlund (eds) *Managing the Global Firm*, London: Routledge.

Doz, Y. L. and Prahalad, C. K. (1980) 'How MNCs cope with host government demands', *Harvard Business Review* 58, 2: 149–160.

Doz, Y. L. and Prahalad, C. K. (1981) 'Headquarters influence and strategic control in MNCs', *Sloan Management Review* 23, 1: 15–29.

Doz, Y. L. and Prahalad, C. K. (1984) 'Patterns of strategic control within multinational corporations', *Journal of International Business Studies* 15, 2: 55–72.

Doz, Y. L. and Prahalad, C. K. (1991) 'Managing DMNCs: A search for a new paradigm', *Strategic Management Journal* 12: 145–164.

Drucker, P. F. (1946) *The Concept of the Corporation*, New York: John Day.

Drucker, P. F. (1986) 'The changed world economy', *McKinsey Quarterly*, Summer issue, 2–26.

Duncan, R. B. (1972) 'Characteristics of organisational environments and perceived environmental uncertainty', *Administrative Science Quarterly* 17, 3: 313–327.

Dunning, J. H. (1977) 'Trade, location of economic activity and the MNE: A search for an eclectic approach', in B. Ohlin *et al.* (eds) *The International Allocation of Economic Activity*, London: Holmes and Meier, 395–418.

Dunning, J. H. (1981) *International Production and the Multinational Enterprise*, London: Allen and Unwin.

Dunning, J. H. (1988a) *Explaining International Production*, London: Unwin Hyman.

Dunning, J. H. (1988b) 'The eclectic paradigm of international production: A restatement and some possible extensions', *Journal of International Business Studies* 19, 1: 1–31.

Dunning, J. H. (1989) 'The study of international business: A plea for a more interdisciplinary approach', *Journal of International Business Studies* 20, 3: 411–436.

Dunning, J. H. (1993a) *Multinational Enterprises and the Global Economy*, Reading, MA: Addison-Wesley.

Dunning, J. H. (1993b) *The Globalisation of Business*, London: Routledge.

Dunning, J. H. (1993c) 'Internationalising Porter's diamond', *Management International Review* 33, 2: 7–15.

Dunning, J. H. (1997) 'The competitive advantage of countries and MNE activity', in H. Vernon-Wortzel and L. H. Wortzel (eds) *Strategic Management in a Global Economy*, 3rd edition, New York: John Wiley & Sons, 186–204.

Dunning, J. H. (1998) 'Location and the multinational enterprise: A neglected factor?', *Journal of International Business Studies* 29, 1: 45–66.

Dunning, J. H. and Rojec, M. (1993) 'Foreign privatisation in Central and Eastern Europe', The Central and Eastern European Privatisation Network Technical Paper Series, No. 2, London: CEEPN.

Dyer, J. H. (1996) 'Specialised supplier networks as a source of competitive advantage: Evidence from the auto industry', *Strategic Management Journal* 17, 4: 271–291.

Dyer, J. H. and Ouchi, W. G. (1993) 'Japanese-style partnerships: Giving companies a competitive edge', *Sloan Management Review* 35, 1: 51–63.

Dymsza, W. A. (1984a), 'Future international business research and multidisciplinary studies', *Journal of International Business Studies* 15, 1: 9–13.

Dymsza, W. A. (1984b) 'Global strategic planning: A model and recent developments', *Journal of International Business Studies* 15, 2: 169–183.

Easterby-Smith, M., Thorpe, R. and Lowe, A. (1991) *Management Research: An Introduction*, London: Sage Publications.

Eccles, R. G. (1991) 'The performance measurement manifesto', *Harvard Business Review* 69, 1: 131–137.

Eccles, R. G. and Nohria, N. (1992) *Beyond the Hype: Rediscovering the Essence of Management*, Cambridge, MA: Harvard Business School Press, 8.

Economist (1993) 'Multinationals: Back in fashion', 326, 7804: S4.

Economist (1995) 'Multinationals: Who wants to be a giant?', 335, 7920: S12.

Economist (1997a) 'Instant coffee as management theory', 342, 8001: 63.

Economist (1997b) 'Europe's tiger economy', 343, 8017: 23–26.

Economist (1998) 'World trade', 349, 8088: S4.

Edstrom, A. and Galbraith, J. R. (1977) 'Transfer of managers as coordination and control strategy in MNCs', *Administrative Science Quarterly* 22, 2: 248–263.

Egelhoff, W. G. (1982) 'Strategy and structure in multinational corporations: An information processing approach', *Administrative Science Quarterly* 27, 3: 435–458.

Egelhoff, W. G. (1988a) 'Strategy and structure in multinational corporations: A revision of the Stopford and Wells model', *Strategic Management Journal* 9, 1: 1–14.

Egelhoff, W. G. (1988b) *Organising the Multinational Enterprise: An Information Processing Perspective*, Cambridge, MA: Ballinger.

EIU (1996) *The European Automotive Components Industry: A Review of the Leading 100 Major Manufacturers*, London: Economist Intelligence Unit.

Emery, F. E. (1969) *Systems Thinking*, vol. 1, Middlesex: Penguin Books.

Emery, F. E. and Trist, E. L. (1965) 'The causal texture of organisational environments', *Human Relations* 18, 1: 21–32.

Ensign, P. C. (1999) 'The multinational corporation as a coordinated network: Organising and managing differently', *Thunderbird International Business Review* 41, 3: 291–322.

Fahy, J. (1994) 'A resource-based perspective on competition in international business', paper presented at the Academy of International Business, Annual Meeting, Boston.

Fahy, J. (1998a), 'The role of resources in global competition', in G. Hooley, R. Loveridge and D. Wilson (eds) *Internationalisation: Process, Context and Markets*, London: Macmillan Press, 122–135.

Fahy, J. (1998b) 'Improving response rates in cross-cultural mail surveys', *Industrial Marketing Management* 27, 6: 459–467.

Fahy, J., Hooley, G., Cox, T., Beracs, J., Fonfara, K. and Snoj, B. (2000) 'The development and impact of marketing capabilities in Central Europe', *Journal of International Business Studies* 31, 1: 63–81.

Farjoun, M. (1994) 'Beyond industry boundaries: Human expertise, diversification and resource-related industry groups', *Organisation Science* 5, 2: 185–199.

Fayerweather, J. (1969) *International Business Management: A Conceptual Framework*, New York: McGraw-Hill.

Feiger, G. M. (1988) 'Managing the new global enterprise', *McKinsey Quarterly*, Summer issue, 25–38.

Financial Times (1995) 'Supply chain hit hard by cost squeeze', S1.

Fleenor, D. (1993) 'The coming and going of the global corporation', *Columbia Journal of Global Business* 28, 4: 6–16.

Fortune (1989) 'How to go global – and why', 70–76.

Fortune (1994) 'The auto industry meets the new economy', 130, 5: 58–63.

Foss, N. J. (1996a) 'Research in strategy, economics and Michael Porter', *Journal of Management Studies* 33, 1: 1–24.

Foss, N. J. (1996b) 'Knowledge-based approaches to the theory of the firm: Some critical comments', *Organisation Science* 7, 5: 470–476.

Foss, N. J. (1996c) 'More critical comments on knowledge-based theories of the firm', *Organisation Science* 7, 5: 519–523.

Fouraker, L. E. and Stopford, J. M. (1968) 'Organisational structure and multi-national strategy', *Administrative Science Quarterly* 13, 1: 47–64.

Franko, L. G. (1976) *The European Multinationals: A Renewed Challenge to American and British Big Business*, Stamford, CT: Greylock Publishing.

Galbraith, J. R. and Nathanson, D. A. (1978) *Strategy Implementation: The Role of Structure and Process*, St Paul, MN: West Publishing Co.

Geringer, J. M., Li, E. and Tallman, S. (1994) 'Internationalisation, multination-alisation, and the resource-based view of the firm: A comparative study of U.S. and Japanese strategies', paper presented at the Strategic Management Society, Annual Conference, Paris.

Ghemawat, P. (1986) 'Sustainable advantage', *Harvard Business Review* 64, 5: 53–58.

Ghoshal, S. (1987) 'Global strategy: An organising framework', *Strategic Management Journal* 8, 5: 425–440.

Ghoshal, S. and Bartlett, C. A. (1990) 'The multinational corporation as an inter-organisational network', *Academy of Management Review* 15, 4: 603–625.

Ghoshal, S. and Moran, P. (1996) 'Bad for practice: A critique of the transaction cost theory', *Academy of Management Review* 21, 1: 13–47.

Ghoshal, S. and Nohria, N. (1993) 'Horses for courses: Organisational forms for multinational corporations', *Sloan Management Review* 34, 2: 23–35.

Ghoshal, S. and Westney, D. E. (1992) *Organisation Theory and the Multi-national Corporation*, London: The Macmillan Press.

Gilbert, X. and Strebel, P. (1989) 'Developing competitive advantage', in H. Mintzberg and J. B. Quinn (eds) *The Strategy Process: Concepts, Contexts, Cases*, 2nd edition, London: Prentice-Hall, 82–93.

Ginsberg, A. (1984) 'Operationalising organisational strategy: Toward an inte-grative framework', *Academy of Management Review* 9, 3: 548–577.

Ginsberg, A. (1988) 'Measuring and modelling changes in strategy: Theoretical foundations and empirical directions, *Strategic Management Journal* 9: 6, 559–575.

Ginsberg, A. and Venkatraman, N. (1985) 'Contingency perspectives of organi-sational strategy: A critical review of the empirical literature', *Academy of Management Review* 10, 3: 421–434.

Gioia, D. A. and Chittepeddi, K. (1991) 'Sensemaking and sensegiving in stra-tegic change initiation', *Strategic Management Journal* 12, 6: 433–448.

Glazer, W. A. (1966) 'International mail surveys of informants', *Human Organ-isation* 25: 78–86.

Gluck, F. W. (1982) 'Meeting the challenge of global competition', *McKinsey Quarterly*, Autumn issue, 2–13.

Glueck, W. F. (1976) *Business Policy: Strategy Formulation and Management Action*, New York: McGraw-Hill.

Godfrey, P. C. and Hill, C. W. (1995) 'The problem of unobservables in strategic management research', *Strategic Management Journal* 16, 7: 519–533.

Gorecki, P. K. (1976) 'The determinants of entry by domestic and foreign enter-prises in Canadian manufacturing industries: Some comments and empirical evidence', *REStat* 58: 485–488.

Graham, E. M. (1978) 'Transatlantic investment by multinational firms: A rival-istic phenomenon?', *Journal of Post Keynesian Economics* 1: 82–99.

Grant, R. M. (1991a) 'The resource-based theory of competitive advantage: Impli-cations for strategy formulation', *California Management Review* 33, 3: 114–135.

Grant, R. M. (1991b) 'Porter's "competitive advantage of nations": An assessment', *Strategic Management Journal* 12, 7: 535–548.

Grant, R. M. (1995) *Contemporary Strategy Analysis*, 2nd edition, Oxford: Basil Blackwell.

Gray, H. P. (1982) 'Macroeconomic theories of foreign direct investment. An assessment', in A. M. Rugman (ed.) *New Theories of the Multinational Enterprise*, London: Croom Helm, 172–195.

Green, R. T. and White, P. D. (1976) 'Methodological considerations in cross-national consumer research', *Journal of International Business Studies* 7, 2: 81–87.

Grimwade, N. (2000) *International Trade: New Patterns of Trade, Production and Investment*, 2nd edition, London: Routledge.

Guido, G. (1992) 'What US marketers should consider in planning a pan-European approach', *Journal of Consumer Marketing* 9, 2: 29–33.

Gunther McGrath, R., MacMillan, I. C. and Venkataraman, S. (1995) 'Defining and developing competence: A strategic process paradigm', *Strategic Management Journal* 16, 4: 251–275.

Gupta, A. K. and Govindarajan, V. (1984) 'Business unit strategy, managerial characteristics, and business unit effectiveness at strategy implementation', *Academy of Management Journal* 27, 1: 25–41.

Gupta, A. K. and Govindarajan, V. (1991) 'Knowledge flows and the structure of control within multinational corporations', *Academy of Management Review* 16, 4: 768–792.

Gupta, A. K. and Govindarajan, V. (2000) 'Knowledge flows within multinational corporations', *Strategic Management Journal* 21, 4: 473–496.

Hagigi, M., Manzon, G. B. and Mascarenhas, B. (1999) 'Increase asset efficiency to gain multinational market share', *Management International Review* 39, 3: 205–222.

Hall, R. (1989) 'The management of intellectual assets: A new corporate perspective', *Journal of General Management* 15, 1: 53–68.

Hall, R. (1992) 'The strategic analysis of intangible resources', *Strategic Management Journal* 13, 2: 135–144.

Hall, R. (1993) 'A framework linking intangible resources and capabilities to sustainable competitive advantage', *Strategic Management Journal* 14, 8: 607–618.

Hall, W. K. (1980) 'Survival strategies in a hostile environment', *Harvard Business Review* 58, 5: 75–85.

Hambrick, D. C. (1980) 'Operationalising the concept of business-level strategy in research', *Academy of Management Review* 5, 4: 567–575.

Hamel, G. and Prahalad, C. K. (1983) 'Managing strategic responsibility in the MNC', *Strategic Management Journal* 4, 4: 341–351.

Hamel, G. and Prahalad, C. K. (1985) 'Do you really have a global strategy?', *Harvard Business Review* 63, 4: 139–148.

Hamel, G. and Prahalad, C. K. (1988) 'Creating global strategic capability', in N. Hood and J. Vahlne (eds) *Strategies in Global Competition*, London: Croom Helm, 5–39.

Hamel, G. and Prahalad, C. K. (1989) 'Strategic intent', *Harvard Business Review* 67, 3: 63–76.

Hamel, G. and Prahalad, C. K. (1996) 'Competing in the new economy: Managing out of bounds', *Strategic Management Journal* 17, 3: 237–242.

Hamel, G. and Sampler, J. (1998) 'The e-corporation: More than just web-based, it's building a new industrial order', *Fortune* 138, 11: 53–82.

Hamilton, R. D. and Kashlak, R. J. (1999) 'National influences on multinational corporation control system selection', *Management International Review* 39, 2: 167–189.

Hampton, G. M. and Buske, E. (1987) 'The global marketing perspective', in S. T. Cavusgil (ed.) *Advances in International Marketing*, Vol. 2, Greenwich, CT: JAI Press, 259–277.

Handy, C. (1989) *The Age of Unreason*, London: Business Books.

Hannan, M. T. and Freeman, J. (1977) 'The population ecology of organisations', *American Journal of Sociology* 82, 5: 929–964.

Hannan, M. T. and Freeman, J. (1984) 'Structural change and organisational inertia', *American Sociological Review* 49: 149–164.

Hansen, G. S. and Wernerfelt, B. (1989) 'Determinants of firm performance: The relative importance of economic and organisational factors', *Strategic Management Journal* 10, 5: 399–411.

Harrigan, K. R. (1983) 'Research methodologies for contingency approaches to business strategy', *Academy of Management Review* 8, 3: 398–405.

Hart, S. (1987) 'The use of mail surveys in industrial market research', *Journal of Marketing Management* 3: 25–38.

Hax, A. C. and Majluf, N. S. (1988) 'The concept of strategy and the strategy formulation process', *Interfaces* 18: 99–109.

Heckscher, E. F. (1919) 'The effects of foreign trade on the distribution of income', *Economics Tidskrift*. Reprinted in H. S. Ellis and L. A. Metzler (eds) *Readings in the Theory of International Trade*, Homewood, IL: Richard D. Irwin.

Hedlund, G. (1986) 'The hypermodern MNC: A heterarchy', *Human Resource Management* 25, 1: 9–35.

Heenan, D. A. and Perlmutter, H. V. (1979) *Multinational Organisation Development: A Social Architecture Perspective*, Reading, MA: Addison-Wesley.

Helfat, C. E. (1994) 'Firm-specificity in corporate applied R&D', *Organisation Science* 5, 2: 173–184.

Helper, S. R. and Sako, M. (1995) 'Supplier relations in Japan and the United States: Are they converging?', *Sloan Management Review* 36, 3: 77–84.

Henderson, R. and Cockburn, I. (1994) 'Measuring competence? Exploring firm effects in pharmaceutical research', *Strategic Management Journal* 15: 63–84.

Henderson, R. and Mitchell, W. (1997) 'The interactions of organisational and competitive influences on strategy and performance', *Strategic Management Journal* 18: 5–14.

Hennart, J. F. (1982) *A Theory of Multinational Enterprise*, Ann Arbor, MI: University of Michigan Press.

Hennart, J. F. and Larimo, J. (1998) 'The impact of culture on the strategy of multinational enterprises: Does national origin affect ownership decisions?', *Journal of International Business Studies* 29, 3: 515–538.

Henzler, H. and Rall, W. (1986) 'Facing up to the globalisation challenge', *McKinsey Quarterly*, Winter issue, 52–68.

Herbert, T. T. (1999) 'Multinational strategic planning: Matching central expectations to local realities', *Long Range Planning* 32, 1: 81–87.

Hibbert, E. P. (1993) 'Global make-or-buy decisions', *Industrial Marketing Management* 22, 2: 67–77.

180   *Bibliography*

Hibbert, E. P. (1997) *International Business: Strategy and Operations*, London: Macmillan Press.

Hill, C. W. and Deeds, D. L. (1996) 'The importance of industry structure for the determination of firm profitability: A neo-Austrian perspective', *Journal of Management Studies* 33, 4: 429–451.

Hill, C. W. and Jones, G. R. (1998) *Strategic Management: An Integrated Approach*, 4th edition, Boston, MA: Houghton Mifflin.

Hilmer, F. G. and Donaldson, L. (1996) 'The trivialisation of management', *McKinsey Quarterly* 4: 26–37.

Hirsch, P. M. (1975) 'Organisational effectiveness and the institutional environment', *Administrative Science Quarterly* 20, 3: 327–344.

Hitt, M. A. and Ireland, R. D. (1985) 'Corporate distinctive competence, strategy, industry and performance', *Strategic Management Journal* 6, 3: 273–293.

Hitt, M. A. and Palia, K. A. (1982) 'Industrial firm's grand strategy and functional importance: Moderating effects of technology and structure', *Academy of Management Journal* 25, 2: 265–298.

Hitt, M. A. and Stadter, G. (1982) 'Functional importance and company performance: Moderating effects of grand strategy and industry type', *Strategic Management Journal* 3, 4: 315–330.

Hodgetts, R. M. (1993) 'Porter's diamond framework in a Mexican context', *Management International Review* 33, 2: 41–54.

Hofer, C. W. and Schendel, D. E. (1978) *Strategy Formulation: Analytical Concepts*, St Paul, MN: West Publishing Co.

Holmstrom, B. R. and Tirole, J. (1989) 'The theory of the firm', in R. Schmalensee and R. D. Willig (eds) *Handbook of Industrial Organisation*, Amsterdam: North Holland, 61–133.

Hood, N. and Young, S. (1979) *The Economics of the Multinational Enterprise*, London: Longman.

Hooley, G., Shipley, D., Fahy, J., Cox, T., Beracs, J. and Kolos, K. (1996) 'Foreign direct investment in Hungary: Resource acquisition and domestic competitive advantage', *Journal of International Business Studies* 27, 4: 683–709.

Horaguchi, H. and Toyne, B. (1990) 'Setting the record straight: Hymer, internalisation theory and transaction cost economics', *Journal of International Business Studies* 21, 3: 487–495.

Hoskisson, R. E., Hitt, M. A., Wan, W. P. and Yiu, D. (1999) 'Theory and research in strategic management: Swings of a pendulum', *Journal of Management* 25, 3: 417–456.

Hout, T., Porter, M. E. and Rudden, E. (1982) 'How global companies win out', *Harvard Business Review* 60, 5: 98–108.

Hrebiniak, L. (1992) 'Implementing global strategies', *European Management Journal* 10, 4: 392–403.

Hrebiniak, L. and Joyce, W. F. (1985) 'Organisational adaptation: Strategic choice and environmental determinism', *Administrative Science Quarterly* 30, 3: 336–349.

Hu, Y. (1992) 'Global or stateless corporations are national firms with international operations', *California Management Review* 34, 2: 107–126.

Hu, Y. (1995) 'The international transferability of the firm's advantages', *California Management Review* 37, 4: 73–88.

Hunt, S. D. and Morgan, R. M. (1995) 'The comparative advantage theory of competition', *Journal of Marketing* 59, 2: 1–15.

Hunt, S. D. and Morgan, R. M. (1996) 'The resource-advantage theory of competition: Dynamics, path dependencies, and evolutionary dimensions', *Journal of Marketing* 60, 4: 107–114.

Hunt, S. D. and Morgan, R. M. (1997) 'Resource-advantage theory: A snake swallowing its tail or a general theory of competition?', *Journal of Marketing* 61, 4: 74–82.

Huszagh, S. M., Fox, R. J. and Day, E. (1986) 'Global marketing: An empirical investigation', *Columbia Journal of World Business* 20, 4: 31–43.

Hymer, S. H. (1976: 1960) *The International Operations of National Firms: A Study of Direct Foreign Investment*, Cambridge, MA: MIT Press.

Hymer, S. H. (1968) 'The large multinational "corporation": An analysis of some motives for the international integration of business' (translated by N. Vacherot from *Revue Economique*, 19 (6), 949–973) in Mark Casson (ed.) *Multinational Corporations*, England: Edward Elgar Publishing (1990), 1–29.

Hyun, J. (1994) 'Buyer–supplier relations in the European automobile component industry', *Long Range Planning* 27, 2: 66–75.

Irvin, R. A. and Michaels, E. G. (1989) 'Core skills: Doing the right things right', *McKinsey Quarterly*, Summer issue, 4–19.

Itaki, M. (1991) 'A critical assessment of the eclectic theory of the multinational enterprise', *Journal of International Business Studies* 22, 3: 445–460.

Itami, H. (1987) *Mobilising Invisible Assets*, Cambrige, MA: Harvard University Press.

Jacobsen, R. (1988) 'Distinguishing among competing theories of the market share effect', *Journal of Marketing* 52, 4: 68–80.

Jacobsen, R. and Aaker, D. A. (1985) 'Is market share all it's cracked up to be?', *Journal of Marketing* 48, 3: 11–22.

Jacoby, J. (1978) 'Consumer research: A state-of-the-art review', *Journal of Marketing* 42, 2: 87–96.

Jain, S. C. (1989) 'Standardisation of international marketing strategy: Some research hypotheses', *Journal of Marketing* 53, 1: 70–79.

JAMA Forum (1993) 'Global, cross-border alliances shape the future of world auto industry', 11, 4: 3–10.

Jeannet, J. P. and Hennessey H. D. (1998) *Global Marketing Strategies*, 4th edition, Boston, MA: Houghton Mifflin.

Jobber, D. (1986) 'Improving response rates in industrial mail surveys', *Industrial Marketing Management* 15: 183–195.

Jobber, D., Mirza, H. and Wee, K. H. (1991) 'Incentives and response rates in cross-national business surveys: A logit model analysis', *Journal of International Business Studies* 22, 4: 711–721.

Jobber, D. and Saunders, J. (1988) 'An empirical investigation into cross-national mail survey response rates', *Journal of International Business Studies* 19, 3: 483–489.

Johanson, J. and Vahlne, J. (1977) 'The internationalisation process of the firm – a model of knowledge development and increasing foreign market commitments', *Journal of International Business Studies* 8, 1: 23–32.

Johanson, J. and Wiedersheim-Paul, F. (1975) 'The internationalisation of the firm: Four Swedish cases', *Journal of Management Studies* 12, 3: 305–322.

Johansson, J. K. and Yip, G. S. (1994) 'Exploiting globalisation potential: U.S. and Japanese Strategies', *Strategic Management Journal* 15, 8: 579–601.

Johnson, H. G. (1970) 'Multinational corporations and international oligopoly: The non-American challenge', in C. P. Kindleberger (ed.) *The International Corporation*, Cambridge, MA: MIT Press, 35–54.

Johnson, J. H. (1995) 'An empirical analysis of the integration–responsiveness framework: U.S. construction equipment industry firms in global competition', *Journal of International Business Studies* 26, 3: 621–635.

Kale, S. H. and Sudharshan, D. (1987) 'A strategic approach to international segmentation', *International Marketing Review* 4, 2: 60–70.

Kamoche, K. (1996) 'Strategic human resource management within a resource-capability view of the firm', *Journal of Management Studies* 33, 2: 213–233.

Kaplan, R. S. and Norton, D. P. (1992) 'The balanced scorecard: Measures that drive performance', *Harvard Business Review* 70, 1: 71–79.

Karakaya, F. and Stahl, M. J. (1989) 'Barriers to entry and market entry decisions in consumer and industrial goods markets', *Journal of Marketing* 53, 2: 80–91.

Kashani, K. (1989) 'Beware the pitfalls of global marketing', *Harvard Business Review* 67, 5: 91–98.

Kay, J. (1993) 'The structure of strategy', *Business Strategy Review* 4, 2: 17–37.

Kay, J. (1994), 'Corporate strategy and corporate accountability', in N. Dimsdale and M. Prevezer (eds) *Capital Markets and Corporate Governance*, Oxford: Clarendon Press, 50–65.

Kay, N. M. (1983) 'Multinational enterprise: A review article', *Scottish Journal of Political Economy* 30: 304–312.

Key Note (1996) *Autoparts: 1996 Market Report*, Middlesex: Key Note Ltd.

Kim, W. C. and Mauborgne, R. A. (1988) 'Becoming an effective global competitor', *Journal of Business Strategy* 9, 1: 33–37.

Kimura, Y. (1989) 'Firm-specific strategic advantages and foreign direct investment behaviour of firms: The case of Japanese semiconductor firms', *Journal of International Business Studies* 19, 2: 296–314.

Kindleberger, C. P. (1969) *American Business Abroad: Six Lectures on Direct Investment*, New Haven and London: Yale University Press.

Kindleberger, C. P. (1984) *Multinational Excursions*, Cambridge, MA: MIT Press, 180–188.

Kircher, D. P. (1964) 'Now the transnational enterprise', *Harvard Business Review* 42, 2: 6–10, 172–176.

Klein, J. A., Edge, G. M. and Kass, T. (1991) 'Skill-based competition', *Journal of General Management* 16, 4: 1–15.

Knickerbocker, F. T. (1973) *Oligopolistic Reaction and Multinational Enterprise*, Boston, MA: Harvard University Press.

Kobrin, S. J. (1991) 'An empirical analysis of the determinants of global integration', *Strategic Management Journal* 12: 17–31.

Koepfler, E. R. (1989) 'Strategic options for global market players', *Journal of Business Strategy* 10, 4: 46–50.

Kogut, B. (1983) 'Foreign direct investment as a sequential process', in C. P. Kindleberger and D. B. Audretsch (eds) *The Multinational Corporation in the 1980s*, Cambridge, MA: MIT Press, 38–56.

Kogut, B. (1984) 'Normative observations on the international value-added chain and strategic groups', *Journal of International Business Studies* 15, 2: 151–167.

Kogut, B. (1985a) 'Designing global strategies: Profiting from operational flexibility', *Sloan Management Review* 27, 1: 27–38.

Kogut, B. (1985b) 'Designing global strategies: Comparative and competitive value-added chains', *Sloan Management Review* 26, 4: 15–28.

Kogut, B. (1989) 'A note on global strategies', *Strategic Management Journal* 10, 4: 383–389.

Kogut, B. (1991) 'Country capabilities and the permeability of borders', *Strategic Management Journal* 12: 33–47.

Kogut, B. and Zander, U. (1992) 'Knowledge of the firm, combinative capabilities, and the replication of technology', *Organisation Science* 3, 2: 383–397.

Kogut, B. and Zander, U. (1993) 'Knowledge of the firm and the evolutionary theory of the multinational corporation', *Journal of International Business Studies* 24, 4: 625–645.

Kogut, B. and Zander, U. (1995) 'Market failure and the multinational enterprise: A reply', *Journal of International Business Studies* 26, 2: 417–426.

Kostova, T. (1999) 'Transnational transfer of strategic organizational practices: A contextual perspective', *Academy of Management Review* 24, 2: 308–324.

Kotler, P. (1988) *Marketing Management: Analysis, Planning, Implementation and Control*, 6th edition, Englewood Cliffs, NJ: Prentice-Hall.

Kotler, P. and Singh, R. (1981) 'Marketing warfare in the 1980s', *McKinsey Quarterly*, Winter issue, 62–81.

Lado, A. A., Boyd, N. G. and Wright, P. (1992) 'A competency-based model of sustainable competitive advantage: Toward a conceptual integration', *Journal of Management* 18, 1: 77–91.

Lado, A. A. and Wilson, M. C. (1994) 'Human resource systems and sustained competitive advantage: A competency-based perspective', *Academy of Management Review* 19, 4: 699–727.

Lall, S. (1980) 'Monopolistic advantages and foreign involvement by U.S. manufacturing industry', *Oxford Economic Papers*, 32: 102–122.

Lawless, M. W. and Finch, L. K. (1989) 'Choice and determinism: A test of Hrebiniak and Joyce's framework on strategy–environment fit', *Strategic Management Journal* 10, 4: 351–365.

Lawrence, P. and Lorsch, J. (1967) *Organisation and Environment*, Boston, MA: Division of Research, Harvard Business School.

Learned, E. P., Christensen, R. C., Andrews, K. R. and Guth, W. D. (1969) *Business Policy*, Homewood, IL: Irwin.

Lemak, D. J. and Bracker, J. S. (1988) 'A strategic contingency model of multinational corporate structure', *Strategic Management Journal* 9, 5: 521–526.

Lenz, R. T. and Engledow, J. L. (1986) 'Environmental analysis: The applicability of current theory', *Strategic Management Journal* 7, 4: 329–346.

Leong, S. M. and Tan, C. T. (1993), 'Managing across borders: An empirical test of the Bartlett and Ghoshal [1989] organisational typology', *Journal of International Business Studies* 24, 3: 449–464.

Lepak, D. P. and Snell, S. A. (1999) 'The human resource architecture: Toward a theory and development', *The Academy of Management Review* 24, 1: 31–48.

Levinthal, D. and Myatt, J. (1994) 'Co-evolution of capabilities and industry: The evolution of mutual fund processing', *Strategic Management Journal* 15: 45–62.

Levitt, T. (1983) 'The globalisation of markets', *Harvard Business Review* 61, 3: 92–102.

Lewis, P. and Thomas, H. (1990) 'The linkage between strategy, strategic groups, and performance in the UK retail grocery industry', *Strategic Management Journal* 11, 5: 385–397.

Lewis, W. W. and Harris, M. (1992) 'Why globalisation must prevail', *McKinsey Quarterly* 2: 114–131.

Lewis, W. W., Gersbach, H., Jansen, T. and Sakate, K. (1993) 'The secret to competitiveness – competition', *McKinsey Quarterly* 4: 29–43.

Lieberman, M. B. and Montgomery, D. B. (1998) 'First-mover (dis)advantages: Retrospective and link with the resource-based view', *Strategic Management Journal* 19, 12: 1111–1125.

Lipparini, A. and Fratocchi, L. (1999) 'The capabilities of the transnational firm: Accessing knowledge and leveraging inter-firm relationships', *European Management Journal* 17, 6: 655–667.

Lippman, S. A. and Rumelt, R. P. (1982) 'Uncertain imitability: An analysis of interfirm differences in efficiency under competition', *Bell Journal of Economics* 13, 1: 418–438.

Lodge, G. C. and Vogel, E. F. (1986) *Ideology and National Competitiveness*, Boston, MA: Harvard Business School Press.

Lorange, P. (1976) 'A framework for strategic planning in multinational corporations', *Long Range Planning* 9, 3: 30–36.

Lorange, P. (1989) 'Challenges to strategic planning processes in multinational corporations', in A. R. Negandhi and A. Savara (eds) *International Strategic Management*, Lexington, MA: Lexington Books, 107–125.

Lorenz, C. (1989) 'Managing in a global environment: The birth of a "transnational"', *McKinsey Quarterly*, Autumn issue, 72–93.

Lorenzoni, G. and Lipparini, A. (1999) 'The leveraging of interfirm relationships as a distinctive organizational capability: A longitudinal study', *Strategic Management Journal* 20, 4: 317–338.

Lowe, J. H. (1995) 'Knowledge, market failure and the multinational enterprise', *Journal of International Business Studies* 26, 2: 399–407.

Luo, Y. (1999) 'International strategy and subsidiary performance in China', *Thunderbird International Business Review* 41, 2: 153–178.

Lyles, M. A. (1990) 'A research agenda for strategic management in the 1990s', *Journal of Management Studies* 27, 4: 363–375.

McClain, D. (1983) 'Foreign direct investment in the United States: Old currents, "new waves" and the theory of direct investment', in C. P. Kindleberger and D. B. Audretsch (eds) *The Multinational Corporation in the 1980s*, Cambridge, MA: MIT Press, 278–333.

McFetridge, D. G. (1995) 'Market failure and the multinational enterprise: A comment', *Journal of International Business Studies* 26, 2: 409–415.

McGahan, A. M. and Porter, M. E. (1997) 'How much does industry matter, really?', *Strategic Management Journal* 18: 15–30.

McGee, J. and Thomas, H. (1986) 'Strategic groups: Theory, research and taxonomy', *Strategic Management Journal* 7, 2: 141–160.

McManus, J. (1972) 'The theory of the international firm', in G. Paquet (ed.) *The Multinational Firm and the Nation State*, Toronto: Collier-Macmillan.

Magee, S. P. (1977) 'Multinational corporations, the industry technology cycle and development', *Journal of World Trade Law*, 11: 297–321.

Mahini, A. (1990) 'A new look at world trade', *McKinsey Quarterly*, Spring issue, 42–53.

Mahoney, J. T. and Pandian, J. R. (1992) 'The resource-based view within the conversation of strategic management', *Strategic Management Journal* 13, 5: 363–380.

Maijoor, S. and Van Witteloostuijn, A. (1996) 'An empirical test of the resource-based theory: Strategic regulation in the Dutch audit industry', *Strategic Management Journal* 17, 7: 549–569.

Makadok, R. and Walker, G. (2000) 'Identifying a distinctive competence: Forecasting ability in the money fund industry', *Strategic Management Journal* 21, 8: 853–864.

Malnight, T. (1995) 'Globalisation of an ethnocentric firm: An evolutionary perspective', *Strategic Management Journal* 16, 2: 119–141.

Malnight, T. (1996) 'The transition from decentralized to network-based MNC structures: An evolutionary perspective', *Journal of International Business Studies* 27, 1: 43–66.

Marcus, A. and Geffen, D. (1998) 'The dialectics of competency acquisition: Pollution prevention in electric generation', *Strategic Management Journal* 19, 12: 1145–1168.

Markides, C. C. and Williamson, P. J. (1994) 'Related diversification, core competences and corporate performance', *Strategic Management Journal* 15: 149–165.

Martinez, J. I. and Jarillo, J. C. (1991) 'Coordination demands of international strategies', *Journal of International Business Studies* 22, 3: 429–512.

Masayoshi, I. (1993) 'Hard-hit parts makers turn to car manufacturing', *Journal of Japanese Trade & Industry* 12, 4: 16–18.

Mascarenhas, B. (1999) 'The strategies of small and large international specialists', *Journal of World Business* 34, 3: 252–266.

Mascarenhas, B., Baveja, A. and Jamil, M. (1998) 'Dynamics of core competencies in leading multinational companies', *California Management Review* 40, 4: 117–132.

Mason, E. S. (1939) 'Price and production policies of large scale enterprises', *American Economic Review* 29: 61–74.

Miles, R. E. and Snow, C. C. (1978) *Organisation Strategy, Structure and Process*, New York: McGraw-Hill.

Miller, D. and Shamsie, J. (1996) 'The resource-based view of the firm in two environments: The Hollywood film studios from 1936–1965', *Academy of Management Journal* 39, 3: 519–543.

Moingeon, B., Ramanantsoa, B., Metais, E. and Orton, J. D. (1998) 'Another look at strategy-structure relationships: The resource-based view, *European Management Journal* 16, 3: 297–305.

Morgan, G. (1986) *Images of Organisation*, London: Sage.

Morgan, G. and Smircich, L. (1980) 'The case for qualitative research', *Academy of Management Review* 5, 4: 491–500.

Morris, J. (1991) 'Japanese car transplants: Implications for the European motor industry', *European Management Journal* 9, 3: 321–328.

Morrison, A. J. and Roth, K. (1989) 'International business-level strategy: The development of a holistic model', in A. R. Negandhi and A. Savara (eds) *International Strategic Management*, Lexington, MA: Lexington Books, 29–51.

Morrison, A. J. and Roth, K. (1992) 'A taxonomy of business level strategies in global industries', *Strategic Management Journal* 13, 6: 399–418.

Morrison, A. J. and Roth, K. (1993) 'Relating Porter's configuration/coordination framework to competitive strategy and structural mechanisms: Analysis and implications', *Journal of Management* 19, 4: 797–818.

Morrison, A. J., Ricks, D. A. and Roth, K. (1991) 'Globalisation versus regionalisation: Which way for the multinational?', *Organisational Dynamics* 19, 3: 17–29.

Moss Kanter, R. and Dretler, D. (1998) 'Global strategy and its impact on local operations: Lessons from Gillette Singapore', *Academy of Management Executive* 12, 4: 60–68.

Muralidharan, R. and Hamilton, R. D. (1999) 'Aligning multinational control systems', *Long Range Planning* 32, 3: 352–361.

Murtha, T. P. and Lenway, S. A. (1994) 'Country capabilities and the strategic state: How national political institutions affect multinational corporations' strategies', *Strategic Management Journal* 15: 113–129.

Naisbitt, J. (1994) *Global Paradox*, London: Nicholas Brealey Publishing.

Naisbitt, J. (2000) 'Multinational networks', *Executive Excellence* 17, 4: 5–6.

Naisbitt, J. and Aburdene, P. (1990) *Megatrends 2000*, London: Sidgwick and Jackson.

Nasif, E. G., Al-Daeaj, H., Ebrahimi, B. and Thibodeaux, M. S. (1991) 'Methodological problems in cross-cultural research: An updated review', *Management International Review* 31, 1: 79–91.

Naylor, T. H. (1985) 'The international strategy matrix', *Columbia Journal of World Business* 20, 2: 11–19.

Nayyar, P. R. (1990) 'Information asymmetries: A source of competitive advantage for diversified service firms', *Strategic Management Journal* 11, 7: 513–519.

Negandhi, A. R. and Savara, A. (1989) *International Strategic Management*, Lexington, MA: Lexington Books.

Nehrt, L. C., Truitt, J. F. and Wright, R. W. (1970) *International Business Research: Past, Present and Future*, Bloomington, IN: Indiana University Bureau of Business Research.

Nelson, R. R. (1991) 'Why do firms differ, and how does it matter?', *Strategic Management Journal* 12: 61–74.

Nelson, R. R. and Winter, S. G. (1982) *An Evolutionary Theory of Economic Change*, Cambridge, MA: Belknap Press.

Nikkei Weekly (1994) 'Auto-parts maker faces profit squeeze' (21 February), 16.

Nikkei Weekly (1995) 'More closures forseen in bloated auto industry' (27 May), 8.

Nikkei Weekly (1996) 'Production moves to U.S. lift auto-parts firms to record profits' (5 February), 9.

Nikko Research Center (1992) *Analysis of Japanese Industries for Investors*, Tokyo: Nikko Research Center.

Nobel, R. and Birkinshaw, J. (1998) 'Innovation in multinational corporations: Control and communication patterns in international R&D operations', *Strategic Management Journal* 19, 5: 479–496.

Nohria, N. and Ghoshal, S. (1997) *The Differentiated Network: Organising Multinational Corporations for Value Creation*, San Francisco, CA: Jossey-Bass Publishers.

O'Grady, S. and Lane, H. W. (1996) 'The psychic distance paradox', *Journal of International Business Studies* 27, 2: 309–333.

Ohlin, B. (1933) *Inter-regional and International Trade*, Cambridge, MA: Harvard University Press.

Ohmae, K. (1985) *Triad Power: The Coming Shape of Global Competition*, New York: The Free Press.

Ohmae, K. (1989a) 'Managing in a borderless world', *Harvard Business Review* 67, 3: 152–161.

Ohmae, K. (1989b) 'Planting for a global harvest', *Harvard Business Review* 67, 4: 136–145.

Oliver, C. (1997) 'Sustainable competitive advantage: Combining institutional and resource-based views', *Strategic Management Journal* 18, 9: 697–713.

Oliver, N., Delbridge, R. and Lowe, J. (1996) 'Lean production practices: International comparisons in the auto components industry', *British Journal of Management* 7: S29–S44.

Oliver, N, Delbridge, R., Jones, D. and Lowe, J. (1994) 'World class manufacturing: Further evidence in the lean production debate', *British Journal of Management* 5: S53–S63.

Oliver, R. (2000) 'New rules for global markets', *Journal of Business Strategy* 21, 3: 7–9.

Padmanabhan, P. and Cho, K. R. (1999) 'Decision specific experience in foreign ownership and establishment strategies: Evidence from Japanese firms', *Journal of International Business Studies* 30, 1: 25–44.

Palich, L. E. and Gomez-Mejia, L. R. (1999) 'A theory of global strategy and firm efficiencies: Considering the effects of cultural diversity', *Journal of Management* 25, 4: 587–606.

Particelli, M. C. (1990) 'A global arena', *Journal of Consumer Marketing* 7, 4: 43–52.

Pascale, R. T. and Athos, A. G. (1982) *The Art of Japanese Management*, London: Allen Lane.

Paxson, M. C. (1992) 'Follow-up mail surveys', *Industrial Marketing Management* 21, 3: 195–201.

Penrose, E. (1959) *The Theory of the Growth of the Firm*, Oxford: Blackwell.

Perlmutter, H. V. (1969) 'The tortuous evolution of the multinational enterprise', *Columbia Journal of World Business* 14: 9–18.

Perrow, C. (1967) 'A framework for the comparative analysis of organisations', *American Sociological Review* 32: 194–208.

Peteraf, M. A. (1993) 'The cornerstones of competitive advantage: A resource-based view', *Strategic Management Journal* 14, 3: 179–191.

Peters, T. J. (1984) 'Strategy follows structure: Developing distinctive skills', *California Management Review* 26, 3: 111–125.

Peters, T. J. (1990) 'Prometheus barely unbound', *Academy of Management Executive* 4, 4: 70–84.

Peterson, R. B. (1993) 'Future directions in international comparative management research', in D. Wong-Rieger and F. Rieger (eds) *International Management Research*, New York: Walter de Gruyter, 13–24.

Petry, G. H. and Quackenbush, S. F. (1974) 'The conservation of the questionnaire as a research resource', *Business Horizons* 17: 43–50.

Pfeffer, J. (1994) 'Competitive advantage through people', *California Management Review* 36, 2: 9–28.

Pitts, R. A. and Lei, D. (1996) *Strategic Management: Building and Sustaining Competitive Advantage*, St Paul, MN: West Publishing Co.

Polanyi, M. (1967) *The Tacit Dimension*, Garden City, NY: Anchor.

Porter, M. E. (1980) Competitive Strategy: Techniques for Analysing Companies and Industries, New York: The Free Press.

Porter, M. E. (1985) *Competitive Advantage*, New York: The Free Press.

Porter, M. E. (1986a) 'Competition in global industries: A conceptual framework', in M. E. Porter (ed.) *Competition in Global Industries,* Boston, MA: Harvard Business School Press, 15–60.

Porter, M. E. (1986b) 'Changing patterns of international competition', *California Management Review* 28, 2: 9–40.

Porter, M. E. (1990) *The Competitive Advantage of Nations*, London: Macmillan Press.

Porter, M. E. (1991) 'Towards a dynamic theory of strategy', *Strategic Management Journal* 12: 95–117.

Porter, M. E. (1996) 'What is strategy?' *Harvard Business Review* 74, 6: 61–78.

Powell, T. C. (1992) 'Organisational alignment as competitive advantage', *Strategic Management Journal* 13, 2: 119–134.

Powell, T. C. (1996) 'How much does industry matter? An alternative empirical test', *Strategic Management Journal* 17, 4: 323–334.

Prahalad, C. K. (1975) 'The strategic process in a multinational corporation', unpublished doctoral dissertation, Graduate School of Business Administration, Harvard University.

Prahalad, C. K. (1976) 'Strategic choices in diversified MNCs', *Harvard Business Review* 54, 4: 67–78.

Prahalad, C. K. and Bettis, R. A. (1986) 'The dominant logic: A new linkage between diversity and performance', *Strategic Management Journal* 7, 6: 485–501.

Prahalad, C. K. and Doz, Y. L. (1987) *The Multinational Misson: Balancing Local Demands and Global Vision*, New York: The Free Press.

Prahalad, C. K. and Hamel, G. (1990) 'The core competence of the corporation', *Harvard Business Review* 68, 3: 79–91.

Prahalad, C. K. and Hamel, G. (1994) 'Strategy as a field of study: Why search for a new paradigm?', *Strategic Management Journal* 15: 5–16.

Prahalad, C. K. and Lieberthal, K. (1998) 'The end of corporate imperialism', *Harvard Business Review* 76, 4: 68–79.

Prescott, J. E. and Smith, D. C. (1987) 'A project-based approach to competitive analysis', *Strategic Management Journal* 8, 5: 411–423.

Quelch, J. A. and Klein, L. R. (1996) 'The internet and international marketing', *Sloan Management Review* 37, 3: 60–75.

Rabstejnek, G. (1989) 'Let's get back to the basics of global strategy', *Journal of Business Strategy* 10, 5: 32–35.

Rangan, S. (1998) 'Do multinationals operate flexibly?', *Journal of International Business Studies* 29, 2: 217–237.

Rau, P. A. and Preble, J. F. (1987) 'Standardisation of marketing strategy by multinationals', *International Marketing Review* 4, 3: 18–28.

Reed, R. and DeFillippi, R. J. (1990) 'Causal ambiguity, barriers to imitation, and sustainable competitive advantage', *Academy of Management Review* 15, 1: 88–102.

Reich, R. B. (1990) 'Who is us?', *Harvard Business Review* 68, 1: 53–64.

Reich, R. B. (1991) *The Work of Nations*, New York: Vintage Books.

Rennie, M. W. (1993) 'Born global', *McKinsey Quarterly* 4: 45–52.

Ricardo, D. (1817) *On the Principles of Political Economy and Taxation*, P. Sraffa (ed.) Cambridge: Cambridge University Press, 1951.

Richard, O. C. (2000) 'Racial diversity, business strategy and firm performance: A resource-based view', *Academy of Management Journal* 43, 2: 164–177.

Richardson, J. (1993) 'Parallel sourcing and supplier performance in the Japanese automobile industry', *Strategic Management Journal* 14, 5: 339–350.

Ricks, D. A. (1985) 'International business research: Past, present and future', *Journal of International Business Studies* 16, 2: 1–4.

Riesenbeck, H. and Freeling, A. (1991) 'How global are global brands?', *McKinsey Quarterly* 4: 3–18.

Rindova, V. P. and Fombrun, C. J. (1999) 'Constructing competitive advantage: The role of firm–constituent interactions', *Strategic Management Journal* 20, 8: 691–710.

Robins, J. and Wiersema, M. F. (1995) 'A resource-based approach to the multi-business firm: Empirical analysis of portfolio interrelationships and corporate financial performance', *Strategic Management Journal* 16, 4: 277–299.

Robinson, J. (1933) *The Economics of Imperfect Competition*, London: Macmillan Press.

Robinson, R. D. (1981) 'Background concepts and philosophy of international business from World War II to the present', *Journal of International Business Studies* 12, 1: 13–21.

Robinson, R. D. (1986) 'Some new competitive factors in international marketing', in S. T. Cavusgil (ed.) *Advances in International Marketing*, vol. 1, Greenwich, CT: JAI Press, 1–20.

Robock, S. H. and Simmonds, K. (1983) *International Business and Multinational Enterprises*, 3rd edition, Homewood, IL: Irwin Publishers.

Rommel, G., Kempis, R. and Kaas, H. (1994) 'Does quality pay?', *McKinsey Quarterly* 1: 51–63.

Root, F. R. and Visudtibhan, K. (1992) 'The current state of research on international strategic management', in F. Root and K. Visudtibhan (eds) *International Strategic Management: Challenges and Opportunities*, London: Taylor & Francis, 249–255.

Rosenzweig, P. M. and Singh, J. V. (1991) 'Organisational environments and the multinational enterprise', *Academy of Management Review* 16, 2: 340–361.

Roth, K. (1992) 'International configuration and coordination archetypes for medium-sized firms in global industries', *Journal of International Business Studies* 23, 3: 533–549.

Roth, K. (1995) 'Managing international interdependence: CEO characteristics in a resource-based framework', *Academy of Management Journal* 38, 1: 200–231.

Roth, K. and Morrison, A. J. (1990) 'An empirical analysis of the integration–responsiveness framework in global industries', *Journal of International Business Studies* 21, 4: 541–564.

Roth, K. and Morrison, A. J. (1992) 'Business-level competitive strategy: A contingency link to internationalisation', *Journal of Management* 18, 3: 473–487.

Roth, K., Schweiger, D. M. and Morrison, A. J. (1991) 'Global strategy implementation at the business unit level: Operational capabilities and administrative mechanisms', *Journal of International Business Studies* 22, 3: 369–402.

Rouse, M. J. and Daellenbach, U. S. (1999) 'Rethinking research methods for the resource-based perspective: Isolating sources of sustainable competitive advantage', *Strategic Management Journal* 20, 5: 487–494.

Rugman, A. M. (1981) *Inside the Multinationals*, London: Croom Helm.

Rugman, A. M. (1986) 'New theories of the multinational enterprise: An assessment of internalisation theory', *Bulletin of Economic Research* 38: 101–118.

Rugman, A. M. (1987) 'The firm-specific advantages of Canadian multinationals', *Journal of International Economic Studies* 2: 1–14.

Rugman, A. M. and D'Cruz, J. R. (1993) 'The "double diamond" model of international competitiveness: The Canadian experience', *Management International Review* 33, 2: 17–39.

Rugman, A. M. and Hodgetts, R. M. (1995) *International Business: A Strategic Management Approach*, New York: McGraw-Hill.

Rugman, A. M. and Verbeke, A. (1992) 'A note on the transnational solution and the transaction cost theory of multinational strategic management', *Journal of International Business Studies* 23, 4: 761–771.

Rugman, A. M. and Verbeke, A. (1993) 'Foreign subsidiaries and multinational strategic management: An extension and correction of Porter's single diamond framework', *Management International Review* 33, 2: 71–84.

Rumelt, R. P. (1982) 'How important is industry in explaining firm profitability?', unpublished working paper, UCLA.

Rumelt, R. P. (1984) 'Towards a strategic theory of the firm', in R. B. Lamb (ed.) *Competitive Strategic Management*, Englewood Cliffs, NJ: Prentice-Hall, 566–570.

Rumelt, R. P. (1987) 'Theory, strategy and entrepreneurship', in D. J. Teece (ed.) *The Competitive Challenge*, New York: Harper & Row, 137–158.

Rumelt, R. P. (1991) 'How much does industry matter?', *Strategic Management Journal* 12, 3: 167–185.

Rumelt, R. P., Schendel, D. and Teece, D. J. (1991) 'Strategic management and economics', *Strategic Management Journal* 12: 5–29.

Russo, J. E. and Schoemaker, P. J. (1989) *Decision Traps: Ten Barriers to Brilliant Decision Making and How to Overcome Them*, New York: Doubleday Publishing Co.

Rybczynski, T. M. (1955) 'Factor endowment and relative commodity prices', *Economica* 22: 336–341.

Samiee, S. and Roth, K. (1992) 'The influence of global marketing standardisation on performance', *Journal of Marketing* 56, 2: 1–17.

Samuelson, P. (1948) 'International trade and equalisation of factor prices', *Economic Journal* 58: 163–184.

Sanchez, D. (1998) 'Global selling with local flavor', *Sales and Marketing Management* 150, 8: 26–28.

Schmalansee, R. (1985) 'Do markets differ much?', *American Economic Review* 75: 341–351.

Schoemaker, P. J. (1990) 'Strategy, complexity and economic rent', *Management Science* 36, 10: 1178–1192.

Schoemaker, P. J. (1992) 'How to link strategic vision to core capabilities', *Sloan Management Review* 34, 1: 67–81.

Schoenecker, T. S. and Cooper, A. C. (1998) 'The role of firm resources and organizational attributes in determining entry timing: A cross-sectional study', *Strategic Management Journal* 19, 12: 1127–1143.

Scholfield, V. and Henry, I. (1996) *The European automotive components industry: A review of the leading 100 manufacturers*, London: The Economic Intelligence Unit.

Schollhammer, H. (1994) 'Strategies and methodologies in international business and comparative management research', *Management International Review* 34, 1: 5–20.

Schumpeter, J. A. (1934) *The Theory of Economic Development*, Cambridge, MA: Harvard University Press.

Segal-Horn, S., Asch, D. and Suneja, V. (1998) 'The globalisation of the European white goods industry', *European Management Journal* 16, 1: 101–109.

Selznick, P. (1957) *Leadership in Administration*, New York: Harper & Row.

Sera, K. (1992) 'Corporate globalisation: A new trend', *Academy of Management Executive* 6, 1: 89–96.

Seth, A. and Thomas, H. (1994) 'Theories of the firm: Implications for strategy research', *Journal of Management Studies* 31, 2: 165–191.

Shan, W. and Hamilton, W. (1991) 'Country-specific advantage and international cooperation', *Strategic Management Journal* 12, 6: 419–432.

Shapiro, D. M. (1983) 'Entry, exit and the theory of the multinational corporation', in C. P. Kindleberger and D. B. Audretsch (eds) *The Multinational Corporation in the 1980s*, Cambridge, MA: MIT Press, 103–122.

Shoham, A. (1995) 'Global marketing standardisation', *Journal of Global Marketing* 9, 1/2: 91–119.

Shrivastava, P. (1987) 'Rigor and practical usefulness of research in strategic management', *Strategic Management Journal* 8, 1: 77–92.

Simon, H. A. (1967) 'The business school: A problem of organisational design', *Journal of Management Studies* 4, 1: 1–14.

Simon, H. (1992) 'Lessons from Germany's midsize giants', *Harvard Business Review* 70, 2: 115–123.

Simon, H. (1995) 'You don't have to be German to be a "hidden champion"', *Business Strategy Review* 7, 2: 1–13.

Singh, J. (1995) 'Measurement issues in cross-national research', *Journal of International Business Studies* 26, 3: 597–619.

Smith, A. (1776) *An Inquiry into the Nature and Causes of the Wealth of Nations*, edited by R. H. Campbell, A. S. Skinner and W. B. Todd, Oxford: Clarendon Press, 1976.

Smitka, M. J. (1991) *Competitive Ties: Subcontracting in the Japanese Automotive Industry*, New York: Columbia University Press.

Snow, C. C. and Hambrick, D. D. (1980) 'Measuring organisational strategies: Some theoretical and methodological problems', *Academy of Management Review* 5, 4: 527–538.

Snow, C. C. and Hrebiniak, L. G. (1980) 'Strategy, distinctive competence, and organisational performance', *Administrative Science Quarterly* 25, 2: 317–336.

Stalk, G., Evans, P. and Schulman, L. E. (1992) 'Competing on capabilities: The new rules of corporate strategy', *Harvard Business Review* 70, 2: 57–69.

Stevenson, H. (1976) 'Defining corporate strengths and weaknesses', *Sloan Management Review* 17, 3: 51–68.

Stopford, J. M. and Wells, L. T. (1972) *Managing the Multinational Enterprise*, New York: Basic Books.

Sullivan, D. (1992) 'Organisation in American MNCs: The perspective of the European regional headquarters', *Management International Review* 32, 3: 237–250.

Sullivan, D. (1998a) 'Cognitive tendencies in international business research: Implications of "a narrow vision"', *Journal of International Business Studies* 29, 4: 837–862.

Sullivan, D. (1998b) 'The ontology of international business: A comment on international business: An emerging vision', *Journal of International Business Studies* 29, 4: 877–886.

Sullivan, D. and Bauerschmidt, A. (1991) 'The "basic concepts" of international business strategy: A review and reconsideration', *Management International Review* 31: 111–124.

Sundaram, A. K. and Black, J. S. (1992) 'The environment and internal organisation of multinational enterprises', *Academy of Management Review* 17, 4: 729–757.

Szymanski, D. M., Bharadwaj, S. G. and Varadarajan, P. R. (1993) 'Standardisation versus adaptation of international marketing strategy: An empirical investigation', *Journal of Marketing* 57, 4: 1–17.

Taggart, J. H. (1997) 'Autonomy and procedural justice: A framework for evaluating subsidiary strategy', *Journal of International Business Studies* 28, 1: 51–76.

Taggart, J. H. (1998) 'Strategy and control in the multinational corporation: Too many recipes?', *Long Range Planning* 31, 4: 571–585.

Tallman, S. B. (1991) 'Strategic management models and resource-based strategies among MNEs in a host market', *Strategic Management Journal* 12: 69–82.

Tallman, S. B. and Fladmoe-Lindquist, K. (1994) 'A resource-based model of the multinational firm', paper presented at the Strategic Management Society, Annual Conference, Paris.

Tallman, S. B. and Fladmoe-Lindquist, K. (1997) 'Resource-based strategy and competitive advantage among multinationals', in H. Vernon-Wortzel and L. H. Wortzel (eds) *Strategic Management in a Global Economy*, 3rd edition, New York: John Wiley & Sons, 149–167.

Taylor, W. (1991) 'The logic of global business: An interview with ABB's Percy Barnevik', *Harvard Business Review* 69, 2: 91–105.

Teece, D. J. (1981) 'The multinational enterprise: Market failure and market power considerations', *Sloan Management Review* 22, 3: 3–17.

Teece, D. J. (1984) 'Economic analysis and strategic management', *California Management Review* 26, 3: 87–110.

Teece, D. J. (1986a), 'Transactions cost economics and the multinational enterprise: An assessment', *Journal of Economic Behaviour and Organisation* 7: 21–45.

Teece, D. J. (1986b) 'Firm boundaries, technological innovation, and strategic management', in L. G. Thomas (ed.) *The Economics of Strategic Planning*, Lexington, MA: Lexington Books, 187–199.

Teece, D. J., Pisano, G. and Shuen, A. (1997) 'Dynamic capabilities and strategic management', *Strategic Management Journal* 18, 7: 509–533.

Theuerkauf, I. (1991) 'Reshaping the global organisation', *McKinsey Quarterly* 3: 102–119.

Theuerkauf, I., Ernst, D. and Mahini, A. (1993) 'Think local, organise ...?', *McKinsey Quarterly* 1: 107–114.

Thomas, A. S., Shenkar, O. and Clarke, L. (1994) 'The globalisation of our mental maps: Evaluating the geographic scope of JIBS coverage', *Journal of International Business Studies* 25, 4: 675–686.

Thomas, H. and Pollock, T. (1999) 'From I–O economics' S–C–P paradigm through strategic groups to competence-based competition: Reflections on the puzzle of competitive strategy', *British Journal of Management* 10, 2: 127–140.

Thomas, H. and Pruett, M (1993) 'Introduction to the special issue: Perspectives on theory building in strategic management', *Journal of Management Studies* 30, 1: 3–10.

Thomas, J. B., Clark, S. M. and Gioia, D. A. (1993) 'Strategic sensemaking and organisational performance: Linkages among scanning, interpretation, action and outcomes', *Academy of Management Journal* 36, 2: 239–270.

Thomas, K. W. and Tymon, W. G. (1982) 'Necessary properties of relevant research: Lessons from recent criticisms of the organisational sciences', *Academy of Management Review* 7, 3: 345–352.

Thompson, A. A. and Strickland, A. J. (1998) *Crafting and Implementing Strategy: Text and Readings*, 10th edition, Boston, MA: McGraw-Hill.

Thompson, J. D. (1967) *Organisations in Action*, New York: McGraw-Hill.

Toffler, A. (1980) *The Third Wave*, London: William Collins Sons & Co.

Tokyo Business Today (1993) 'The Japanese auto industry: Where is it headed?' (April), 8–15.

Toyne, B. (1989) 'International exchange: A foundation for theory building in international business', *Journal of International Business Studies* 19, 1: 1–17.

Toyne, B. and Nigh, D. (1998) 'A more expansive view of international business', *Journal of International Business Studies* 29, 4: 863–876.

Tsang, E. W. (1997) 'Choice of international technology transfer mode: A resource-based view', *Management International Review* 37, 2: 151–168.

Turnbull, P., Delbridge, R., Oliver, N. and Wilkinson, B. (1993) 'Winners and losers – The "tiering" of component suppliers in the UK automotive industry', *Journal of General Management* 19, 1: 48–63.

Turnbull, P., Oliver, N. and Wilkinson, B. (1992) 'Buyer–supplier relations in the UK automotive industry: Strategic implications of the Japanese manufacturing model', *Strategic Management Journal* 13, 2: 159–168.

Ulrich, D. and Lake, D. (1991) 'Organisational capability: Creating competitive advantage', *Academy of Management Executive* 5, 1: 77–91.

Van de Ven, A. H. (1989) 'Nothing is quite as practical as good theory', *Academy of Management Review* 14, 4: 486–489.

van Wolferen, K. (1989) *The Enigma of Japanese Power*, Tokyo: Charles E. Tuttle Co.

Venkatraman, N. and Grant, J. H. (1986) 'Construct measurement in organisational strategy research: A critique and proposal', *Academy of Management Review* 11, 1: 71–87.

Venkatraman, N. and Ramanujam, V. (1986) 'Measurement of business performance in strategy research: A comparison of approaches', *Academy of Management Review* 11, 4: 801–814.

Vernon, R. (1966) 'International investment and international trade in the product cycle', *Quarterly Journal of Economics* 80: 190–207.

Vernon, R. (1977) *Storm Over the Multinationals: The Real Issues*, London: Macmillan Press.

Verona, G. (1999) 'A resource-based view of product development', *Academy of Management Review* 24: 1, 132–142.

von Neumann, J. and Morgenstern, O. (1944) *The Theory of Games and Economic Behavior*, Princetown, NJ: Princetown University Press.

Walker, B. J., Kirchmann, W. and Conant, J. S. (1987) 'A method to improve response to industrial mail surveys', *Industrial Marketing Management* 16, 4: 305–314.

Weick, K. E. (1979) *The Social Psychology of Organising*, Reading, MA: Addison-Wesley.

Welch, L. S. and Luostarinen, R. (1988) 'Internationalisation: Evolution of a concept', *Journal of General Management* 14, 2: 34–55.

Wells, L. T. (1972) 'The multinational business enterprise: What kind of international organisation?', in *Transnational Relations and World Politics*, Cambridge, MA: Harvard University Press, 97–114.

Wernerfelt, B. (1984) 'A resource-based view of the firm', *Strategic Management Journal* 5, 2: 171–180.

Wernerfelt, B. (1989) 'From critical resources to corporate strategy', *Journal of General Management* 14, 3: 4–12.

Wernerfelt, B. (1995) 'The resource-based view of the firm: Ten years after', *Strategic Management Journal* 16, 3: 171–174.

Wernerfelt, B. and Montgomery, C. A. (1988) 'Tobin's q and the importance of focus in firm performance', *American Economic Review* 78: 246–251.

Whittington, R. (1993) *What is Strategy – and Does it Matter?*, London: Routledge.

Williams, J. R. (1992) 'How sustainable is your competitive advantage?', *California Management Review* 34, 3: 29–51.

Williamson, O. E. (1975) *Markets and Hierarchies*, New York: The Free Press.

Williamson, O. E. (1985) *The Economic Institutions of Capitalism*, New York: The Free Press.

Wind, Y. and Douglas, S. (1981) 'International portfolio analysis and strategy: The challenges of the 80s', *Journal of International Business Studies* 12, 2: 69–80.

Winter, S. G. (1987) 'Knowledge and competence as strategic assets', in D. J. Tecce (ed.) *The Competitive Challenge*, New York: Harper & Row, 159–184.

Womack, J. P., Jones, D. T. and Roos, D. (1990) *The Machine That Changed the World*, New York: Harper Perennial.

Wong-Rieger, D. (1993) 'Why relevance in international management research?', in D. Wong-Rieger and F. Rieger (eds) *International Management Research*, New York: Walter de Gruyter, 1–6.

Woo, C. Y. and Willard, G. (1983) 'Performance representation in strategic management research', paper presented at the annual meeting of the Academy of Management, Dallas.

Wortzel, Lawrence H. (1991) 'Global strategies: Standardization versus flexibility', in Heidi Vernon-Wortzel and Lawrence H. Wortzel (eds) *Global Strategic Management: The Essentials*, 2nd edition, New York: John Wiley & Sons, 135–149.

Wright, R. W. and Ricks, D. A. (1994) 'Trends in international business research: Twenty-five years later', *Journal of International Business Studies* 25, 4: 687–701.

WTO (1999): http://www.wto.org/english/res_e/statis_e/statis_e.htm

Yeoh, P. L. and Roth, K. (1999) 'An empirical analysis of sustained advantage in the U.S. pharmaceutical industry: Impact of firm resources and capabilities', *Strategic Management Journal* 20, 7: 637–653.

Yip, G. S. (1989) 'Global strategy … in a world of nations?', *Sloan Management Review* 31, 1: 29–41.

Yip, G. S. (1992) *Total Global Strategy: Managing for Worldwide Competitive Advantage*, Englewood Cliffs, NJ: Prentice-Hall.

Yip, G. S. and Coundouriotis, G. A. (1991) 'Diagnosing global strategy potential: The world chocolate confectionery industry', *Planning Review* 19, 1: 4–14.

Yip, G. S., Johansson, J. K. and Roos, J. (1997) 'Effects of nationality on global strategy', *Management International Review* 37, 4: 365–385.

Yu, J. and Cooper, H. (1983) 'A quantitative review of research design effects on response rates to questionnaires', *Journal of Marketing Research* 20: 36–44.

Zajac, E. (1995) 'SMJ 1994 best paper prize to Birger Wernerfelt', *Strategic Management Journal* 16, 3: 169–170.

Index

advantages: comparative 31, 75; cost of acquisition 37; 'diamonds' of national advantage 79–80, 138; domestically derived 115–116; efficiency-derived 25; factor-related 78; firm-specific 23, 25, 26–27, 74, 141, 142; in global environment 2; goods-related 78; idiosyncratic 22–23, 87–88, 132; internalisation 25, 27; locational 25, 26, 140; ownership 25–26, 27; resource-based 53, 99, 135, 137, 139; *see also* competitive advantages; sustainable competitive advantages

American Showa Inc. 117

arbitrage 6, 31, 113

assets: and competencies 58; firm-specific 69, 81, 106, 120; intangible 27, 54, 58, 59, 65, 69, 77, 78, 81, 82, 84–85, 99, 106–111, 114, 116, 120, 122–123, 125, 147–148, 154; stock accumulation 54, 62, 63, 77, 85, 86, 106, 145; strategic 77, 80; tangible 58, 59, 60, 78, 81, 82, 84–86, 99, 106–109, 120, 122–123, 125, 137, 147–148, 154; *see also* capabilities; resources

automotive components industry 9, 92–126; competitive advantage 137–138, 147–148; conceptual model 124, convergence toward Japanese model 93, 95, 96; dynamics of the industry 95–97; firm size 98–99; global consolidation 97; global environment 13, 92–126; hypothesis testing 12–14, 106–109, 111–117, 120–123, 125–126; investment intensity 98; Japanese management practices 137; JIT (just-in-time) systems 94, 103, 117; multifunctional teams 105, 108, 148, 166; Nissan

collaboration with suppliers 94; parallel sourcing 94; profitability 118, 119, 121; quality, importance of 100, 103; research findings 99–126; research study limitations 133–136; resource pools 12–13, 99–109; restructuring 96; selected for research 97–99; structure of industry 93–95; supply chain organisation 93–95, 104–105; transfer of Japanese best practice 96; vertical integration 93–94, 95

automotive components manufacturers: affected by worldwide recession 117; cooperative activity 97; cost reduction pressures 97, 105, 117, 151; global sourcing of parts 97–98; international expansion 98; large global suppliers 98; performance figures 117–118; supplier/buyer relationships 104–105, 108; *see also* automotive components industry; performance; suppliers

Bain/Mason industrial organisation (IO) theory 22–27, 31, 39, 44–45, 47, 128, 132, 133, 142

Bartlett and Ghoshal typology of strategic orientation 12, 83, 87, 114, 136, 146–147, 156

behaviouralism 28

biotechnology industry 77, 86

BMW AG 97

business, international 4–5, 8, 9–10, 13, 15–41, 83; economic perspective 19–28, 39–41; environment changes 129; global environment 15–19; interdisciplinary approach 8, 14, 74, 140–141; management perspective 28–41; multi-disciplinary nature 8;